Sir David Lindsay, David Laing

Poetical Works

With Memoir, Notes and Glossary

Sir David Lindsay, David Laing

Poetical Works
With Memoir, Notes and Glossary

ISBN/EAN: 9783337777982

Printed in Europe, USA, Canada, Australia, Japan

Cover: Foto ©Thomas Meinert / pixelio.de

More available books at **www.hansebooks.com**

THE POETICAL WORKS

OF

SIR DAVID LYNDSAY

WITH MEMOIR, NOTES AND GLOSSARY

BY DAVID LAING, LL.D

IN THREE VOLUMES.—VOL. II

EDINBURGH: WILLIAM PATERSON
MDCCCLXXIX.

TABLE OF CONTENTS.

	PAGE
Ane Pleasant Satyre of the thrie Estaitis, Part I.,	1
The first Interlude,	69
An Interlude of the puir man and the Pardoner,	99
Ane Pleasant Satyre, &c., Part II.,	118
An Interlude: the Sermon of Foly,	206
Ane Dialog betuix Experience and ane Courteour of the miserabyll Estait of the World, Part I.,	223
The Epistil to the Redar,	225
Ane Dialog, &c., Buke i.,	237
Ane Exclamatioun to the Redar, &c.,	246
The creatioun of Adam and Eve,	252
Of the miserabyll Transgressioun of Adam,	258
Quhow God distroyit all leveand creature, &c.,	269
Notes and Various Readings,	285
Appendix,	325
No. 1. The auld man and his wife,	327
No. 2. Various Readings, &c.,	340

ANE PLEASANT SATYRE OF
THE THRIE ESTAITIS.

VOL. II. A

ANE SATYRE

OF THE THRIE ESTAITIS.

Lyndsay's Satyre or Play is known to have been represented on at least three occasions, at an interval of several years, and each time probably with considerable modifications. Chalmers says, "It was first acted on the Playfield at Coupar in Fife, during the year 1535; and indeed much of the scene is laid in Fife, where several men and things are mentioned which must have been familiar to the people of that shire." In a previous sentence he states that "this remarkable drama of a rude age was undoubtedly presented, at Epiphany 1539-40, before the King and Queen, the court, and country, on the Playfield near Linlithgow. It must necessarily have been written some years before. The King is everywhere spoken of, as still unmarried; but he changed his unmarried state in 1537, so that this play must have been written before that year both of joy and of sorrow."[1] No doubt the general character of Rex Humanitas in the Play may be supposed to have some resemblance to that of James the Fifth—well disposed in his youth, but led into vicious courses by

[1] Vol. 1., p. 60, 61.

his profligate advisers; but it is mere assumption to apply the language of the Play to the Scottish Monarch, and in so doing to draw any conclusion either respecting the date of its composition, or its first representation. In this place it is sufficient to observe that no evidence exists of its having been represented at Cupar so early as 1535.

In a letter addressed to Thomas Lord Cromwell, Lord Privy Seal, Sir William Eure on the 26th of January 1539-40, relates his communings with Mr Thomas Bellenden, Justice Clerk, who was then at Berwick, as one of the Commissioners for settling some of the disputes of the Borders. To illustrate the disposition which the Scottish King and the temporal lords of his Council are supposed to have entertained in favour of some reformation in matters of religion, he communicates a detailed account of the representation of Lyndsay's Play at Linlithgow in the presence of the King, Queen, and the Lords of Council, spiritual and temporal, on the feast of Epiphany (sometimes called the Twelfth Day), or the 6th of January 1540. Had this been a repetition of its performance, the fact must have been well known, and would have been stated. It is therefore of importance, as the Play in its original state is not known to exist, that we should introduce the description alluded to, which is entitled:[1]—

[1] Eure's Letter is preserved in the British Museum (MSS. Reg. 7 C. XVI. fol. 168), and is printed in Pinkerton's History, vol. ii., p. 494; and in Ellis's Original Letters, Third Series, vol. iii., p. 275. In the State Papers, vol. v., p. 170; the "Notes of the Interlude" are not given.

THE COPIE OF THE NOOTES OF THE INTERLUYDE.

"In the firste entres come in SOLAICE (whose parte was but to make mery, sing balletts with his fellowes, and drinke at the interluyds of the Play), whoe shewede FIRST to all the Audiance the Playe to be played, whiche was a generall thing, meanyng nothing in speciall to displeas noe man, praying therfore noe man to be angre with the same. NEXTE come in a KING whoe passed to his throne, having noe speche to thende of the Playe (and thene to raitefie and approve as in playne Parliament all things doon by the reste of the players whiche represented the Three [ESTATES]). Withe hym come his courtiours PLACEBO, PIK-THANKE, and FLATERYE; and suche a like garde, one swering he was the lustieste, starkeste, best proporcioned, and moste valiaunte man that ever was; an other sweare he was the beste with longe bowe, crose bowe, and culverin, in the world; an other sweare he was the best juster and man of armes in the world; and soe furthe during thaire parts. THERAFTER came a MAN, armed in harnes, withe a sword drawen in his hande. A BUSSHOPE, a BURGES man, and EXPERIENCE clede like a Doctor, whoe sete thaym all down on the deis vnder the King. After thayme come a POOR MAN, whoe did goe upe and downe the scaffald, making a hevie complaynte that he was heryed throughe the Courtiours taking his fewe in one place, and alsoe his tacks in an other place; where throughe he hade scayled his house, his wif and chil-

deren beggyng thaire brede, and soe of many thousands
in Scotlande, whiche wolde make the Kyngs Grace lose
of men if his Grace stod neide; saying, Thaire was noe
remedye to be gotten, for thoughe he wolde suyte to
the Kyngs Grace, he was naither acquaynted with
Controuller nor Treasourer, and withoute thaym myght
noe man gete noe goodenes of the King. And after
he spered for the King, and whene he was shewed to
the MAN that was KING in the playe, he answered
and said, he was noe King, for there is but one
King, whiche made all and gouernethe all, whoe is
Eternall; to whome he and all erthely Kings ar but
officers, of the whiche thay muste make recknyng; and
soe furthe much moor to that effecte. And thene he
loked to the KING, and saide he was not the King of
Scotlande, for ther was an other King in Scotlande,
that hanged John Armestrang with his fellowes, and
Sym the larde, and many other moe which had paci-
fied the countrey, and stanched thifte, but he had
lefte one thing vndon, which perteynede aswell to his
charge as th' other. And whene he was asked what
that was, he made a long narracion of the oppression
of the poor, by the taking of the Corsepresaunt beists,
and of the herying of poore men by Concistorye lawe,
and of many other abussions of the Spiritualitie and
Churche, withe many long stories and auctorities. And
thene the BUSSHOPE roise and rebuked hym, saying it
effered not to hym to speake such matiers; commaunded of hym scilence, or ells to suffer dethe for it
by thair lawe. THERAFTER roise the Man of Armes,
alledginge the contrarie and commaunded the poore man

to speake, saying thair abusion hade been over longe suffered withoute any lawe. Thene the Poore Man shewed the greate abusion of Busshopes, Preletts, Abbotts, reving menes wifs and doughters, and holding thaym, and of the maynteynyng of thair childer; and of thair over bying of Lords and Barrons eldeste sones to their doughters, wherethoroughe the nobilitie of the blode of the realme was degenerate. And of the greate superfluous rents that perteyned to the Churche by reason of over muche temporall lands given to thaym, whiche thaye proved that the Kinge might take boothe by the Canon Lawe and Civile Lawe. And of the greate abomynable vices that reiague in cloistures; and of the common bordelles that was keped in closturs of Nunnes. All this was provit by EXPERIENCE, and alsoe was shewed the office of a Busshope, and producit the Newe Testament, with the auctorities to that effecte. And then roise the MAN OF ARMES, and the BURGES, and did saye that all that was producit by the Poor Man and Experience was reasonable, of veritie and of greate effecte, and very expedient to be reafourmede withe the consent of Parliament. And the BUSSHOPE said, he wold not consent therunto. The MAN OF ARMES and BURGESS saide thay were twoe, and he bot one, wherfor thair voice shuld have mooste effecte. Theraftre the KING in the Playe ratefied, approved, and confermed all that was rehersed."

Names of Persons in the Play.

Part the First.—(*Page* 11 to 69 and 77 to 98.)

Rex Humanitas.
Diligence, *the Messenger.*
Wantonnes.
Placebo.
Solace, *called* Sandie.
The Vyces *in the habit of Friars* :—
    Flatterie (*alias* Devotioun).
    Falset (*alias* Sapience).
    Dissait (*alias* Discretioun).
Divyne Correctioun (*or* King Correctioun).
Correctioun's Varlet.
Gude Counsall.
Spiritualitie :—
    The Bishop.
    The Abbot.
    Schir Parson, a Persone.
Temporalitie.
Sensualitie.
Hamelines.
Danger.
Fund Jonet.
Dame Chastitie.
Dame Veritie.
Prioress or Abbess.

THE FIRST INTERLUDE.—(*Page* 69 to 76.)

Dame Chastitie.
The Sowtar.
The Sowtar's Wyfe.
The Taylour.
The Taylour's Wyfe.
Jennie the Taylour's Daughter.
Diligence.

THE SECOND INTERLUDE.—(*Page* 99 to 117.)

Pauper, the Pure Man.
Diligence.
The Pardoner, *called* Schir Robert Rome-raker.
The Sowtar.
The Sowtar's Wyfe.
Wilkin, the Pardoner's Boy.

PART THE SECOND.—(*Page* 118 to 205.)

Rex Humanitas.
Diligence, *the Messenger*.
THE THREE ESTAITIS :—
    Spiritualitie (or the Clergy).
    Temporalitie (or Landholders).
    The Burgesses (or Merchants.)
Johne the Common-weill.
Divyne Correctioun.
Pauper.

The Abbot.
The Parson.
Placebo.
Wantones.
Solace.
Covetice.
Sensualitie.
Gude Counsell.
First and Second Sarjeant.
The Scrybe, or Notar.
Commoun Thift.
Oppressioun.
Doctour of Divinity.
First Licentiate.
Batchelor.
Flatterie, the Freir.
The Taylor.
The Sowtar.
Dissait.
Dame Veritie.
Dame Chastitie.
The Abbess or Prioress.

THE THIRD INTERLUDE.—(*Page* 206.)

Rex Humanitas.
Folie.
Diligence.

ANE PLEASANT SATYRE OF THE THRIE ESTAITIS IN COMMENDATIOUN OF VERTEW AND VITUPERATIOUN OF VYCE, AS FOLLOWIS.

[PART THE FIRST.]

DILIGENCE.

THE FATHER, and founder of faith, and felicitie,
    That your fassioun formed to his similitude;
And his SONE, our Saviour, scheild in necessitie,
    That bocht yow from baillis, ransonit on the Rude,
    Repleadgeand his presonaris with his hart blude;
The HALIE GAIST, governour, and grounder of grace,
    Of wisdome and weilfair baith fontane and flude,
Saif yow all that I sie seisit in this place,
    And scheild yow from sinne;
And with his spreit yow inspyre,   10
Till I have shawin my desyre:
Silence, Soveraine, I requyre:
    For now I begin.   [*Pausa.*]

TAK tent to me, my freinds, and hald yow coy,
    For I am sent to yow, as messingeir,
From ane nobill and rycht redoubtit Roy,
    The quhilk hes bene absent this monie yeir;
Humanitie, give ye his name wald speir,
Quha bade me shaw to yow, but variance,

> That he intendis amang yow to compeir,   20
> With ane triumphand awfull ordinance:
> With crown, and sword, and scepter, in his hand,
> > Temperit with mercie, quhen penitence appeiris:
> Howbeit, that he lang tyme hes bene sleipand,
> > Quhairthrow misreull hes rung thir monie yeiris;
> > That innocentis hes bene brocht on thair beiris,
> Be fals reporteris of this natioun;
> > Thocht young oppressouris at the elder leiris;
> Be now assurit of reformatioun.

> Sie no misdoeris be sa bauld,   30
> As to remaine into this hauld:
> For quhy, be him that Judas sauld,
> > They will be heich hangit;
> Now faithfull folk for joy may sing:
> For quhy, it is the just bidding
> Of my soveraine lord the King,
> > That na man be wrangit.
> Thocht he ane quhyll into his flouris,
> Be governit be vile trompouris,
> And sumtyme lufe his paramouris,   40
> > Hauld ye him excusit;
> For quhen he meittis with Correctioun,
> With Veritie, and Discretioun,
> Thay will be banisched aff the toun,
> > Quhilk hes him abusit.

> And heir, be oppin Proclamatioun,
> > I wairne, in name of his magnificence.
> The THRIE ESTAITIS of this Natioun,

That thay compeir, with detfull diligence,
 And till his Grace mak thair obedience.   50
And first, I wairne the Spiritualitie,
 And se the Burgessis spair not for expence,
Bot speid thame heir, with Temporalitie.

Als I beseik yow, famous Auditouris,
 Conveinit in this congregatioun,
To be patient, the space of certaine houris,
 Till ye have hard our schort narratioun :
And als we mak yow supplicatioun,
 That na man tak our wordis intill disdaine ;
  Althocht ye heir be declamatioun,   60
The Common-weill richt pitiouslie complaine.
Richt so the verteous ladie Veritie
 Will mak ane pitious lamentatioun :
Als for the treuth scho will impresonit be,
 And banisched lang tyme out of the Toun :
And Chastitie will mak narratioun,
 How scho can git na lugeing in this land,
Till that the heavinlye king Correctioun
Meit with the King, and commoun hand for hand.

Prudent Peopill I pray yow all,   70
 Tak na man greif, in speciall ;
For wee sall speik in generall,
 For pastyme, and for play :
Thairfoir till all our rymis be rung,
And our mistoinit sangis be sung,
Let everie man keip weill ane toung,
 And everie woman tway.

REX HUMANITAS.

O Lord of lords, and King of kingis all,
    Omnipotent of power, Prince but peir,
Ever ringand, in gloir celestiall,   80
    Quha be great micht, and haifing na mateir,
    Maid heavin, and eird, fyre, air, and watter cleir;
Send me thy grace, with peace perpetuall,
    That I may rewll my realme to thy pleaseir,
Syne bring my saull to joy angelicall.

Sen thow hes givin mee dominatioun,
    And rewll of pepill subject to my cure,
Be I nocht rewlit be counsall, and reasoun,
    In dignitie I may nocht lang indure.
    I grant my stait my self may nocht assure,   90
Nor yit conserve my lyfe in sickernes:
    Have pitie, Lord, on mee, thy creature,
Supportand me in all my busines.

I thé requeist, quha rent was on the Rude,
    Me to defend from the deids of defame;
That my pepill report of me bot gude,
    And be my saifgaird baith from sin, and shame.
    I knaw my dayis induris bot as ane dreame;
Thairfor, O Lord, I hairtlie thé exhort,
    To gif me grace to use my diadeame   100
To thy pleasure, and to my gret comfort.

    [*Heir sall the King pass to the Royall suit, and sit with
    ane grave countenance, till Wantonnes cum.*]

WANTONNES.

My Soveraine Lord, and Prince but peir,
Quhat garris yow mak sic dreirie cheir?
Be blyth, sa lang as ye ar heir,
    And pas tyme, with pleasure:
For als lang leifis the mirrie man,
As the sorie for ocht he can,
His banis full sair, Sir, sall I ban,
    That dois yow displeasure.
Sa lang as Placebo, and I,   110
Remaines into your company,
Your Grace sal leif richt mirrely;
    Of this haif ye na dout.
Sa lang as ye haif us in cure,
Your Grace, Sir, sall want na pleasure:
War Solace heir, I yow assure,
    He wald rejoyce this rout.

PLACEBO.

Gude brother myne, quhair is Solace?
The mirrour of all mirrines?
I have gret mervell, be the Mess,   120
    He taries sa lang.
Byde he away, wee ar bot shent,
I ferlie how he fra us went:
I trow he hes impediment,
    That lettis him nocht gang.

WANTONNES.

I left Solace, that same greit loun.

Drinkand into the burrows toun,
It will cost him halfe of ane croun,
   Althocht he had na mair.
And als hee said, he wald gang see   130
Fair Ladie Sensualitie,
The beriall of all bewtie,
   And portratour preclair.

PLACEBO.

Be God, I see him at the last,
As he war chaist, rynnand richt fast,
He glowris, evin as he war agast,
   Or fleyit of ane gaist.
Na, he is wod drunkin, I trow,
Sie ye not that he is wod fow :
I ken weill, be his creischie mow,   140
   He hes bene at ane feast.

SOLACE.

Now, quha saw ever sic ane thrang?
Me thocht sum said I had gaine wrang;
Had I help, I wald sing ane sang,
   With ane richt mirrie noyse.
I have sic pleasure at my hart,
That garris me sing the tribill pairt,
Wald sum gude fallow fill the quart,
   It wald my hart rejoyce.
Howbeit, my coat be short, and nippit,   150
Thankis be to God I am weill hippit,
Thocht all my gold may sone be grippit
   Intill ane pennie pursse ;

Thocht I ane servand lang haif bene,
My purchais is nocht worth ane preine;
I may sing, Peblis on the Greine,
    For ocht that I may tursse.
Quhat is my name? can ye not gesse,
Sirs, ken ye nocht Sandie Solace?
Thay callit my mother bonie Besse,   160
    That dwelt betwene the Bowis.
Of twelf yeir auld scho lernit to swyve,
Thankit be the great God on lyve!
Scho maid me fatheris four, or fyve,
    But dout this is na mowis.
Quhen ane was deid scho gat ane uther,
Was never man had sic ane mother,
Of fatheris scho maid me ane futher,
    Of lawit men, and leirit.
Scho is baith wyse, worthie, and wicht,   170
For, scho spairis nouther kuik nor knycht;
Yea, four and twentie on ane nicht,
    And ay thair eine scho bleirit.
And gif I lie, sirs, ye may speir:
Bot, saw ye nocht the King cum heir?
I am ane sportour, and playfeir
    To that royall young King.
He said, he wald within schort space,
Cum pas his tyme into this place:
I pray the Lord to send him grace,   180
    That he lang tyme may ring.

PLACEBO.

Solace, quhy taryit ye sa lang?

SOLACE.

The feind a faster I micht gang :
I micht not thrist out throw the thrang,
    Of wyfes fyftein fidler :
Than for to rin I tuik ane rink,
Bot I felt never sik ane stink :
For our Lordis luif gif me ane drink,
    Placebo, my deir brother.

[*Heir sall Placebo gif Solace ane drink.*]

REX HUMANITAS.

My servant Solace, quhat gart you tarie ?   190

SOLACE.

I wait nocht, Sir, be sweit Saint Marie !
I have bene in ane feirie farie,
    Or ellis intill ane trance :
Sir, I have sene, I yow assure,
The fairest earthlie creature,
That ever was formit be nature,
    And maist for to advance.
To luik on hir is great delyte,
With lippis reid, and cheikis quhyte,
I wald renunce all this warld quyte,   200
    For till stand in hir grace :
Scho is wantoun, and scho is wyse ;
And cled scho is on the new gyse,
It wald gar all your flesche up ryse,
    To luik upon hir face.

War I ane king it sould be kend,
I sould not spair on hir to spend;
And this same nicht for hir to send,
  For my pleasure.
Quhat rak of your prosperitie, 210
Gif ye want Sensualitie?
I wald nocht gif ane sillie flie,
  For your treasure.

REX HUMANITAS.

Forsuith, my freinds, I think ye ar nocht wyse,
  Till counsall me to break commandement,
Directit be the Prince of Paradyse:
  Considdering ye knaw that my intent
  Is for till be to God obedient,
Quhilk dois forbid men to be lecherous:
  Do I nocht sa, perchance, I will repent; 220
Thairfoir, I think your counsall odious,
  The quhilk ye gaif mee till;
  Because I haif bene, to this day,
  Tanquam tabula rasa:
  That is als mekill as to say,
  Redie for gude, and ill.

PLACEBO.

Beleive ye, that we will begyll yow?
Or from your vertew we will wyle yow?
Or with evill counsall overseyll yow?
  Both, into gude and evill: 230
To tak your Graces part wee grant,
In all your deidis participant;

Sa that ye be nocht ane young sanct,
And syne ane auld devill.

WANTONNES.

Beleive ye, Sir, that lecherie be sin?
    Na, trow nocht that, this is my ressoun quhy;
First, at the Romane Kirk will ye begin,
    Quhilk is the lemand lamp of lechery:
    Quhair Cardinalis, and Bischopis, generally,
To luif ladies, thay think ane pleasand sport,   240
    And out of Rome hes baneist Chastity,
Quha with our Prelats can get na resort.

SOLACE.

Sir, quhill ye get ane prudent Queine,
I think your Majestie serein
Sould haif ane lustie concubein,
    To play yow withall:
For, I knaw, be your qualitie,
Ye want the gift of chastitie;
Fall to *in nomine Domini:*
    This is my counsall.   250
I speik, Sir, under protestatioun,
That nane at me haif indignatioun:
For all the Prelats of this natioun,
    For the maist part,
Thay think na schame to have ane huir,
And sum hes thrie under thair cuir:
This to be trew, I'le yow assuir,
    Ye sall heir efterwart.

Sir, knew ye all the mater throch,
 To play ye wald begin ;   260
Speir at the Monks of Bamirrinoch,
 Gif lecherie be sin.

PLACEBO.

Sir, send ye for Sandie Solace,
Or ells your monycoun Wantonnes,
And pray my ladie Priores,
 The suith till declair:
Gif it to be sin to tak Kaity,
Or to leif like ane bummill baty ?
The buik sayis, *Omnia probate*,
 And nocht for to spair.   270

[*Heir sall entir Dame Sensualitie, with hir Madynnis Hamelines and Danger.*]

SENSUALITIE.

Luifers awalk! behald the fyrie spheir,
 Behauld the naturall dochter of Venus :
Behauld luifers, this lustie Ladie cleir,
 The fresche fonteine of knichtis amorous,
 Repleit with joyis dulce and delicious.
Or quha wald mak to Venus observance,
 In my mirthfull chalmer melodious,
There sall thay find all pastyme, and pleasance ;

Behauld my heid, behauld my gay attyre,
 Behauld my halse, lusum and lilie quhyte ;   280
Behauld my visage, flammand as the fyre,

Behauld my papis, of portratour perfyte.
To luik on mee luiffers hes greit delyte,
Rycht sa hes all the kinges of Christindome;
To thame I haif done pleasouris infinyte,
And speciallie unto the Court of Rome.

Ane kis of me war worth, in ane morning,
A milyioun of gold to knicht, or king:
And yit, I am of nature sa towart,
I lat na luiffer pas with ane sair hart. 290
Of my name, wald ye wit the veritie,
Forsuith thay call me Sensualitie.
I hauld it best now, or we farther gang,
To dame Venus let us go sing ane Sang.

HAMELINESS.

Madame but tarrying,
    For to serve Venus deir,
We sall fall to, and sing,
    Sister Danger, cum neir.

DANGER.

Sister, I was nocht sweir,
    To Venus observance, 300
Howbeit, I mak Dangeir,
    Yit, be continuance,
    Men may have thair pleasance:
Thairfoir let na man fray,
    We will tak it, perchance,
Howbeit that wee say nay.

HAMELINES.

Sister, cum on your way,
    And let us nocht think lang,
In all the haist wee may,
    To sing Venus ane Sang.   310

DANGER.

Sister, sing this Sang I may not,
Without the help of gude Fund-Jonet.
Fund-Jonet, hoaw! cum tak a part.

FUND-JONET.

That sall I do, with all my hart,
Sister, howbeit, that I am hais,
I am content to beir a bais.
Ye twa suld luif me as your lyfe,
Ye knaw I lernit yow baith to swyfe:
In my chalmer, ye wait weill quhair,
Sen syne the feind ane man ye spair.   320

HAMELINES.

Fund-Jonet, fy, ye ar to blame!
To speik foull wordis, think ye not schame?

FUND-JONET.

Thair is ane hundreth heir sittand by,
That luiftis geaping als weill as I,
Micht they get it in privitie:
Bot, quha begins the Sang, let se.

                                [*Exeunt.*]

REX HUMANITAS.

Up, Wantonnes, thow sleipis too lang!
Me thocht I hard ane mirrie sang:
I thee command, in haist to gang,
    Se quhat yon mirth may meine.   330

WANTONNES.

I trow, Sir, be the Trinitie,
Yon same is Sensualitie,
Gif it be scho, sune sall I sie
    That Soverane sereine.

[*Heir sall Wantonnes go spy thame, and come agane to the King.*]

REX HUMANITAS.

Quhat war thay yon, to me declair.

WANTONNES.

Dame Sensuall, baith gude and fair.

PLACEBO.

Sir, scho is mekill to avance,
For scho can baith play, and dance:
That perfyt patron of plesance,
    Ane perle of pulchritude: 340
Soft as the silk is hir quhite lyre,
Hir hair is like the goldin wyre:
My hart burnis in ane flame of fyre.
    I sweir yow, be the Rude!

I think scho is sa wonder fair,
That in earth scho hes na compair,
War ye weill lernit at luifis lair
    And syne had hir anis sene :
I wait, be cokis passioun,
Ye wald mak supplicatioun,   350
And spend on hir ane millioun,
    Hir lufe for till obteine.

SOLACE.

Quhat say ye, Sir, ar ye content,
That scho cum heir incontinent?
Quhat vails your kingdome, and your rent,
    And all your great treasure ;
Without ye haif ane mirrie lyfe,
And cast asyde all sturt, and stryfe?
And sa lang as ye want ane wyfe,
    Fall to, and tak your pleasure.   360

REX HUMANITAS.

Gif that be trew, quhilk ye me tell,
    I will not langer tarie :
Bot will gang preif that play my sell,
    Howbeit the warld me warie.
    Als fast as ye may carie,
        Speid with all diligence :
    Bring Sensualitie,
        Fra hand to my presence.
Forsuth, I wait not how it stands,
Bot sen I hard of your tythands,   370
My bodie trimblis, feit and hands,

And quhiles is hait as fyre:
I trow Cupido, with his dart,
Hes woundit me out-throw the hart;
My spreit will fra my bodie part,
    Get I nocht my desyre.
Pas on away, with diligence,
And bring hir heir, to my presence:
Spair nocht for travell, nor expence,
    I cair not for na cost.   380
Pas on your way schone Wantonnes,
And tak with you Sandie Solace,
And bring that Ladie to this place,
    Or els I am bot lost.
Commend me to that sweitest thing,
And present hir with this same ring,
And say, I ly in languisching,
    Except scho mak remeid.
With siching sair, I am bot schent,
Without scho cum incontinent,   390
My heavie langour to relent,
    And saif me now fra deid.

WANTONNES.

Or ye tuke skaith, be Gods goun,
I lever thair war not, up nor doun,
Ane tume cunt into this toun,
    Nor twentie myle about.
Dout ye nocht, Sir, bot wee will get hir,
Wee sall be feirie for till fetch hir,
Bot faith wee wald speid all the better
    Till gar our pursses rout.   400

SOLACE.

Sir, let na sorrow in yow sink,
Bot gif us ducats for till drink,
And wee sall never sleip ane wink
    Till it be back, or eadge :
Ye ken weill, Sir, we haif no cunzie.

REX HUMANITAS.

Solace, sure that sall be no sunzie,
Beir ye that bag upon your lunzie,
    Now sirs, win weill your wage ;
I pray yow speid yow sone agane.

WANTONNES.

Ye, of this sang, Sir, we are fane,   410
Wee sall nether spair [for] wind, nor raine,
    Till our days wark be done :
Fairweill, for wee are at the flicht,
Placebo rewll our Roy at richt :
We sall be heir, man, or midnicht,
    Thocht wee marche with the Mone.

[*Heir sall thay depairt, singand mirrely.*]

WANTONNES.

Pastyme, with pleasance, and greit prosperitie,
Be to yow, soveraine Sensualitie.

SENSUALITIE.

Sirs, ye ar welcum : quhair go ye ? eist or west

WANTONNES.

In faith, I trow we be at the farrest. 420

SENSUALITIE.

Quhat is your name, I pray you, sir, declair?

WANTONNES.

Marie! Wantonnes, the Kings Secretair!

SENSUALITIE.

Quhat King is that, quhilk hes sa gay a boy?

WANTONNES.

Humanitie, that richt redoutit Roy,
Quhilk dois commend him to yow hartfullie,
And sendis yow heir ane ring with ane rubie,
In takin, that abuife all creatour,
He hes chosen yow to be his paramour:
He bade me say, that he will be bot deid,
Without that ye mak haistelie remeid. 430

SENSUALITIE.

How can I help him, althocht he suld forfair,
Ye ken richt weill, I am na medcinair.

SOLACE.

Yes, lustie Ladie, thocht he war never sa seik,
I wait ye beare his health into your breik:
Ane kis of your sweit mow, in ane morning,
Till his seiknes micht be greit comforting,

And als he maks yow supplicatioun,
This nicht, to mak with him collatioun.

SENSUALITIE.

I thank his Grace, of his benevolence,
   Gude sirs, I sall be reddie evin fra hand :   440
In me, thair sall be fund na negligence,
   Baith nicht, and day, quhen his Grace will demand.
   Pas ye befoir, and say, I am cummand,
And thinks richt lang to haif of him ane sicht :
   And I to Venus do mak ane faithfull band,
That in his arms I think to ly all nicht.

WANTONNES.

That sal be done, bot yit, or I hame pass,
Heir I protest for Hamelynes, your lass.

SENSUALITIE.

Scho sal be at command, sir, quhen ye will,
I traist, scho sall find yow flinging your fill.   450

WANTONNES.

Now hay for joy, and mirth, I dance.
Tak thair ane gay gamond of France :
Am I nocht worthie till avance,
   That am sa gude a page ?
And that sa spedelie can rin,
To tyst my maister unto sin :
The feind a penny he will win
   Of this his mariage.
I rew richt sair, be Sanct Michell,

Nor I had pearst hir my awin sell: 460
For quhy, yon King, be Bryd's bell,
    Kennis na mair of ane cunt,
Nor dois the noveis of ane freir:
It war bot almis to pull my eir,
That wald not preif yon gallant geir:
    Fy! that I am sa blunt.
I think, this day, to win greit thank,
Hay! as an brydlit cat I brank:
Alace! I haif wrestit my schank,
    Yit I gang, be Sanct Michaell. 470
Quhilk of my leggis, Sirs, as ye trow,
Was it that I did hurt evin now?
Bot, quhairto sould I speir at yow,
    I think thay baith ar haill.

Gude morrow, Maister, be the Mes!

REX HUMANITAS.

Welcum, my minyeon, Wantonnes,
How hes thow speid, in thy travell?

WANTONNES.

Rycht weill, be Him that herryit hell:
    Your erand is weill done.

REX HUMANITAS.

Then, Wantonnes, how weill is mee,
Thow hes deservit baith meit, and fie, 480
    Be him that maid the Mone:
Thare is ane thing that I wald speir,

Quhat sall I do quhen scho cums heir!
For I knaw nocht the craft perqueir
   Of lufferis gyn:
Thairfoir, at lenth, ye mon me leir,
   How to begin.

WANTONNES.

To kis hir, and clap hir, Sir, be not affeard,
Scho will not schrink, thocht ye kis hir, ane span
   within the baird: [490
Gif ye think, that scho thinks shame, then hyd the
   bairns eine,
With hir taill, and tent hir weill, ye wait quhat I meine.
Will ye leif me, Sir, first for to go to,
And I sall leirne yow all kewis how to do.

REX HUMANITAS.

God forbid, Wantonnes, that I gif thé leife;
Thou art ouer perillous ane page, sic practiks to preife.

WANTONNES.

Now, Sir, preife as ye pleis: I se hir cumand,
Use yourself gravelie, wee sall by yow stand.

[*Heir sall Sensualitie cum to the King, and say.*]

SENSUALITIE.

O Queene Venus! unto thy celsitude,   500
   I gif gloir, honour, laud, and reverence,
Quha grantit me sic perfite pulchritude,
   That Princes of my persone have pleasance.

I mak ane vow, with humbill observance,
Richt reverentlie thy tempill to visie
With sacrifice unto thy dyosie.
Till everie stait I am so greabill,
    That few or nane refuses me at all;
Paipis, patriarks, or prelats venerabill,
    Common pepill, and princes temporall,   510
    Ar subject all to me Dame Sensuall :
Sa sall it be ay quhill the warld indures,
And speciallie quhair youthage hes the cures.
        Quha knawis the contrair?
    I traist few in this companie.
    Wald thay declair the veritie,
    How thay use Sensualitie,
        Bot with me maks repair.
    And now my way I man avance,
    Unto ane Prince of great puissance,   520
    Quhom young men hes in governance,
        Rolland into his rage :
    I am richt glaid, I yow assure,
    That potent Prince to get in cure ;
    Quhilk is of lustines the luir,
        And greitest of curage.

      [*Heir sall scho mak reverence, and say
               to the King.*]

O potent Prince, of pulchritude preclair,
    God Cupido, preserve your celsitude !
And Dame Venus mot keip your Court from cair ;
    As I wald scho suld keip my awin hart-blud.   530

REX HUMANITAS.

Welcum to me peirles in pulchritude ;
  Welcum to me thow sweiter nor the lamber,
Quhilk hes maid me of all dolour denude.
  Solace, convoy this Ladie to my chamber.

[Heir sall scho pass to the chalmer, and say,]

SENSUALITIE.

I gang this gait with richt gude will ;
Sir Wantonnes, tarie ye still,
And Hamelines the cap yeis fill,
  And beir him cumpanie.

[HAMELINES.]

That sall I do, withoutin dout,
And he, and I sall play cap out.   540

WANTONNES.

Now, Ladie, len me that batye tout ;
  Fill in for I am dry.
  Your Dame, be this trewlie,
Hes gotten upon the gumis ;
  Quhat rak thocht ye, and I,
Go junne our justing lumis.

HAMELINES.

Content I am, with gude will,
  Quhenever ye ar reddie,
  Your pleasure to fulfill.

WANTONNES.

Now, weill said, be our Ladie;   550
 I'le bair my maister cumpanie,
  Till that I may indure :
 Gif ye be quhisland wantounlie,
  We sall fling on the flure.

[*Heir sall thay pass all to the chalmer; and Gude Counsall sall say:*]

GUDE COUNSALL.

Immortall God ! maist of magnificence,
 Quhais Majestie na clark can comprehend :
Must save yow all that givis sic audience,
 And grant yow grace Him never till offend,
 Quhilk on the Croce did willinglie ascend,
And sched his pretious blude, on everie side : 560
 Quhais pitious passioun from danger yow defend,
And be your gratious governour, and gyde.

Now my gude friendis considder, I yow beseik,
 The caus maist principall of my cumming,
Princes, or potestatis, ar nocht worth ane leik,
 Be thay not gydit, be my gude governing;
 Thair was never Empriour, Conquerour, nor King,
Without my wisdome, that micht thair wil avance,
 My name is GUDE COUNSALL, without feinzeing,
Lords, for lack of my lair, ar brocht to mischance. 570

 Finallie, for conclusioun,
 Quha haldis me at delusioun

Sall be brocht to confusioun:
    And this I understand,
For I have maid my residence,
With hie Princes of greit puissance,
In Ingland, Italie, and France,
    And monie uther land.
Bot, out of Scotland, wa, alace!
I haif bene fleimit lang tyme space,   580
That garris our gyders all want grace,
    And die, befoir thair day;
Becaus thay lichtlyit Gude Counsall,
Fortune turnit on thame hir saill,
Quhilk brocht this Realme to meikill baill,
    Quha can the contrair say!
My Lords, I came nocht heir to lie:
Wais me! for King Humanitie,
Overset with Sensualitie,
    In th' entrie of his ring.   590
Throw vicious counsell insolent,
Sa thay may get riches, or rent,
To his weilfair thay tak na tent,
    Nor quhat sal be th' ending.
Yit, in this Realme, I wald mak sum repair,
Gif I beleifit my name suld nocht forfair,
For wald this King be gydit yit with ressoun,
And on misdoars mak punitioun:
Howbeit, I haif lang tyme bene exyllit,
I traist in God my name suld yit be styllit: 600
Sa till I se God send mair of his grace,
I purpois till repois me in this place.

[*How enteris Flatterie, new landit out of France; and stormesteid at the May.*]

FLATTERIE.

Mak roume, sirs, hoaw! that I may rin,
Lo se quhair I am new cum [in],
   Begaryit all with sindrie hewis:
Let be your din, till I begin,
   And I sall schaw yow of my newis.
Throuchout all Christindome I have past,
And am cum heir now at the last,
   Tostit on sea, ay sen Yuill day:
That wee war faine to hew our mast,   610
   Nocht half ane myle beyond the May.
Bot, now amang yow, I will remaine,
I purpois never to sail againe;
   To put my lyfe, in chance of watter:
Was never sene sic wind, and raine,
   Nor of schipmen sic clitter clatter:
Sum bade haill, and some bade stand by,
On steirburd, hoaw! aluiff! fy! fy!
   Quhill all the raipis beguith to rattil:
Was never Roy sa fleyd as I,   620
   Quhen all the sails playd brittill brattill.
To see the wavis it was ane wonder,
And wind that raif the sails in sunder,
   Bot, I lay braikand like ane brok:
And shot sa fast above, and under,
   The Devill durst not cum neir my dok.

Now, am I scapit fra that effray,
Quhat say ye, Sirs; am I nocht gay?
 Se ye not, Flatterie, your awin fuill,
That yeid to mak this new array,   630
 Was I not heir with yow at Yuill?
Yes, be my faith, I think on weill.
Quhair ar my fallows that wald nocht faill?
 We suld have cum heir for ane cast.
Hoaw! Falset, hoaw!

FALSET.

   Wa sair the Devill!
Quha is that, that cryis for me sa fast?

FLATTERIE.

Quhy Falset, brother knawis thou not me?
Am I nocht thy brother Flattrie?

FALSET.

Now, welcome, be the Trinitie,   640
 This meitting cums for gude:
Now, let me bresse thé in my armis,
Quhen freinds meits hartis warmis,
 Quod Jok, that frelie fude.
How happinit yow into this place?

FLATTERIE.

Now, be my saul, evin on a cace,
I come in sleipand at the port,
Or ever I wist, amang this sort.
Quhair is Dissait, that limmer loun?

FALSET.

I left him drinkand in the Toun: 650
He will be heir incontinent.

FLATTERIE.

Now, be the haly Sacrament,
That tydingis comforts all my hart:
I wait Dissait will tak my part.
He is richt craftie, as ye ken,
And counsallour to the Merchandmen:
Let us ly doun heir baith, and spy,
Gif wee persave him cummand by.

[*Heir sall Dissait entir.*]

DISSAIT.

Stand by the gait, that I may steir,
I say, Koks bons! how cam I heir? 660
I can not mis, to tak sum feir,
    Into sa greit ane thrang:
Marie! heir ane cumlie congregatioun,
Quhat ar ye, sirs, all of ane natioun?
Maisters, I speik be protestatioun,
    In dreid ye tak me wrang.
Ken ye nocht, sirs, quhat is my name?
Gude faith! I dar nocht schaw it for schame:
Sen I was clekit of my dame,
    Yit was I never leill; 670
For, Katie unsell was my mother,
And Common Theif my father brother;

Of sic freindship I had ane fither,
    Howbeit I can not steill.
Bot yit, I will borrow, and len,
As be my cleathing ye may ken,
That I am cum of nobill men;
    And als I will debait,
That querrell with my feit, and hands:
And I dwell amang the merchands,   680
My name, gif onie man demands,
    Thay call me Dissait.
Bon jour! brother, with all my hart!
Heir I am cum to tak your part.
    Baith into gude, and evill:
I met Gude Counsall be the way,
Quha pat me in ane felloun fray,
    I gif him to the Devill!

FALSET.

How chaipit ye, I pray yow tell?

DISSAIT.

I slipit into ane bordell,   690
And hid me in ane bawburds bed;
Bot, suddenlie hir schankis I sched,
With hoch hurland amang hir howis,
God wait, gif wee maid monie mowis.
How came ye heir, pray yow tell me!

FALSET.

Marie! to seik King Humanitie.

DISSAIT.

Now, be the gude ladie, that me bair,
That samin hors is my awin mair.
Now, with our purpois, let us mell.
Quhat is your counsall, I pray yow tell? 700
Sen we thrie seiks yon nobill King,
Let us devyse sum subtill thing:
And als I pray yow, as my brother,
That we ilk ane be trew to uther.
I mak ane vow, with all my hart,
In gude, and evill to tak your part.
I pray to God, nor I be hangit,
Bot I sall die, or ye be wrangit.

FALSET.

Quhat is my counsall that wee do?
Marie! Sirs, this is my counsall lo, 710
Till tak our tyme, quhill wee may get it,
For now thair is na man to let it;
Fra tyme, the King begin to steir him,
Marie! Gude Counsall, I dreid cum neir him,
And be wee knawin with Correctioun,
It will be our confusioun:
Thairfoir, my deir brother, devyse,
To find sum toy of the new gyse.

FLATTERIE.

Marie! I sall finde ane thousand wyles,
Wee man turne our claithis, and change our styles:
And disagyse us that na man ken us: [720

Hes na man Clarkis cleathing to len us?
And let us keip grave countenance,
As wee war new cum out of France.

DISSAIT.

Now, be my saull! that is weill devysit,
Ye sall se me sone disagysit.

FALSET.

And sa sall I man, be the Rude!
Now sum gude fallow len me ane hude.

[*Heir sall Flatterie help his twa marrowis.*]

DISSAIT.

Now, am I buskit, and quha can spy,
The Devill stik me, gif this be I!   730
If this be I, or not, I can not weill say;
Or hes the Feind, or Farie folk, borne me away.

FALSET.

And gif my hair war up in ane how,
The feind ane man wald ken me, I trow.
Quhat sayis thou of my gay garmoun?

DISSAIT.

I say, thou luiks evin like ane loun.
Now, brother Flatterie, quhat do ye,
Quhat kynde of man schaip ye to be?

FLATTERIE.

Now be my faith! my brother deir,
I will gang counterfit the Freir.   740

DISSAIT.

A Freir! quhairto? ye can not preiche!

FLATTERIE.

Quhat rak, bot I can richt weill fleich!
Perchance I'le cum to that honour,
To be the Kings Confessour.
Pure Freirs ar free at any feist,
And marchellit ay amang the best.

Als God hes lent to them sic graces,
That Bischops puts them in thair places,
Out-throw thair dioceis to preich,
Bot ferlie nocht howbeit thay fleich: 750
For schaw thay all the veritie,
Thai'll want the Bischops charitie.
And thocht the corne war never sa skant,
The gudewyfis will not let Freiris want:
For quhy, thay ar thair confessours,
Thair heavinlie prudent counsalours:
Thairfor the wyfis plainlie taks thair parts,
And schawis the secreits of thair harts
To Freirs, with better will, I trow,
Nor thay do to thair bed-fallow.   760

DISSAIT.

And I reft anis ane Freirs coull,
Betwixt Sanct Johnestoun, and Kinnoull:
I sall gang fetch it, gif ye will tarie.

FLATTERIE.

Now play me that of companarie:
Ye saw him nocht, this hundreth yeir,
That better can counterfeit the Freir.

DISSAIT.

Heir is thy gaining, all and sum,
This is ane koull of Tullilum.

FLATTERIE.

Quha hes ane portouns for to len me?
The feind ane saull, I trow, will ken me.   770

FALSET.

Now gang thy way quhairever thow will,
Thow may be fallow to freir Gill:
Bot, with Correctioun, gif wee be kend,
I dreid wee mak ane schamefull end.

FLATTERIE.

For that mater, I dreid nathing,
Freiris ar exemptit fra the King:
And Freiris will reddie entreis get,
Quhen Lords are haldin at the yet.

FALSET.

Wee man do mair yit, be Sanct James!
For wee mon all thrie change our names; 780
Hayif me, and I sall baptize thee.

DISSAIT.

Be God! and thair-about may it be.
How will thou call me, I pray thé tell?

FALSET.

I wait not how to call my sell.

DISSAIT.

Bot, yit anis name the bairns name!

FALSET.

Discretioun, Discretioun, in God's name!

DISSAIT.

I neid nocht now to cair for thrift,
Bot quhat sal be my God bairne gift?

FALSET.

I gif yow all the devillis of hell.

DISSAIT.

Na Brother, hauld that to thysell: 790
Now, sit doun, let me baptize thé,
I wait not quhat thy name sould be.

FALSET.
Bot, yit anis name the bairns name.

DISSAIT.
Sapience, in ane warlds-schame.

FLATTERIE.
Brother Dissait, cum baptize me.

DISSAIT.
Then sit doun lawlie on thy knè.

FLATTERIE.
Now, brother, name the bairns name.

DISSAIT.
Devotioun, in the Devillis name!

FLATTERIE.
The Devill resave thé, lurdoun loun!
Thow hes wet all my new schavin croun.   800

DISSAIT.
Devotioun, Sapience, and Discretioun,
Wee thrie may rewll this Regioun:
Wee sall find monie craftie things,
For to begyll ane hundreth kings;
For thow can richt weil crak, and clatter,
And I sall feinze, and thow sall flatter.

FLATTERIE.

Bot, I wald have, or wee depairtit,
Ane drink to mak us better hartit.

DISSAIT.

Weill said, be Him that herryit hell!
I was evin thinkand that mysell.　　　　　　　　810
Now, till we get the Kings presence,
Wee will sit doun, and keip silence.

[*Heir sall they drink; till the King sall cum furth of his chamber, and call for Wantonnes.*]

I se ane yonder, quhat ever he be,
I'le wod my lyfe, yon same is he.
Feir nocht Brother, bot hauld yow still,
Till wee have hard quhat is his will.

[*Heir the King has bene with his Concubyne, and thairefter returns to his young company.*]

REX HUMANITAS.

Now quhair is Placebo, and Solace?
Quhair is my minzeoun Wantonnes?
Wantonnes, hoaw! cum to me sone.

WANTONNES.

Quhy cryit ye, Sir, till I had done!　　　　　　　　820

REX HUMANITAS.

Quhat was ye doand, tell me that?

WANTONNES.

Mary! leirand how my father me gat.
I wait nocht how it stands, but doubt,
Me think the warld rinnis round about.

REX HUMANITAS.

And sa think I, man, be my thrift,
I se fyfteine Mones in the lift.

HAMELINES.

Gat ye nocht that, quhilk ye desyrit?
Sir, I beleif, that ye ar tyrit.

[WANTONNES.

Lat Hamelines my lass allane;　　　　　830
Scho bendyt up aye twa for ane.]

DANGER.

Bot, as for Placebo, and Solace,
I held them baith in mirriness.
[Howbeit I maid it sumthing teuch,
I fand thame chalmer glew aneweh.

SOLACE.

Mary! thow wald gar ane hundreth tyre,
Thow hes ane cunt lyk ane quaw myre.

DANGER.

Now fowll fall yow! it is na bourdis
Befoir the King to speik fowll wourdis:

Or evir ye cum that gate agane,
To kiss my claff ye sall be fane.] 840

SOLACE.

Now, schaw me, Sir, I yow exhort,
How ar ye of your luif content;
Think ye not this ane mirrie sport?

REX HUMANITAS.

Yea! that I do, in verament.
Quhat bairnis ar yon upon the bent?
I did nocht se them all this day.

WANTONNES.

Thay will be heir incontinent:
Stand still, and heir quhat thay will say.

[*Now the Vycis cums, and maks salutatioun to the King, saying,*]

DISSAIT.

Laud, honor, gloir, triumph, and victory,
Be to your maist excellent Majestie. 850

REX HUMANITAS.

Ye ar welcum, gude freinds, be the Rude!
Appeirandlie ye seime sum men of gude;
Quhat ar your names? tell me without delay.

DISSAIT.

Discretioun, Sir, is my name, perfay.

REX HUMANITAS.

Quhat is your name, Sir, with the clippit croun?

FLATTRIE.

But dout, my name is callit Devotioun.

REX HUMANITAS.

Welcum Devotioun, be Sanct Jame.
Now, sirray, tell quhat is your name?

FALSET.

Marie! Sir, thay call me, quhat call thay me,
[I wait not weill, but gif I lie!]   860

REX HUMANITAS.

Can ye nocht tell, quhat is your name.

FALSET.

I kend it, quhen I cam fra hame.

REX HUMANITAS.

Quhat gars ye can nocht schaw it now?

FALSET.

Marie! thay call me Thin Drink, I trow.

REX HUMANITAS.

Thin Drink! quhat kynde of name is that?

DISSAIT.

Sapiens, thow servis to beir ane plat:
Me think thow schawis thé not weill wittit.

FALSET.

Sypeins, Sir, Sypeins, Marie! now ye hit it.

FLATTRIE.

Sir, gif ye pleis to let him say,
His name is Sapientia.   870

FALSET.

That same is it, be Sanct Michell.

REX HUMANITAS.

Quhy could thou not tell it thy sell?

FALSET.

I pray your Grace appardoun me,
And I sall schaw the veritie:
I am sa full of Sapience,
That sumtyme, I will tak ane trance.
My spreit was reft fra my bodie,
Now heich abone the Trinitie.

REX HUMANITAS.

Sapience suld be ane man of gude.

FALSET.

Schir, ye may ken that be my hude.   880

REX HUMANITAS.

Now have I Sapience, and Discretioun ;
How can I faill, to rewll this Regioun ?
And Devotioun, to be my confessour,
Thir thrie came in ane happie hour.
Heir, I mak thé my Secretar ;
And thow salbe my Thesaurar ;
And thow salbe my Counsallour
In sprituall things, and Confessour.

FLATTRIE.

I sweir to yow, Sir, be Sanct An,
Ye met never with ane wyser man,   890
For monie a craft, Sir, do I can,
    War thay weill knawin :
Sir, I have na feill of flattrie,
Bot fosterit with philosophie,
Ane strange man in astronomie,
    Quhilk sal be schawin.

FALSET.

And I have greit intelligence,
In quelling of the quintessence ;
Bot to preif my experience,
    Sir, len me fourtie crownes,   900
To mak multiplicatioun,
And tak my obligatioun :
Gif wee mak fals narratioun,
    Hauld us for verie lownes.

DISSAIT.

Sir, I ken, be your physnomie,
Ye sall conqueis, or els I lie,
Danskin, Denmark, and Almane,
Spittelfeild, and the realme of Spane.
Ye sall have at your governance,
Ranfrow, and all the realme of France,   910
Yea, Rugland, and the toun of Rome,
Corstorphine, and all Christindome.
Quhairto, Sir, be the Trinitie,
Ye ar ane verie A per se.

FLATTRIE.

Sir, quhen I dwelt in Italie,
I leirit the craft of palmistrie,
Schaw me the lufe, Sir, of your hand,
And I sall gar yow understand,
Gif your Grace be infortunat,
Or gif ye be predestinat.   920
I see ye will haif fyfteine Queenes,
And fyfteine scoir of concubeines:
The Virgin Marie saife your Grace!
Saw ever man sa quhyte ane face,
Sa greit ane arme, sa fair ane hand,
Thair's nocht sic ane leg in al this land,
War ye in armis, I think na wonder,
Howbeit, ye dang doun fyfteine hunder.

DISSAIT.

Now, be my saull, that's trew thow sayis,

Wes never man set sa weill his clais :	930
Thair is na man in Christintie,
Sa meit to be ane King as ye.

FALSET.

Sir, thank the Haly Trinitie,
That send us to your cumpanie :
For, God, nor I gaip in ane gallows,
Gif ever.ye fand thrie better fallows.

REX HUMANITAS.

Ye ar richt welcum, be the Rude !
Ye seime to be thrie men of gude.

[*Heir sall Gude Counsell schaw himself in the feild.*

Bot, quha is yon, that stands sa still ?
Ga spy, and speir quhat is his will :	940
And, gif he yearnis my presence,
Bring him to mee, with diligence.

DISSAIT.

That sall wee do, be God's breid,
We's bring him eather quick, or deid.

REX HUMANITAS.

I will sit still heir, and repois :
Speid yow agane to me, my jois.

FALSET.

Ye, hardlie, Sir, keip yow in clois

And quyet, till wee cum againe.
Brother, I trow, be Coks toes!
Yon bairdit bogill cums fra ane traine.   950

DISSAIT.

Gif he dois sa, he salbe slaine,
　I doubt him nocht, nor yit ane uther:
Trowit I that he come for ane traine,
　Of my friendis, I sould rais ane futher.

FLATTRIE.

I doubt full sair, be God him sell!
That yon auld churle be Gude Counsell:
Get he anis to the King's presence,
We thrie will get na audience.

DISSAIT.

That matter, I sall tak on hand,
And say, it is the King's command,   960
That he anone devoyd this place,
And cum nocht neir the King's grace;
And that under the paine of tressoun.

FLATTRIE.

Brother, I hauld your counsell ressoun.
Now, let us heir quhat he will say:
Auld lyart beird, gude day, gude day!

GUDE COUNSELL.

Gude day againe, Sirs, be the Rude,
The Lord mot mak yow men of gude.

DISSAIT.

Pray nocht for us to Lord, nor Ladie,
For we ar men of gude alreadie.   970
Sir, schaw to us, quhat is your name?

GUDE COUNSELL.

Gude Counsell, thay call me at hame.

FALSET.

Quhat says thow, Carle, ar thow Gude Counsell?
Swyith! pak thé sone, unhappie unsell,
Gif ever thou cum this gait againe,
I vow to God thou sall be slaine.

GUDE COUNSELL.

I pray yow, Sirs, gif me licence,
To cum anis to the King's presence:
To speik bot twa words to his Grace.

FLATTRIE.

Swyith! hursone Carle, devoyd this place.   980

GUDE COUNSELL.

Brother, I ken yow weill aneuch,
Howbeit ye mak it never sa teuch:
Flattrie, Dissait, and Fals Report,
That will not suffer to resort
Gude Counsall to the King's presence.

DISSAIT.

Swyith! hursone Carle, gang pak thé hence:

Gif ever thou cum this gait agane,
I vow to God thou sall be slane!

[*Heir sall thay hurle away Gude Counsall.*

[GUDE COUNSALL.]

Sen, at this tyme, I can get na presence,
Is na remeid bot tak in patience: 990
Howbeit Gude Counsell haistelie be nocht hard,
With young Princes, yit sould thay nocht be skard:
Bot, quhen youthheid hes blawin his wanton blast,
Then sall Gude Counsell rewll him at the last.

[*Now the Vycis gangs to ane counsall.*

FLATTRIE.

Now quhill Gude Counsall is absent,
Brother, wee mon be diligent:
And mak betwix us sikker bands,
Quhen vacauds fallis in onie lands;
That everie man help weill his fallow.

DISSAIT.

I hauld, deir brother, be Alhallow! 1000
Sa, ye fische nocht within our bounds.

FLATTRIE.

That sall I nocht, be God's wounds!
Bot, I sall plainlie tak your partis.

FALSET.

Sa, sall wee thyne, with all our hartis.

Bot, haist us, quhill the King is young,
Lat everie man keip weill ane toung;
And, in ilk quarter have ane spy,
Us till adverteis haistelly,
Quhen ony casualities
Sall happin into our countries;　　　　　　　　1010
And lat us mak provisioun,
Or he cum to discretioun:
Na mair he waits now, nor ane Saut,
Quhat thing it is to haif, or want.
Or he cum till his perfyte age,
We sall be sikker of our wage:
And then, lat everie carle craif uther.

DISSAIT.

That mouth speik mair, my awin dear brother;
For God, nor I rax in ane raip!
Thow may gif counsall to the Paip.　　　　　　　1020

   [*Now thay returne to the King.*

REX HUMANITAS.

Quhat gart you byde sa lang fra my presence?
I think it lang since ye depairtit thence.
Quhat man was yon, with an greit bostous beird;
Me thocht he maid yow all thrie very feard.

DISSAIT.

It was ane laidlie lurdan loun,
Cumde to break buithis into this toun:
Wee have gart bind him with ane poill,
And send him to the theifis hoill.

REX HUMANITAS.

Let him sit thair with ane mischance ;
And let us go to our pastance.   1030

WANTONNES.

Better go revell at the rackat,
Or ellis go to the hurlie hackat ;
Or then, to schaw our curtlie corsses,
Ga se, quha best can rin thair horsses.

SOLACE.

Na, Soveraine, or wee farther gang,
Gar Sensualitie sing ane sang.

> [*Heir sall the Ladies sing ane sang, the King
> sall ly doun amang the Ladies, and then
> Veritie sall enter.*

VERITIE.

Diligite justitiam qui judicatis terram.
Luif justice, ye quha hes ane judges cure,
   In earth, and dreid the awfull judgement
Of Him, that sall cum judge baith rich and pure,
   Rycht terribilly, with bludy woundis rent.   1040
   That dreidfull day into your harts imprent :
Belevand weill how, and quhat maner, ye
   Use justice heir til uthers, thair at lenth
That day, but doubt, sa sall ye judgit be.

Wo than, and duill, be to yow Princes all !
   Sufferand the pure anes, for till be opprest :

In everlasting burnand fyre, ye sall,
  With Lucifer, richt dulfullie be drest;
Thairfoir in tyme, for till eschaip that nest,
Feir God, do law, and justice equally   1050
  Till everie man; se that na puir opprest
Up to the Hevin, on yow ane vengence cry.

Be just judges, without favour or fead,
  And hauld the ballance evin till everie wicht;
Let not the fault be left into the head,
  Then sall the members reulit be at richt:
For quhy, subjects do follow, day and nicht,
Thair governours in vertew, and in vyce.
  Ye ar the lamps that sould schaw them the licht,
To leid thame on this sliddrie rone of yce.   1060

    Mobile mutatur semper cum Principe vulgus.
And gif ye wald your subjectis war weill gevin,
  Then verteouslie begin the dance your sell:
Going befoir; then they anone, I wein,
  Sal follow yow, eyther till hevin, or hell.
Kings sould of gude exempils be the well;
Bot, gif that your strands be intoxicate,
  Insteid of wyne, thay drink the poyson fell:
Thus pepill followis ay thair principate.

    Sic luceat lux vestra coram hominibus, ut videant
        opera vestra bona.
And, specially, ye Princes of the preists;
  That of peopill hes Spiritual cuir,   1070
Dayly ye sould revolve into your breistis,

How that thir haly words ar still maist sure,
  In verteous lyfe, gif that ye do indure,
The pepill wil tak mair tent to your deids,
  Then to your words, and als baith rich, and puir,
Will follow yow baith in your warks, and words.

    [*Heir sall Flattrie spy Veritie, with ane dum
      countenance.*

Gif men of me wald haif intelligence,
  Or knaw my name, thay call me Veritie:
Of Christis law I haif experience,
  And hes over saillit many stormie sey.   1080
  Now, am I seikand King Humanitie;
For, of his Grace, I have gude esperance,
  Fra tyme that he acquaintit be with mee,
His honour, and heich gloir, I sall avance.

    [*Heir sall Veritie pas to hir sait.*

DISSAIT.

Gude day, Father, quhair have ye bene?
  Declair till us of your novells.

FLATTRIE.

Thare is now lichtit on the grene,
  Dame Veritie, be buiks and bells.
Bot cum scho to the King's presence,
  Thair is na buit for us to byde;   1090
Tharfoir, I red us all go hence.

FALSET.

That will we nocht yit be Sanct Bryde,

Bot, wee sall ather gang, or ryde,
  To Lords of Spiritualitie ;
And gar them trow, yon bag of pryde,
  Hes spokin manifest heresie.

[*Heir thay cum to the Spiritualitie.*

FLATTRIE.

O reverent Fatheris of the Sprituall State,
  Wee counsall yow, be wyse, and vigilant :
Dame Veritie hes lychtit now of lait,   [1100
  And, in hir hand, beirand the New Testament :
Be scho ressavit, but dout, wee ar bot schent,
  Let hir nocht ludge, thairfoir, into this Land,
And this wee reid yow do incontinent,
Now, quhill the King is with his luif sleipand.

SPIRITUALITIE.

Wee thank yow, Freindis, of your benevolence :
  It sall be done evin as ye haif devysit ;
Wee think ye serve ane gudlie recompence,
  Defendand us, that wee be nocht supprysit.
  In this mater, wee man be weill avysit,
Now, quhill the King misknawis the Veritie :   1110
  Be scho ressavit, then wee will be deprysit ;
Quhat is your counsell, Brother, now let se ?

ABBOT.

I hauld it best, that wee incontinent,
  Gar hauld hir fast into captivitie,
Untill the thrid day of the Parlament :
  And then, accuse hir of hir heresie ;

Or than banische hir out of this cuntrie;
For, with the King, gif Veritie be knawin,
  Of our greit gloir we will degradit be,
And all our secreits to the commouns schawin.   1120

PERSONE.

Ye se the King is yit effeminate,
  And gydit be Dame Sensualitie,
Richt sa with young counsall intoxicate;
  Swa at this tyme ye haif your libertie,
  To tak your tyme, I hauld it best for me,
And go distroy all thir Lutherians;
  In speciall, yon ladie Veritie.

SPIRITUALITIE.

Schir Persone, ye sall be my commissair,
  To put this matter till executioun;
And ye, Sir Freir, becaus ye can declair   1130
  The haill processe, pas with him in commissioun;
  Pas all togidder, with my braid bennisoun,
And gif scho speiks against our libertie,
  Then, put hir in perpetuall presoun,
That scho cum nocht to King Humanitie.

  [*Heir sall thay pas to Veritie.*

PERSONE.

Lustie Ladie, we wald faine understand
  Quhat earand ye haif in this Regioun?
To preich, or teich, quha gaif to yow command;
  To counsall kingis, how gat ye commissioun?
  I dreid, without ye get ane remissioun,   1140

And syne renunce your New Opiniones,
  The Sprituall Stait sall put yow to perditioun;
And, in the fyre, will burne yow flescho and bones.

VERITIE.

I will recant nathing that I have schawin,
  I have said nathing bot the veritie;
Bot, with the King, fra tyme that I be knawin,
  I dreid, ye spaiks of Sprituralitie
  Sall rew, that ever I came in this cuntrie:
For, gif the veritie plainlie war proclamit,
  And speciallie to the King's Majestie, 1150
For your traditions ye wilbe all defamit.

FLATTRIE.

Quhat buik is that, harlot, into thy hand?
  Out, walloway! this is the New Test'ment,
In Englisch toung, and printit in England:
  Herisie, herisie! fire, fire! incontinent.

VERITIE.

Forsuith, my friend, ye have ane wrang judgement,
For, in this Buik, thair is na heresie:
  Bot our Christ's word, baith dulce and redolent,
Ane springing well of sinceir veritie.

DISSAIT.

Cum on your way, for all your yealow locks, 1160
  Your wantoun words, but doubt ye sall repent:
This nicht ye sall forfair ane pair of stocks,
  And syne the morne be brocht to thoill judgement.

VERITIE.

For our Christ's saik, I am richt weill content
To suffer all thing that sall pleis his Grace,
  Howbeit, ye put ane thousand till torment,
Ten hundreth thowsand sall ryse into thair place.

    [*Veritie sits down on hir knies, and sayis;*

Get up, thow sleipis all too lang, O Lord!
  And mak sum ressonabill reformatioun,
On thame that dois tramp doun thy gracious
    word,   1170
  And hes ane deidlie indignatioun,
    At them, quha maks maist trew narratioun:
Suffer me not, Lord, mair to be molest,
  Gude Lord, I mak thé supplicatioun,
With thy unfriends let me nocht be supprest.

    Now, Lordis, do as ye list,
      I have na mair to say.

FLATTRIE.

Sit doun, and tak yow rest,
  All nicht till it be day.

    [*Thay put Veritie in the stocks and returne to
      Spiritualitie.*

DISSAIT.

My Lord, wee have, with diligence,   1180
  Bucklit up weill yon bledrand baird.

SPIRITUALITIE.

I think ye serve gude recompence :
  Tak thir ten crowns, for your rewaird.

VERITIE.

The Prophesie of the Propheit Esay
Is practickit, alace ! on mee this day ;
Quha said, the Veritie sould be trampit doun
Amid the streit, and put in strang presoun :
His fyve and fyftie chapter, quha list luik,
Sall find thir wordis, writtin in his buik.
Richt sa, Sanct Paull wrytis to Timothie,   1190
That men sall turne thair earis from veritie.
Bot in my Lord God, I have esperance,
He will provide for my deliverance.
Bot, ye Princes of Spiritualitie,
Quha sould defend the sinceir veritie,
I dreid the plagues of Johnes Revelatioun
Sall fall upon your generatioun.
I counsall yow this misse to amend.
Sa that ye may eschaip that fatall end.

    [Heir sall Chastitie entir, and say,]

CHASTITIE.

How lang sall this inconstant warld indure,   1200
  That I sould bancist be, sa lang, alace !
Few creatures, or nane, takis on me cure,
  Quhilk gars me monie nicht ly harbrieles,
  Thocht I have past all yeir, fra place to place,

Amang the Temporall, and Spirituall Staits;
   Nor, amang Princes, I can get na grace:
Bot, boustuouslie am halden at the yetis.

DILIGENCE.

Ladie, I pray yow schaw me your name,
   It dois me noy your lamentatioun.

CHASTITIE.

My freind, thairof I neid not to think shame,   1210
   Dame Chastitie, baneist from town to town.

DILIGENCE.

   Then, pas to Ladeis of Religioun,
Quhilk maks thair vow, to observe chastitie;
   Lo! quhair thair sits ane Priores of renown,
Amangs the rest of Spiritualitie.

CHASTITIE.

I grant, yon Ladie hes vowit chastitie,
   For hir professioun thairto sould accord:
Scho maid that vow, for ane Abesie,
   Bot nocht for Christ Jesus, our Lord.   [1220
   Fra tyme, that thay get thair vows, I stand for'd,
Thay banische hir out of thair companie;
   With Chastitie, thay can mak na concord,
Bot leids thair lyfis in sensualitie.
   I sall observe your counsall, gif I may,
Cum on, and heir quhat yon Ladie will say?

    [*Chastitie passis to the Ladie Priores, and sayis,*

My prudent, lustic Ladie Priores,
    Remember how ye did vow chastitie :
Madame, I pray yow of your gentilnes,
    That ye wald pleis to haif of me pitie,
    And, this ane nicht, to gif me harberie ;   1230
For this I mak yow supplicatioun,
    Do ye nocht sa, Madame, I dreid perdie,
It will be caus of depravatioun.

PRIORES.

Pas hynd, Madame, be Christ, ye cum nocht heir,
    Ye ar contrair to my complexioun :
Gang seik ludging at sum auld monk, or freir,
    Perchance, thay will be your protectioun ;
    Or to Prelats, mak your progressioun,
Quhilks ar obleist to yow, als weill as I :
    Dame Sensuall hes gevin directioun,   1240
Yow till exclude out of my cumpany.

CHASTITIE.

Gif ye wald wit mair of the veritie,
    I sall schaw yow, be sure experience,
How that the Lords of Spiritualitie
    Hes baneist me, alace ! fra thair presence.

[Chastitie passis to the Lords of Spiritualitie.

My Lords ! laud, gloir, triumph, and reverence,
    Mot be unto your halie Sprituall Stait :
I yow beseik, of your benevolence,

To harbry mee, that am sa desolait.
Lords, I have past throw mony uncouth schyre, 1250
  Bot in this Land, I can get na ludgeing:
  Of my name, gif ye wald haif knawledging,
Forsuith, my Lords, they call me Chastitie:
  I yow besoik, of your graces bening,
Gif me ludging this nicht for charitie?

SPIRITUALITIE.

Pas on, Madame, we knaw yow nocht,
Or, be Him that the warld wrocht,
Your cumming sall be richt deir coft,
    Gif ye mak langer tarie.

ABBOT.

But dout, wee will baith leif and die,   1260
With our luif Sensualitie,
Wee will haif na mair deall with thee,
    Then with the Queene of Farie.

PERSONE.

Pas hame amang the Nunnis, and dwell,
Quhilks ar of chastitie the well:
I traist thay will, with buik and bell,
    Ressave yow in thair closter.

CHASTITIE.

Sir, quhen I was the Nunnis amang,
Out of thair dortour thay mee dang,
And wald nocht let me bide sa lang,   1270
    To say my Pater Noster.

I se na grace, thairfoir to get,
I hauld it best, or it be lait,
For till go prove the Temporall Stait,
    Gif thay will mee ressaif.

Gud-day, my lord Temporalitie,
And yow merchant of gravitie,
Ful faine wald I haif harberie,
    To ludge amang the laif.

TEMPORALITIE.

Forsuith, wee wald be weil content,   1280
To harbrie yow with gude intent,
War nocht, we haif impediment
    For quhy, we twa ar maryit
Bot wist our wyfis that ye war heir,
Thay wald mak all this town on steir,
Thairfoir, we reid yow rin areir,
    In dreid ye be miscaryit.

[THE FIRST INTERLUDE.]

[*Heir sall Dame Chastitie pas, and seik luging athort all the Spirituall Estait, and Temporall Estait, quhill scho cum to the Sowttar, and Tailyeour, and say:*]

CHASTITIE.

Ye men of craft of greit ingyne,
Gif me harbrie, for Christis pyne,

And win God's bennesone and myne,   1290
    And help my hungrie hart.

SOWTAR.

Welcum, be him that maid the Mone,
Till dwell with us, till it be June :
We sall mend baith your hois and schone,
    And plainlie tak your part.

TAYLOUR.

Is this fair ladie Chastitie ?
Now, welcum, be the Trinitie :
I think it war ane great pitie,
    That thou sould ly thair out :
Your great displesour, I forthink,   1300
Sit doun, Madame, and tak ane drink ;
And let na sorrow in yow sink,
    Bot let us play cap'out.

SOWTAR.

Fill in, and play cap'out,
    For, I am wonder dry :
The Devill snyp aff thair snout,
    That haits this company.

[*Heir sall thay gar Chastitie sit doun and drink.*]

JENNIE.

Hoaw ! mynnie, mynnie, mynnie !

TAYLOUR'S WYFE.

Quhat wald thow, my deir dochter, Jennie ?

Jennie, my joy, quhair is thy dadie? 1310

JENNIE.

Mary, drinkand with ane lustic Ladie,
Ane fair young mayden cled in quhyte,
Of quhom my dadie taks delyte,
Scho hes the fairest forme of face,
Furnischit with all kynd of grace:
I traist gif I can reckon richt,
Scho schaips to ludge with him all nicht.

SOWTAR'S WYFE.

Quhat dois the Sowtar, my gudman?

JENNIE.

Mary, fillis the cap and turnes the can,
Or he cum hame, be God, I trow, 1320
He will be drunkin lyke ane sow.

TAYLOUR'S WYFE.

This is ane greit dispyte, I think,
For to resave sic ane kow-clink:
Quhat is your counsell, that wee do?

SOWTAR'S WYFE.

Cummer, this is my counsall, lo!
Ding ye the tane, and I the uther.

TAYLOUR'S WYFE.

I am content, be God's Mother,
I think for mee thay huirsone smaiks;

Thay serve richt weill, to get thair paiks.
Quhat maister feind neids all this haist ? 1330
For, it is half ane yeir almaist,
Sen ever that loun laborde my ledder.

SOWTAR'S WYFE.

God, nor my trewker mence ane tedder,
For, it is mair nor fourtie dayis
Sen ever he cleikit up my clayis :
And last quhen I gat chalmer glew,
That foull Sowter began till spew.
And now thay will sit doun, and drink,
In company, with ane kow-clink,
Gif thay haif done us this dispyte, 1340
Let us go ding thame till thay dryte.

[*Heir the Wyfis shall chase away Chastitie.*

TAYLOURS WYFE.

Go hence, harlot, how durst thow be sa bauld,
  To ludge with our gudemen, but our licence :
I mak ane vow to Him that Judas sauld,
  This rock of myne sall be thy recompence.
  Schaw me thy name, dudroun, with diligence ?

CHASTITIE.

Marie, Chastitie is my name, be Sanct Blais.

TAYLOURS WYFE.

I pray God, nor he work on thee vengence ;
For I luifit never Chastitie all my dayes.

SOWTAR'S WYFE.

Bot, my gudeman, the treuth I sall thé tell,   1350
Gars me keip chastitie sair aganis my will :
Becaus that monstour hes maid sic ane mint,
With my bedstaf, that dastard beirs ane dint.
And als I vow, cum thow this gait againe,
Thy buttoks sal be beltit, be Sanct Blaine.

   [*Heir sall thay speik to thair Gudemen, and ding them.*

TAYLOUR'S WYFE.

Fals horson carle, but dout thou sall forthink,
That ever thow eat or drink with yon kow-clink.

SOWTAR'S WYFE.

I mak ane vow to Sanct Crispine,
Ise be revengit on that graceles grume :
And to begin the play, tak thair ane flap.   1360

SOWTAR.

The Feind ressave the hands that gaif mee that.

SOWTAR'S WYFE.

Quhat now, huirsun, begins thow for till ban ?
Tak thair ane uther upon thy peil'd harne pan.
Quhat now, cummer, will thow nocht tak my part ?

TAYLOUR'S WYFE.

That sal I do, cummer, with all my hart.

[*Heir sall thay ding thair Gudemen, with silence.*

TAYLOUR.

Alace! gossop, alace! how stands with yow?
Yon cankart carling, alace! hes brokin my brow.
Now, weill's yow preistis, now weill's yow all your lyfes,
That ar nocht weddit with sic wickit wyfes.

SOWTAR.

Bischops ye ar blist, howbeit that thay be waryit, 1370
For, thay may fuck thair fill, and be unmaryit.
Gossop, alace, that blak band we may wary,
That ordanit sic puir men as us to mary.
Quhat may be done bot tak in patience?
And on all wyfis we'ill cry ane loud vengence.

[*Heir sall the Wyfis stand be the watter syde, and say,*

SOWTAR'S WYFE.

Sen, of our Cairls, we have the victorie,
Quhat is your counsell, cummer, that be done?

TAYLOUR'S WYFE.

Send for gude wine, and hald our selfis merie,
I hauld this ay best, cummer, be Sanct Clone.

SOWTAR'S WYFE.

Cummer, will ye draw aff my hois, and schone, 1380
To fill the quart, I sall rin to the toun.

TAYLOUR'S WYFE.

That sal I do, be him that made the Mone,
With all my hart, thairfoir, cummer sit doun.
    Kilt up your claithis, abone your waist,
    And speid yow hame againe in haist,
    And I sall provyde for ane paist,
        Our corsses to comfort.

SOWTAR'S WYFE.

Then help me, for to kilt my clais,
Quhat gif the padoks nip my tais,
I dreid to droun heir, be Sanct Blais,   1390
    Without I get support.

    [*Scho lifts up hir clais above hir waist, and
    enters in the water.*

Cummer, I will nocht droun my sell ;
    Go East about the Nether mill.

TAYLOUR'S WYFE.

I am content, be Bryd's bell,
    To gang with yow, quhair ever ye will.

    [*Heir sall thay depairt, and pas to the palzeoun.*

DILIGENCE *to* CHASTITIE.

Madame, quhat gars yow gang sa lait?
Tell me, how ye have done debait,
With the Temporall, and Spirituall Stait ;
    Quha did yow maist kyndnes?

CHASTITIE.

In faith, I fand bot ill, and war ;   1400
Thay gart mee stand fra thame askar,
Evin lyk ane begger, at the bar,
    And fleimit mair and lesse.

DILIGENCE.

I counsall yow, but tarying,
Gang tell Humanitie, the King,
Perchance, hee of his grace bening,
    Will mak to yow support.

CHASTITIE.

Of your counsell, I am content,
To pas to him incontinent,
And my service till him present,   1410
    In hope of sum comfort.

[*Heir sall thay pass to the King.*

[END OF THE INTERLUDE.]

DILIGENCE.

Hoaw! Solace, gentil Solace declair unto the King,
   How thair is heir ane Ladie fair of face,
That in this cuntrie can get na ludging,
   Bot pitifullie flemit from place to place,
   Without the King, of his speciall grace,
As ane sarvand, hir in his Court ressaif.
   Brother Solace, tell the King all the cace,
That scho may be resavit amang the laif.

SOLACE.

Soverane, get up, and se ane hevenlie sicht;   1420
   Ane fair Ladie, in quhyt abuilzement:
Scho may be peir unto ane king or knicht,
   Most lyk ane angell, be my judgment.

REX HUMANITAS.

I sall gang se that sicht, incontinent:
Madame, behauld, gif ye have knawledging
   Of yon Ladie, or quhat is hir intent;
Thairefter, wee sall turne but tarying.

SENSUALITIE.

Sir, let me se quhat you mater may meine,
   Perchance, that I may knaw hir be hir face:
But doubt, this is Dame Chastitie, I weine;   1430
   Sir, I and scho cannot byde in ane place,
   But, gif it be the pleasour of your Grace,
That I remaine, into your cumpany,
   This woman richt haistelie gar chace,
That scho na mair be sene in this cuntrie.

REX HUMANITAS.

As ever ye pleis, Sweit hart, sa sall it be;
   Dispone hir, as ye think expedient:
Evin as ye list, to let hir live or die,
   I will refer that thing to your judgement.

SENSUALITIE.

I will that scho be flemit incontinent,   1440

And never to cum againe in this cuntrie :
  And gif scho dois, but doubt scho sall repent,
As als perchance, a duilfull deid sall die.

Pas on, sir Sapience, and Discretioun,
  And banische hir out of the King's presence.

DISSAIT.

That sall we do, Madame, be God's passioun,
  Wee sall do your command with diligence ;
  And at your hand, serve gudely recompence :
Dame Chastitie, cum on, be not agast ;
  Wee sall rycht sone upon your awin expence, 1450
Into the stocks your bony fute mak fast.

    [*Heir sall thay harll Chastitie to the stocks,
      and scho sall say,*

  I pray yow, Sirs, be patient,
  For I sall be obedient
    Till do quhat ye command ;
  Sen I se thair is na remeid.
  Howbeit, it war to suffer deid,
    Or flemit furth of the land.
  I wyte the Empreour Constantine,
  That I am put to sic ruine,
    And baneist from the Kirk : 1460
  For, sen he maid the Paip ane King,
  In Rome I could get na ludging ;
    Bot, heidlangs, in the mirk.
  Bot Ladie Sensualitie,

Sensyne hes gydit this cuntrie,
    And monie of the rest:
And now, scho reulis all this land,
And hes decryit, at hir command,
    That I suld be supprest.
Bot, all comes for the best,   1470
   Til him that lovis the Lord:
Thocht I be now molest,
   I traist to be restorde.

[*Heir sall thay put hir in the stocks.*

Sister, alace! this is ane cairful cace,
   That wee, with Princes, sould be sa abhorde.

VERITIE.

Be blyth, Sister, I trust, within schort space,
   That we sall be richt honorablie restorde,
   And with the King wee sall be at concorde;
For [I] heir tell, Divyne Correctioun
   Is new landit, thankit be Christ our Lord!   1480
I wait hee will be our protectioun.

[*Heir sall enter Correctiouns Varlet.*

VARLET.

Sirs, stand abak, and hauld yow coy,
I am the King Correctioun's boy;
   Cum heir to dres his place:
Se that ye mak obedience,
Untill his nobill excellence,
   Fra tyme ye se his face.

For, he maks reformatiouns,
Out-throw all Christin Natiouns,
    Quhair he finds gret debaits: 1490
And sa far as I understand,
He sall reforme into this Land,
    Evin all the Thrie Estaits.
God, furth of heavin, hes him send,
To punische all that dois offend
    Against his Majestie;
As lyks him best, to tak vengence,
Sumtyme, with sword, and pestilence,
    With derth, and povertie.
Bot, quhen the peopill dois repent,   1500
And beis to God obedient,
    Then will he gif them grace:
Bot, thay that will nocht be correctit,
Rycht sudanlie will be dejectit,
    And fleimit from his face.

Sirs, thocht wee speik in generall,
Let na man, into speciall,
    Tak our wordis at the warst:
Quhat ever wee do, quhat ever wee say,
I pray yow tak it all in play,   1510
    And judge ay to the best:
For silence, I protest,
Baith of Lord, Laird, and Ladie:
    Now, I will rin, but rest,
And tell that all is ready.

DISSAIT.

Brother, heir ye yon proclamatioun;

I dreid full sair of reformatioun,
    Yon message maks me mangit:
Quhat is your counsell, to me tell,
Remaine wee heir, be God him sell,   1520
    Wee will be all thrie hangit.

FLATTERIE.

I'le gang to Spiritualitie,
And preich out-throw his dyosie,
    Quhair I wald be unknawin:
Or keip me closse into sum closter,
With mony piteous Pater Noster,
    Till all thir blasts be blawin.

DISSAIT.

I'le be weill treitit, as ye ken,
With my masteris, the Merchand men,
    Quhilk can mak small debait: 1530
Ye ken richt few of them that thryfes,
Or can begyll the landwart wyfes,
    But me thair man, Dissait.

Now, Falset, quhat sall be thy schift?

FALSET.

Na cuir thow nocht, man, for my thrift,
    Trows thou, that I be daft?
Na, I will leif ane lustie lyfe,
Withoutin ony sturt and stryfe,
    Amang the men of craft.

FLATTERIE.

I na mair will remaine besyd yow;   1540
Bot counsell yow, rycht weill to gyde yow,
    Byde nocht on Correctioun:
Fair-weils, I will na langer tarie.
I pray the alrich Queene of Farie,
    To be your protectioun.

DISSAIT.

Falset, I wald wee maid ane band,
Now, quhill the King is yit sleipand,
    Quhat rack to steill his box?

FALSET.

Now, weill said, be the Sacrament,
I sall it steill incontinent,   1550
    Thocht it had twentie lox.

[*Heir sall Falset steill the King's Box, with silence.*

Lo! heir the Box, now let us ga,
    This may suffice, for our rewairds.

DISSAIT.

Yea, that it may, man, be this day
    It may weill mak of landwart lairds:
Now, let us cast away our clais,
    In dreid, sum follow on the chase.

FALSET.

Richt weill devysit, man, be Sanct Blais,

Wald God! wee war out of this place.

DAISSIT.

Now, sen thair is na man to wrang us,   1560
  I pray yow, brother, with my hart,
Let us ga part this pelf amang us;
  Syne, haistely, we sall depart.

FALSET.

Trows thou, to get als mekill as I?
  That sall thow nocht, I staw the box
Thou did nathing bot luikit by,
  Ay lurkeand, lyke ane wylie fox.

DISSAIT.

Thy heid sall beir ane cuppill of knox,
  Pellour, without I get my part:
Swyith, huirsun smaik, ryfe up the lox,   1570
  Or, I sall stick thé throuch the hart.

[Heir sall thay fecht, with silence.

FALSET.

Alace! for ever, my eye is out,
  Walloway! will na man red the men?

DISSAIT.

Upon thy craig, tak thair ane clout,
  To be courtesse, I sall thé ken.
Fare-weill! for I am at the flicht,
  I will nocht byde on ma demands;

And wee twa meit againe this nicht,
Thy feit salbe worth fourtie hands.

[*Heir sal Dissait rin away, with the Box, through the water.*]

DIVYNE CORRECTIOUN.

" *Beati qui esuriunt et sitiunt Justitiam:*"
Thir ar the wordis of the redoutit Roy,   1580
   The Prince of peace, above all kings, King:
Quhilk hes me sent all cuntreis to convoye,
   And all misdoars dourlie to doun thring.
     I will do nocht, without the conveining
Ane Parliament of the Estaits all;
     In their presence, I sall, but feinzeing,
Iniquitie, under my sword, doun thrall.

Thair may no Prince do acts honorabill,
   Bot gif, his Counsall thairto will assist:
How may he knaw the thing maist profitabil,   1590
   To follow vertew, and vycis to resist,
     Without he be instructit, and solist?
And quhen the King standis at his Counsell sound,
   Then welth sall wax, and plentie, as he list,
And policie sall in his Realme abound.

Gif ony list my name for till inquyre,
   I am callit Divyne Correctioun.
I fled throch mony uncouth land, and schyre,
   To the greit profit of ilk Natioun:
     Now am I cum into this Regioun,   1600
To teill the ground, that hes bene lang unsawin,

To punische tyrants, for thair transgressioun,
And to caus leill men live upon thair awin.

Na realme, nor land but my support may stand;
   For I gar kings live into royaltie:
To rich, and puir, I beir ane equall band,
    That thay may live into thair awin degrie:
    Quhair I am nocht, is no tranquilitie.
Be me, tratours, and tyrants, ar put doun;
    Quha thinks na schame of thair iniquitie,   1610
Till thay be punisched be mee Correctioun.

Quhat is ane King? nocht bot ane officiar,
   To caus his leiges live in equitie:
And, under God, to be ane punischer
    Of trespassouris against His Majestic.
    Bot, quhen the king dois law in tyrannie,
Breakand justice for feare or affectioun;
    Then, is his realme in weir, and povertie,
With schamefull slauchter, but correctioun.

I am ane Judge richt potent, and seveir,   1620
   Cum, to do justice, monie thowsand myle:
I am sa constant baith in peace and weir,
    Na bud, nor favour, may my sicht ouersyle,
    Thair is thairfoir richt monie in this Ile,
Of my repair, but doubt, that dois repent:
    Bot verteous men, I traist, sall on me smyle,
And of my cumming sall be richt weill content.

        [GUDE COUNSALL.]
Welcum, my Lord, welcum ten thousand tymes
   Till all faithfull men of this regioun;

Welcum, for till correct all falts, and crymes, 1630
   Amang this cankerd congregatioun.
Lowse Chastitie, I mak supplicatioun ;
Put till fredome fair Ladie Veritie,
   Quha, be unfaithfull folk of this Natioun,
Lyis bund full fast into captivitie.

CORRECTIOUN.

I mervel, Gude Counsell, how that may be,
   Ar ye nocht with the King familiar ?

GUDE COUNSALL.

That I am nocht, my Lord, full wa is me,
   Bot, lyke ane begger, am halden at the bar :
   Thay play Bo-keik, evin as I war ane skar : 1640
Thair came thrie knaves, in cleithing counterfeit,
   And, fra the King, thay gart me stand affar ;
Quhais names war Flatterie, Falset, and Dissait :

Bot, quhen thay knavis hard tell of your cumming,
   Thay staw away, ilk ane ane sindrie gait ;
And cuist fra them thair counterfit cleithing,
   For thair leving full weill thay can debait :
   The merchandmen, thay haif resavit Dissait.
As for Falset, my Lord, full weill I ken,
   He will be richt weill treitit, air and lait, 1650
Among the maist part of the craftis men.

Flattrie has taine the habite of ane Freir,
   Thinkand to begyll Spiritualitie.

CORRECTIOUN.

But dout, my freind, and I live half ane yeir,

I sall search out that great iniquitie.
Quhair lyis yon Ladyes in captivitie?
How now, Sisters, quha hes yow sa disgysit?

VERITIE.

Unfaithfull members of iniquitie,
Dispytfullie, my Lord, hes us supprysit.

CORRECTIOUN.

Gang, put yon Ladyis to thair libertie   1660
  Incontinent, and break doun all the stocks:
But doubt, thay ar full deir welcum to mee;
  Mak diligence, me think ye do bot mocks;
  Speid hand, and spair nocht for to break the locks,
And tenderlie, tak thame up be the hand;
  Had I thame heir, thay knaves suld ken my knocks,
That them opprest, and baneist aff the land.

    [*Thay tak the Ladyis furth of the stocks; and
      Veritie sall say:*

VERITIE.

Wee thank you, Sir, of your benignitie,
  Bot, I beseik your Majestie royall,
That ye wald pas to King Humanitie,   1670
  And fleime from him, yon Ladie Sensuall,
  And enter in his service Gude Counsall:
For ye will find him verie counsalabill.

CORRECTIOUN.

Cum on, Sisters, as ye haif said, I sall,
And gar him stand with yow thrie, firme and stabill.

[*Correctioun passis towards the King, with
Veritie, Chastitie, and Gude Counsell.*

WANTONNES.

Solace, knawis thou not quhat I se?
Ane knicht, or ellis ane king, thinks me,
With wantoun wings as he wald fle;
    Brother, quhat may this meine?
I understand nocht, be this day,   1680
Quhidder that he be freind or fay,
Stand still, and heare quhat he will say,
    Sic ane I haif nocht seine.

SOLACE.

You is ane stranger, I stand forde,
He semes to be ane lustie lord,
Be his heir-cumming, for concorde,
    And be kinde till our King:
He sall be welcome to this place,
And treatit with the King's grace;
Be it nocht sa, we sall him chace,   1690
    And to the Divell him ding.

PLACEBO.

I reid us put upon the King,
And walkin him of his sleiping.
Sir, rise, and se ane uncouth thing:
    Get up, ye ly too lang!

SENSUALITIE.

Put on your hude, Johne Fule, ye raif.

How dar ye be so pert, Sir knaif,
    To tuich the King ! sa Christ me saif,
        Fals huirsone, thow sall hang.

CORRECTIOUN.

Get up, Sir King ! ye haif sleipit aneuch   1700
    Into the armis of Ladie Sensual ;
Be suir, that mair belangis to the pleuch,
    As efterwards perchance, rehears I sall :
Remember how the king Sardanapall,
Amang fair ladyes tuke his lust sa lang ;
    Sa that, the maist pairt of his leiges all
Rebeld, and syne him duilfully doun thrang.

Remember how into the tyme of Noy,
    For the foull stinckand sin of lechery,
God, be my wande, did al the Warld destroy.   1710
    Sodome and Gomore, richt sa full rigorously,
    For that vyld sin, war brunt maist cruelly :
Thairfoir, I thé command incontinent,
    Banische from thé that huir Sensualitie,
Or els, but dout, rudlie thow sall repent.

REX HUMANITAS.

Be quhom, haif ye sa greit authoritie ?
    Quha dois presume, for till correct ane King ?
Knaw ye nocht me, greit King Humanitie ?
    That in my Regioun royally dois ring.

CORRECTIOUN.

I have power greit Princes to doun thring,   1720

That lives contrair the Majestie Divyne,
   Against the treuth quhilk plainelie dois maling,
Repent thay nocht, I put them to ruyne.

I will begin at thee, quhilk is the head,
   And mak on thee first reformatioun,
Thy leiges than, will follow thee but pleid,
   Swyith, harlot ! hence without dilatioun.

SENSUALITIE.

My Lord, I mak yow supplicatioun,
Gif me licence, to pas againe to Rome ;
Amang the princes of that natioun,   1730
   I lat yow wit, my fresche beautie will blume.

Adew, Sir King, I may na langer tary,
   I cair nocht that, als gude luife cumis as gais ;
I recommend yow to the Queene of Farie,
   I se ye will be gydit, with my fais.
   As for this King, I cure him nocht twa strais :
War I amang bischops, and cardinals,
   I wald get gould, silver, and precious clais :
Na earthlie joy, but my presence, availis.

   [*Heir sall scho pas to Spiritualitie.*

My Lords of the Sprituall Stait ;   1740
   Venus preserve yow, air and lait ;
For, I can mak na mair debait,
      I am partit with your King ;
And am baneischt this regioun,

Be counsell of Correctioun ;
Be ye nocht my protectioun,
   I may seik my ludgeing.

SPIRITUALITIE.

Welcum, our dayis darling,
   Welcum, with all our hart :
Wee all, but feinzeing,   1750
   Sall plainly tak your part.

[*Heir sall the Bischops, Abbots, and Persons, kiss the Ladies.*

CORRECTIOUN.

Sen ye ar quyte of Sensualitie,
  Resave into your service Gude Counsall,
And richt sa this fair ladie Chastitie,
  Till ye mary sum Queene of blude-royall ;
  Observe then Chastitie matrimoniall ;
Richt sa, resave Veritie be the hand ;
  Use thair counsell, your fame sall never fall :
With thame, thairfoir, mak ane perpetuall band.

[*Heir sall the King resave [Gude] Counsall, Veritie, and Chastitie.*

Now, Sir, tak tent, quhat I will say,   1760
Observe thir same baith nicht and day,
And let thame never part yow fray,
   Or els, withoutin doubt,
Turne ye to Sensualitie,
To vicious lyfe, and rebaldrie,

Out of your Realme richt schamefullie,
    Ye sall be ruttit out;
As was Tarquine, the Romane king,
    Quha was, for his vicious living,
And for the schamefull ravisching   1770
    Of the fair chaist Lucres:
He was degraidit of his croun,
    And baneist aff his regioun;
I maid on him correctioun,
    As storeis dois expres.

REX HUMANITAS.

I am content to your counsall to inclyne,
    Ye beand of gude conditioun.
At your command sall be all that is myne,
    And heir I gif you full commissioun,
    To punische faults, and gif remissioun.   1780
To all vertew, I sal be consociabill,
    With yow, I sall confirme ane unioun,
And, at your counsall, stand ay firme and stabill.

[*The King imbraces Correctioun with a humbill countenance.*]

CORRECTIOUN.

I counsall yow, incontinent,
    To gar proclame ane Parliament,
        Of all the Thrie Estaits:
That thay be heir, with diligence,
To mak to yow obedience,
        And syne dres all debaits.

REX HUMANITAS.

That salbe done, but mair demand.   1790

Hoaw! Diligence, cum heir fra hand,
   And tak your informatioun;
Gang warne the Spiritualitie,
Rycht sa the Temporalitie,
   Be oppin proclamatioun,
In gudlie haist, for to compeir,
In thair maist honorabill maneir,
   To gif us thair counsails:
Quha that beis absent to them schaw,
That thay sall underly the law,   1800
   And punischt be, that fails.

DILIGENCE.

Sir, I sall baith in bruch and land,
With diligence, do your command,
   Upon my awin expens:
Sir, I have servit yow all this yeir,
Bot, I gat never ane denneir
   Yit, for my recompence.

REX HUMANITAS.

Pas on, and thou sall be regairdit,
And, for thy service, weill rewairdit;
   For quhy, with my consent,   1810
Thou sall haif yeirly, for thy hyre,
The teind mussellis of the Ferrie myre,
   Confirmit in Parliament.

DILIGENCE.

I will get riches throw that rent,
    Efter the day of Dume,
Quhen, in the colpots of Tranent,
    Butter will grow on brume!
Or I proclame ocht with my mouth,
    I micht nocht sleip ane wink;   1820
All nicht, I had sa meikill drouth,
    But doubt, I man haif drink.

CORRECTIOUN.

Cum heir Placebo, and Solace,
With your companzeoun, Wantonnes,
    I knaw weill your conditioun:
For tysting King Humanitie,
To resave Sensualitie,
    Ye man suffer punitioun.

WANTONNES.

We grant, my Lord, we have done ill;
Thairfoir, wee put us in your will,
    Bot, wee haife bene abusit;   1830
For, in gude faith, Sir, wee beleifit
That lecherie had na man greifit,
    Becaus it is sa usit.

PLACEBO.

Ye sé how Sensualitie,
With Principals of ilk cuntrie,
    Bene glaidlie lettin in,

And, with our Prelatis, mair and les :
Speir at my ladie Priores,
    Gif lechery be sin?

SOLACE.

Sir, wee sall mend our conditioun,   1840
Sa ye give us remissioun,
    Bot, give us leave to sing ;
To dance, to play at chesse, and tabills,
To reid stories, and mirrie fabils,
    For pleasure of our King.

CORRECTIOUN.

Sa that ye do na uther cryme,
Ye sall be pardonit, at this tyme,
    For quhy? as I suppois,
Princes may sumtyme seik solace,
With mirth, and lawfull mirrines,   1850
    Thair spirits to rejoyis.
And richt sa, halking, and hunting,
Ar honest pastymes, for ane king,
    Into the tyme of peace :
And leirne to rin ane heavie spear,
That he, into the tyme of wear,
    May follow at the cheace.

REX HUMANITAS.

Quhair is Sapience, and Discretioun !
    And quhy cums nocht Devotioun nar?

VERITIE.

Sapience, Sir, was ane verie loun,   1860

And Discretioun was nathing war:
The suith, Sir, gif I wald report,
   Thay did begyle your Excellence;
And wald not suffer to resort
   Ane of us thrie to your presence.

CHASTITIE.

Thay thrie war Flattrie, and Dissait,
   And Falset, that unhappie loun,
Against us thrie quhilk maid debait,
   And baneischt us from town to town,
   Thay gart us twa fall into sowne,   1870
Quhen thay us lockit in the stocks:
   That dastart knave, Discretioun,
Full thifteouslie did steill your box.

REX HUMANITAS.

The Devill tak them, sen thay ar gane,
   Me thocht them ay thrie verie smaiks,
I mak ane vow to Sanct Mavane,
   Quhen I them finde thays bear thair paiks:
   I se thay haif playit me the glaiks.
Gude Counsall, now schaw me the best;
   Quhen I fix on yow thrie my staiks,   1880
How I sall keip my Realme in rest.

   Initium sapientiæ est timor Domini.

GUDE COUNSALL.

Sir, gif your Hienes yearnis lang to ring,
First dread your God abuif all uther thing:

For ye ar bot ane mortall instrument,
To that great God and King Omnipotent:
Preordinat be his Divine Majestie,
To reull his peopill intill unitie.
The principall point, Sir, of ane King's office,
Is for to do to everilk man justice;
And for to mix his justice with mercie,　　　　1890
But rigour, favour, or parcialitie.
Forsuith, it is na littill observance,
Great regions to have in governance:
Quha ever takis on him that kinglie cuir,
To get ane of thir twa, he suld be suir,
Great paine, and labour, and that continuall,
Or ellis till have defame perpetuall:
Quha guydis weill they win immortall fame,
Quha the contrair, they get perpetuall schame;
Efter quhais deith, but doubt, ane thousand yeir,　1900
Thair life, at lenth, rehearst sall be, perqueir.
The Chroniklis to knaw, I yow exhort,
Thair sall ye finde baith gude and evill report:
For everie Prince, efter his qualitie,
Thocht he be deid, his deidis sall never die.
Sir, gif ye please, for to use my counsall,
Your fame and name sall be perpetuall.

　　　[*Heir sall the messinger Diligence returne; and
　　　　cry a Hoyzes, a Hoyzes, a Hoyzes, and say;*

At the command of King Humanitie,
　I wairne, and charge, all members of Parliament,
Baith Sprituall Stait, and Temporalitie,　　　　1910

That till his Grace, thay be obedient,
  And speid them to the Court incontinent,
In gude ordour arrayit royally;
  Quha beis absent, or inobedient,
The King's displeasure they sall underly.

And als I mak yow exhortatioun,
  Sen ye haif heard the FIRST PAIRT of our Play,
Go tak ane drink, and mak collatioun;
  Ilk man drink till his marrow, I yow pray,
  Tarie nocht lang, it is lait in the day;   1920
Let sum drink ayle, and sum drink claret wine,
  Be gret Doctors of Physick, I heare say,
That michtie drink comforts the dull ingine.

    And ye Ladies, that list to pisch,
    Lift up your taill, plat in ane disch;
    And gif that your mawkine cryis quhisch,
        Stop in ane wusp of stray.
    Let nocht your bladder burst, I pray yow,
    For that war evin aneuch to slay yow:
    For yit thair is to cum, I say yow,   1930
        The best pairt of our Play.

THE END OF THE FIRST PART OF THE SATYRE.

  [*Now sall the Pepill mak collatioun: then beginnis
    the Interlude; the Kings, Bischops, and princi-
    pall Players, being out of their seats.*

[AN INTERLUDE OF
THE PUIR MAN AND THE PARDONER.]

[*Heir sall entir Pauper the puir man.*]

PAUPER.

OF your almis, gude folks, for God's luife of heavin,
For I have motherles bairns either sax, or seavin:
Gif ye'ill gif me na gude, for the luife of Jesus,
Wische me the richt way till Sanct-Androes.

DILIGENCE.

Quhair haif wee gottin this gudly companzeoun?
Swyith! out of the feild, [thow] fals raggit loun.
God wait, gif heir be ane weill keipit place,
Quhen sic ane vilde begger Carle may get entres.
Fy on yow officiars! that mends nocht thir failyies, 1940
I gif yow all till the Devill baith Provost, and Bailzies:
Without ye cum, and chase this Carle away,
The devill a word ye'is get mair of our Play.
    Fals huirsun, raggit Carle, quhat Devill is that thou
       rugs?

PAUPER.

Quha Devill maid thee ane gentill man, that wald cut
    not thy lugs?

DILIGENCE.

Quhat now! me thinks the Carle begins to crack,
Swyith! Carle away, or be this day, Is'e break thy
    back.

> [*Heir sall the Carle clim up and sit in the
>   King's tchyre.*

Cum doun, or be God's croun, fals loun, I sall slay
    thee.

PAUPER.

Now sweir be thy brunt schinnis, the Devill ding
    thame fra thee.
Quhat say ye till thir court dastards? be thay get
    hail clais,   1950
Sa sune as thay leir to sweir, and trip on thair tais.

DILIGENCE.

Me thocht, the Carle callit me knave, evin in my face.
Be Sanct Fillane, thou sal be slane, bot gif thou ask
    grace:
Loup doun, or be the gude Lord, thow sall lose thy
    heid.

PAUPER.

I sall anis drink or I ga, thocht thou had sworne my
    deid.

> [*Heir Diligence castis away the ledder.*

DILIGENCE.

Loup now, gif thou list, for thou hes lost the ledder:
It is full weill thy kind, to loup, and licht in a tedder.

PAUPER.

Thou sall be faine, to fetch agane the ledder, or I loup;
I sall sit heir, into this tcheir, till I have tumde the stoup.

[Heir sall the Carle loup aff the scaffald.

[DILIGENCE.]

Swyith! beggar, bogill, haist thé away; 1960
Thow art over pert to spill our Play.

PAUPER.

I will not gif, for al your Play, worth an sowis fart:
For, thair is richt lytill play, at my hungrie hart.

DILIGENCE.

Quhat devill ails this cruckit Carle?

PAUPER.

Marie! meikill sorrow:
I can not get, thocht I gasp, to beg, nor to borrow.

DILIGENCE.

Quhair devill is this thou dwels? or quhat's thy intent?

PAUPER.
I dwell into Lawthiane, ane myle fra Tranent.

DILIGENCE.
Quhair wald thou be, Carle? the suth to me schaw.

PAUPER.
Sir, evin to Sanct-Androes, for to seik law.

DILIGENCE.
For to seik law, in Edinburgh was the neirest
    way.   1970

PAUPER.
Sir, I socht law thair this monie deir day :
Bot, I culd get nane at Sessioun, nor Seinzie ;
Thairfor, the meikill din Devill droun all the meinzie.

DILIGENCE.
Schaw me thy mater, man, with all the circumstances,
How that thou hes happinit on thir unhappie chances.

PAUPER.
Gude man, will ye gif me of your charitie,
And I sall declair yow the black veritie.
My Father was ane auld man, and ane hoir,
And was of age fourscoir of yeirs and moir.
And Mald, my mother, was fourscoir and fyfteine, 1980
And with my labour I did thame baith susteine.
Wee had ane meir, that caryit salt and coill,
And everie ilk yeir, scho brocht us hame ane foill.
Wee had thrie ky, that was baith fat and fair,

Nane tydier into the toun of Air.
My Father was sa waik of blude, and bane,
That he deit, quhairfoir my Mother maid gret maine:
Then scho deit, within ane day or two;
And thair began my povertie, and wo.
Our gude gray meir was baittand on the feild,   1990
And our Land's laird tuik hir, for his hyreild,
The Vickar tuik the best cow be the heid,
Incontinent, quhen my father was deid.
And quhen the Vickar hard tel how that my mother
Was deid, fra hand, he tuke to him ane uther:
Then Meg, my wife, did murne baith evin, and
    morow,
Till at the last scho deit for veric sorow:
And quhen the Vickar hard tell my wyfe was dead,
The thrid cow he cleikit be the heid.
Thair umest clayis, that was of rapploch gray,   2000
The Vickar gart his Clark bear them away.
Quhen all was gane, I micht mak na debeat,
Bot with my bairns, past for till beg my meat.
  Now, haif I tald yow the blak veritie,
  How I am brocht into this miserie.

DILIGENCE.

How did the Person? was he not thy gude freind?

PAUPER.

The Devil stick him! he curst me for my teind:
And halds me yit under that same proces,
That gart me want the Sacrament at Pasche.
In gude faith, Sir, thocht he wald cut my throt, 2010
I have na geir, except ane Inglis grot,

Quhilk I purpois to gif ane man of law.

DILIGENCE.

Thou art the daftest fuill, that ever I saw ;
Trows thou, man, be the law, to get remeid
Of men of Kirk ! Na, nocht till thou be deid.

PAUPER.

Sir, be quhat law, tell me, quhairfoir, or quhy
That ane Vickar suld tak fra me thre ky ?

DILIGENCE.

Thay have na law, exceptand consuetude,
Quhilk law, to them, is sufficient and gude.

PAUPER.

Ane consuetude against the common weill,   2020
Suld be na law, I think, be sweit Sanct Geill.
Quhair will ye find that law, tell gif ye can,
To tak thrie ky, fra ane pure husband man ?
Ane for my father, and for my wyfe ane uther,
And the thrid cow, he tuke fra Mald my mother.

DILIGENCE.

It is thair law, all that thay have in use,
Thocht it be cow, sow, ganer, gryse, or guse.

PAUPER.

Sir, I wald speir at yow ane questioun :
Behauld sum Prelats of this regioun,
Manifestlie, during thair lustie lyfis,   2030
Thay swyfe ladyis, madinis, and uther men's wyfis ;

And sa, thair cunts thay have in consuetude;
Quhidder say ye, that law is evill, or gude?

DILIGENCE.

Hald thy toung, man, it seims that thou war mangit,
Speik thou of Preists, but doubt, thou will be hangit.

PAUPER.

Be Him, that buir the cruell croun of thorne,
I cair nocht to be hangit, evin the morne.

DILIGENCE.

Be sure, of Preistis thou will get na support.

PAUPER.

Gif that be trew, the Feind resave the sort?
Sa, sen I se, I get na uther grace,   2040
I will ly down, and rest mee in this place.

    [*Heir sall the Puirman ly doun in the feild: and
    the Pardoner sall cum in and say:*

PARDONER.

Bona dies! Bona dies!
Devoit pepill, gude day, I say yow,
Now tarie ane lytill quhyll, I pray yow.
    Till I be with yow knawin:
Wat ye weill how I am namit?
Ane nobill man, and undefamit,
    Gif all the suith war schawin.
I am Sir Robert Rome-raker,

Ane perfyte publike Pardoner,
    Admittit be the Paip :   2050
Sirs, I sall schaw yow, for my wage,
My pardons, and my pilgramage,
    Quhilk ye sall se, aad graip:
I give to the Devill, with gude intent,
This unsell wickit New Testament,
    With thame that it translaitit :
Sen layik men knew the veritie,
Pardoners gets no charitie,
    Without that thay debait it.
Amang the wives with wrinks and wyles,   2060
As all my marrowis, men begyles,
    With our fair fals flattrie :
Yea, all the crafts I ken perqueir,
As I was teichit, be ane Freir,
    Callit Hypocrisie.
Bot now, allace ! our greit abusioun
Is cleirlie knawin till our confusioun,
    That we may sair repent :
Of all credence, now I am quyte,
For, ilk man halds me at dispyte,   2070
    That reids the New Test'ment,
Duill fell the braine, that hes it wrocht,
Sa fall them that the Buik hame brocht :
    Als I pray to the Rude,
That Martin Luther, that fals loun,
Black Bullinger, and Melancthoun,
    Had bene smorde in their cude.
Be Him, that buir the crowne of thorne,
I wald Sanct Paull had never bene borne,

And als, I wald his buiks, 2080
War never red in the kirk,
Bot amangs freirs, into the mirk,
    Or riven amang ruiks.

> *Heir sall he lay doun his geir upon ane baird, and say.*

My patent Pardouns, ye may se,
Cum fra the Cane of Tartarie,
    Weill scald with oster-schellis.
Thocht ye have na contritioun,
Ye sall have full remissioun,
    With help of buiks, and bellis.
Heir is ane relict, lang and braid 2090
Of Fine Macoull the richt chaft blaid,
    With teith, and al togidder :
Of Colling's cow, heir is ane horne,
For eating of Makconnal's corne,
    Was slaine into Baquhidder.
Heir is ane coird, baith great and lang,
Quhilk hangit Johne the Armistrang :
    Of gude hemp soft, and sound :
Gude, halie peopill, I stand for'd
Quha ever beis hangit with this cord, 2100
    Neids never to be dround.
The culum of Sanct Bryd's kow,
The gruntill of Sanct Antonis sow,
    Quhilk buir his haly bell :
Quha ever he be heiris this bell clinck,
Gif me ane ducat for till drink,
    He sall never gang to hell,

Without he be of Baliell borne:
Maisters, trow ye, that this be scorne!
  Cum win this Pardoun, cum.   2110
Quha luifis thair wyfis nocht, with thair hart,
I have power thame for till part,
  Me think yow deif and dum.
Hes naine of yow curst wickit wyfis,
That halds yow intill sturt and stryfis,
  Cum tak my dispensatioun:
Of that cummer, I sall mak yow quyte,
Howbeit your selfis be in the wyte,
  And mak ane fals narratioun.
Cum win the Pardoun, now let se,   2120
For meill, for malt, or for monie,
  For cok, hen, guse, or gryse.
Of relicts, heir I haif ane hunder;
Quhy cum ye nocht? this is ane wonder:
  I trow ye be nocht wyse.

SOWTAR.

Welcum hame, Robert Rome-raker,
Our halie patent pardoner:
  Gif ye have dispensatioun,
To pairt me, and my wickit wyfe,
And me deliver from sturt and stryfe,   2130
  I mak yow supplicatioun.

PARDONER.

I sall yow pairt, but mair demand,
Sa, I get mony in my hand;
  Thairfor let se sum cunzie.

SOWTAR.

I have na silver, be my lyfe,
Bot fyve schillings, and my schaipping knyfe,
   That sall ye have, but sunzie.

PARDONER.

Quhat kynd of woman is thy wyfe?

SOWTAR.

Ane quick devill, Sir, ane storme of stryfe,
   Ane frog, that fyles the winde;   2140
Ane fistand flag, a flagartie fuffe,
At ilk ane pant, scho lets ane puffe,
   And hes na ho behind.
All the lang day, scho me dispyts,
And all the nicht, scho flingis, and flyts,
   Thus sleip I never ane wink:
That cockatrice, that commoun huir,
The mekill Devill may nocht induir
   Hir stuburness, and stink.

SOWTAR'S WYFE.

Theif Carle, thy wordis I hard rycht weill,   2150
In faith, my friendschip, ye sall feill,
   And I thee fang.

SOWTAR.

Gif I said ocht, Dame, be the Rude,
Except ye war baith fair and gude,
   God nor I hang.

PARDONER.

Fair dame, gif ye wald be ane wower,
To part yow twa, I have ane power,
    Tell on, ar ye content?

SOWTAR'S WYFE.

Ye, that I am, with all my hart,
Fra that fals huirsone till depart,   2160
    Gif this theif will consent.
Causses to part I haif anew;
Becaus I gat na chamber-glew,
    I tell yow verely;
I mervell nocht, sa mot I lyfe,
Howbeit that swingeour can not swyfe,
    He is baith cauld and dry.

PARDONER.

Quhat will ye giff me, for your part?

SOWTAR'S WYFE.

Ane cuppill of sarks, with all my hart,
    The best claith, in the land.   2170

PARDONER.

To part, sen ye ar baith content,
I sall yow part incontinent,
    Bot, ye mon do command:
My will, and finall sentence is,
Ilk ane of yow uthers arsse kiss.
Slip doun your hois! me thinkis the carle is glaikit,
Set thou not by, howbeit scho kisse, and slaik it.

[*Heir sall scho kis hiss arsse, with silence.*

Lift up hir clais, kiss hir hoill with your hart.

SOWTAR.

I pray yow, Sir, forbid hir for to fart.

[*Heir sall the Carle kiss hir arsse, with silence,*

PARDONER.

Dame, pas ye to the east end of the toun; 2180
And pas ye west, evin lyke ane cuckald loun;
Go hence ye baith, with Baliel's braid blissing!
Schirs, saw ye ever mair sorrowles pairting?

[*Heir sall the Boy cry aff the hill, and say:*

WILKIN.

Hoaw! Maister, hoaw! quhair ar ye now?

PARDONER.

I am heir, Wilkin widdiefow.

WILKIN.

Sir, I have done your bidding;
For, I have fund ane greit hors bane,
Ane fairer saw ye never nane,
   Upon dame Flescher's midding.
Sir, ye may gar the wyfis trow, 2190
It is ane bane of Sanct Bryd's cow;

  Gude for the fever quartane:
Sir, will ye reull this relict weill,
All the wyfis will baith kiss, and kneill,
  Betuixt this and Dumbartane.

PARDONER.

Quhat say thay of me, in the Toun?

WILKIN.

Some sayis, ye ar ane verie loun,
  Sum sayis, *Legatus Natus*;
Sum sayis ye ar ane fals Saracene;
And sum sayis, ye ar for certaine   2200
  Diabolus Incarnatus.
Bot keip yow fra subjectioun
Of the curst King Correctioun;
  For be ye with him fangit
Becaus ye ar ane Rome-raker,
Ane common publick cawsay-paker,
  But doubt ye will be hangit.

PARDONER.

Quhair sall I ludge into the toun?

WILKIN.

With gude kynde Cristiane Anderson,
  Quhair ye will be weill treatit.   2210
Gif ony limmer yow demands,
Scho will defend yow with hir hands,
  And womaulie debait it.
Bawburdie sayis, be the Trinitie,

That scho sall beir yow cumpanie,
    Howbeit ye byde ane yeir.

PARDONER.

Thou hes done weill, be God's mother,
Tak ye the taine, and I the tother,
    Sa sall we mak greit cheir.

WILKIN.

I reid yow, speid yow heir,   2220
    And mak na langer tarie;
Byde ye lang thair, but weir,
    I dreid your weird yow warie.

[Heir sall Pauper rise, and rax him.

PAUPER.

Quhat thing was yon that I heard crak and cry?
I have bene dreamand, and dreveland of my ky,
With my richt hand my haill bodie I saine,
Sanct Bryd, Sanct Bryd, send me my ky againe!
I se standand yonder ane halie man,
To mak me help, let me se gif he can.
Halie Maister, God speid yow! and gude morne. 2230

PARDONER.

Welcum to me, thocht thou war at the horne,
Cum win the pardoun, and syne I sall thé saine.

PAUPER.

Will that pardon get me my ky againe?

PARDONER.

Carle, of thy ky, I have nathing ado :
Cum, win my pardon, and kis my relicts to.

[*Heir sall he saine him with his relictis:*

PARDONER.

Now lows thy pursse, and lay doun thy offrand,
And thou sall have my pardoun evin fra hand.
With raipis, and relicts, I sall thé saine againe ;
Of gut, or gravell, thou sall never have paine ;
Now, win the pardoun, limmer, or thou art lost. 2240

PAUPER.

My haly Father, quhat wil that pardon cost ?

PARDONER.

Let se quhat mony thou bearest in thy bag.

PAUPER,

I haif ane grot heir, bund into ane rag.

PARDONER.

Hes thou na uther silver bot ane groat ?

PAUPER.

Gif I have mair, Sir, cum and rype my coat.

PARDONER.

Gif me that groat, man, gif thou hest na mair.

PAUPER.

With all my hart, Maister, lo tak it thair:
Now let me se your pardon, with your leif.

PARDONER.

Ane thousand yeir of pardons, I thee geif.

PAUPER.

Ane thousand yeir! I will nocht live sa lang;　2250
Delyver me it, maister, and let me gang,

PARDONER.

Ane thousand yeir, I lay upon thy head,
With *totiens quotiens:* now, mak me na mair plead:
Thou hast resaifit thy pardon now already.

PAUPER.

Bot, I can se na thing, Sir, be Our Lady:
Forsuith, Maister, I trow I be nocht wyse,
To pay ere I have sene my marchandryse.
That ye have gottin my groat full sair I rew;
Sir, quhidder is your pardon black, or blew?
Maister, sen ye have tain fra me my cunzie,　2260
My marchandryse schaw me, withouttin sunzie;
Or, to the Bischop I sall pas, and pleinzie,
In Sanct-Androis, and summond yow to the Seinzie.

PARDONER.

Quhat craifis the Carle? me thinks thou art not wise.

PAUPER.

I craif my groat, or ellis my marchandrise.

PARDONER.

I gaif thé pardon for ane thowsand yeir.

PAUPER.

How sall I get that pardon, let me heir.

PARDONER.

Stand still, and I sall tell the haill storie:
Quhen thow art deid, and gais to Purgatorie,
Being condempnit to paine a thowsand yeir,   2270
Then sall thy pardoun thee releif but weir:
Now be content, ye ar ane mervelous man.

PAUPER,

Sall I get nathing, for my groat, quhill than?

PARDONER.

That sall thou not, I mak it to yow plaine.

PAUPER.

Na than, gossop, gif me my groat againe,
Quhat say ye, Maisters? call ye this gude resoun,
That he suld promeis me ane gay pardoun,
And he resave my mony, in his stead;
Syne mak me na payment till I be dead?
Quhen I am deid, I wait full sikkerlie,   2280
My sillie saull will pas to Purgatorie:

Declair me this, now God, nor Baliell, bind thé,
Quhen I am thair, curst Carle, quhair sall I find thé?
Not into heavin, but rather into hell:
Quhen thou art thair, thou cannot help thy sell.
Quhen will thou cum my dolours till abait?
Or I thee find, my hippis will get ane hait.
Trowis thou, butchour, that I will buy blind lambis?
Gif me my groat, the Devill dryte in thy gambis.

PARDONER.

Swyith! stand abak! I trow this man be mangit: 2290
Thou gets not this, Carle, thocht thou suld be hangit.

PAUPER.

Gif me my groat, weill bund into ane clout,
Or, be Godis breid, Robin sall beir ane rout.

> [*Heir sall thay fecht with silence; and Pauper sal cast doun the buird, and cast the relicts in the water.*

DILIGENCE.

Quhat kind of daffing is this al day?
Swyith, smaiks! out of the feild, away:
Intill ane presoun put them sone,
Syne hang them, quhen the PLAY is done.

[ANE PLEASANT SATYRE OF THE THRIE ESTAITIS IN COMMENDATIOUN OF VERTEW AND VITUPERATIOUN OF VYCE.

Part the Second.]

[Heir sall Diligence mak his Proclamatioun.

DILIGENCE.

Famous Peopill, tak tent, and ye sall se
   The Thrie Estaits of this Natioun
Cum to the Court, with ane strange gravitie;   2300
   Thairfoir, I mak yow supplicatioun,
   Till ye have heard our haill narratioun,
To keip silence, and be patient, I pray yow,
   Howbeit we speik be adulatioun,
Wee sall say nathing bot the suith, I say yow :

Gude, verteous men, that luifis the veritie,
   I wait thay will excuse our negligence :
Bot vicious men, denude of charitie,
   As fenzeit, fals, flattrand Saracens ;
   Howbeit thay cry on us ane loud vengence,   2310
And of our pastyme mak ane fals report :
   Quhat may wee do, bot tak in patience?
And us refer unto the faithfull sort.

Our Lord Jesus, Peter, nor Paull,

Culd nocht compleis the peopill all,
    But sum war miscontent:
Howbeit thay schew the veritie,
Sum said, that it war herisie,
    Be thair maist fals judgement.

    [*Heir sall The Thrie Estaits cum fra the palzeoun;
      gangand backwart, led be thair Vyces.*

WANTONNES.

Now braid Benedicite!   2320
Quhat thing is yon that I se?
    Luke Solace, my hart.

SOLACE.

Brother Wantonnes, quhat thinkis thow?
You ar The Thrie Estaits, I trow,
    Gangand backwart.

WANTONNES.

Backwart, backwart! out wallaway!
It is gret schame for them, I say,
    Backwart to gang;
I trow the King Correctioun,
Man mak ane reformatioun,   2330
    Or it be lang.
Now let us go, and tell the King.   [*Pausa.*

Sir, we have sene ane mervelous thing,
    Be our judgement:
The Thrie Estaits of this Regioun

Ar cummand backwart, throw this toun,
To the Parliament.

REX HUMANITAS.

Backwart, backwart! how may that be?
Gar speid them haistelie to me;
   In dreid, that thay ga wrang.   2340

PLACEBO.

Sir, I se them yonder cummand,
Thay will be heir evin fra hand
   Als fast as thay may gang.

GUDE COUNSEL.

Sir, hald you stil, and skar them nocht,
Till ye persave quhat be thair thocht,
   And se quhat men them leids:
And let the King Correctioun,
Mak ane scharp inquisitioun,
   And mark thame be the heids.
Quhen ye ken the occasioun,   2350
That makis them sic persuasioun,
   Ye may expell the caus:
Syne them reforme, as ye think best,
Sua that the Realme may live in rest,
   According to God's lawis.

[*Heir sall The Thrie Estaits cum and turne thair faces to the King.*

SPIRITUALITIE.

Gloir, honour, laud, triumph, and victorie,

Be to your michtie, prudent, Excellence!
Heir ar we cum, all The Estaits Thrie,
   Readie to mak our dew obedience,
   At your command, with humbill observance,   2360
As may pertene to Spiritualitie,
With counsell of the Temporalitie.

TEMPORALITIE.

Sir, we with michtie curage, at command
   Of your superexcellent Majestie,
Sall mak service, baith with our hart and hand,
   And sall not dreid in thy defence to die:
   Wee ar content, but doubt, that wee may se
That nobyll heavenlie King Correctioun,
Sa he, with mercie, mak punitioun.

MERCHAND.

Sir, we ar heir, your burgessis, and merchands,   2370
   Thanks be to God, that we may se your face:
Traistand wee may now, into divers lands,
   Convoy our geir, with support of your Grace:
   For now, I traist, wee sall get rest, and peace,
Quhen misdoars ar, with your sword, overthrawin;
Then, may leil merchandis live upon thair awin.

REX HUMANITAS.

Welcom to me, my prudent Lordis all.
   Ye ar my members, suppois I be your head:
Sit doun, that we may, with your just counsall,
   Aganis misdoars find soveraine remeid: 2380
   Wee sall nocht spair, for favour nor for feid,

With your avice to mak punitioun,
And put my sword to executioun.

CORRECTIOUN.

My tender friends, I pray yow, with my hart,
   Declair to me the thing that I wald speir,
Quhat is the caus, that ye gang all backwart?
   The veritie thairof faine wald I heir.

SPIRITUALITIE.

Soveraine, we have gaine sa, this mony a yeir;
Howbeit ye think we go undecently,
Wee think wee gang richt wonder pleasantly.   2390

DILIGENCE.

Sit doun, my Lords, into your proper places:
Syne let the King consider all sic caces.
Sit doun, sir Scribe; and sit doun Dampster to,
And fence the Court, as ye war wont to do.

    [*Thay ar set doun, and Gud Counsell sall pas to his seat.*

    [*Heir sall The Thrie Estaitis compeir to the Parliament; and the King sall say.*]

REX HUMANITAS.

My prudent Lords of The Thrie Estaits,
   It is our will abuife all uther thing,
For to reforme all thame that maks debaits
   Contrair the richt, quhilk daylie dois maling;

And thay, that dois the Common-weil doun thring,
With help, and counsell, of King Correctioun,   2400
    It is our will, for to mak punisching;
And plaine oppressours put to subjectioun.

SPIRITUALITIE.

Quhat thing is this, Sir, that ye have devysit?
Schirs, ye have neid, for till be weill advysit:
Be nocht haistie into your executioun,
And be nocht ouer extreime in your punitioun.
And gif ye please to do, Sir, as wee say,
Postpone this Parlament till ane uther day:
For quhy! the peopill of this Regioun
May nocht indure extreme correctioun.   2410

CORRECTIOUN.

Is this the part, my Lords, that ye will tak?
To mak us supportatioun to correct:
It dois appeir, that ye ar culpabill,
That ar nocht to Correctioun applyabill.
Swyith, Diligence, ga schaw it is our will,
That everilk man opprest, geif in his bill.

DILIGENCE.

All maneir of men, I wairne, that be opprest.
Cum and complaine, and thay sall be redrest.
For quhy, it is the nobill Prince's will,
That ilk compleiner sall gif in his bill.   2420

JOHNE THE COMMON-WEILL.

Out of my gait, for God's saik let me ga:

Tell me againe, gude Maister, quhat ye say.

DILIGENCE.

I warne al that be wrangouslie offendit,
Cum, and complaine, and thay sall be amendit.

JOHNE.

Thankit be Christ, that buir the croun of thorne,
For I was never sa blyth, sen I was borne.

DILIGENCE.

Quhat is thy name, fallow, that wald I feill?

JOHNE.

Forsuith, thay call me Johne the Common-weill.
Gude maister, I wald speir at you ane thing,
Quhair, traist ye, I sall find yon new-cumde
   King?   2430

DILIGENCE.

Cum over, and I sall schaw thee to his Grace.

JOHNE.

God's bennesone licht on that luckie face!
Stand by the gait: let se, gif I can loup,
I man rin fast in cace I get ane coup.

   [*Heir sall Johne loup the stank, or els fall in it.*

DILIGENCE.

Speid thee away, thou taryis all to lang.

JOHNE.

Now, be this day, I may na faster gang.

[*Johne to the King.*
Gude day, gude day! greit God saif baith your Graces!
Wallie, wallie, fall thay twa weill fairde faces.

REX HUMANITAS.

Shaw me thy name, gude man, I thee command.

JOHNE.

Marie, Johne the Common-weill of fair Scotland. 2440

REX HUMANITAS.

The Commoun-weill hes bene amang his fais.

JOHNE.

Yea, Sir, that gars the Commoun-weil want clais.

REX HUMANITAS.

Quhat is the caus the Common-weill is crukit?

JOHNE.

Becaus the Common-weill hes bene overlukit.

REX HUMANITAS.

Quhat gars thé luke sa, with ane dreirie hart?

JOHNE.

Becaus The Thrie Estaitis gangs all backwart.

REX HUMANITAS.

Sir Common-weill, knaw ye the limmers, that them leids?

JOHNE.

Thair canker cullours, I ken them be the heads:
As for our reverent fathers of Spiritualitie,
They ar led be Coveticc, and cairles Sensualitie. 2450
And as ye se Temporalitie hes neid of correctioun,
Quhilk hes lang tyme bene led be Publick Oppres-
 sioun:
Loe! quhair the loun lyis lurkand, at his back;
Get up, I think to se thy craig gar ane raip crack.
Loe! heir is Falset, and Dissait, weill I ken,
Leiders of the Merchants, and sillie crafts-men.
Quhat mervell thocht The Thrie Estaits backwart
 gang?
Quhen sic an vyle cumpanie dwels them amang;
Quhilk hes reulit this rout monie deir dayis,
Quhilk gars Johne the Common-weill want his warme
 clais: 2460
Sir, call them befoir yow, and put them in ordour,
Or els Johne the Common-weil man beg on the Bor-
 dour.
Thou feinzeit Flattrie, the Feind fart in thy face,
Quhen ye was guyder of the Court we gat litill grace;
Ryse up Falset, and Dissait, without ony sunzie,
I pray God! nor the Devil's dame dryte on thy grunzie.
Behauld, as the loun lukis evin lyke a theif,
Monie wicht warkman, thow brocht to mischeif.

My soveraine Lord Correctioun, I mak yow supplication,
Put thir tryit truikers from Christis congregation. 2470

CORRECTIOUN.

As ye have devysit, but doubt, it sal be done :
Cum heir, my Sergeants, and do your debt sone :
Put thir thrie pellours into pressoun strang,
Howbeit ye sould hang thame, ye do them na wrang.

FIRST SERGEANT.

Soverane Lordis, wee sall obey your commands.
Brother, upon thir limmers, lay on thy hands;
Ryse up sone, loun, thou luiks evin lyke ane lurden,
Your mouth war meit to drink an wesche jurden.

SECUND SERGEANT.

Cum heir, gossop, cum heir, cum heir,
   Your rackles lyfe ye sall repent :   2480
Quhen was ye wont to be sa sweir?
   Stand still, and be obedient.

FIRST SERGEANT.

Thare is nocht in all this toun,
   (Bot, I wald nocht this taill war tald,)
Bot I wald hang him for his goun,
   Quhidder that it war laird, or laid.
I trow this pellour be spur-gaid
   Put in thy hand into this cord,
Howbeit, I se thy skap skyre skaid ;
   Thou art ane stewat I stand foir'd.   2490

[*Heir sall the Vycis be led to the stocks.*

SECUND SERGEANT.

Put in your leggis into the stocks,
   For, ye had never ane meiter hois:
Thir stewats stinks as thay war broks,
   Now ar ye sikker, I suppois.   [*Pausa.*

My Lordis, wee have done your commands;
   Sall wee put Covetice in captivitie?

CORRECTIOUN.

Yea, hardlie lay on them your hands;
   Richt sa upon Sensualitie.

SPIRITUALITIE.

This is my graniter and my chalmerlaine;
   And hes my gould, and geir, under hir curis: 2500
I mak ane vow to God, I sall complaine
   Unto the Paip, how ye do me injuris.

COVETICE.

My reverent Fathers, tak in patience,
I sall nocht lang remaine from your presence,
Thocht for ane quhyll, I man from yow depairt,
I wait my spreit sall remaine in your hart:
And quhen this King Correctioun beis absent,
Then sall we twa returne incontinent;
Thairfoir adew!—

SPIRITUALITIE.

   Adew, be Sanct Mavene!

Pas quhair ye will, we ar twa naturall men. 2510

SENSUALITIE.

Adew, my Lord!

SPIRITUALITIE.

Adew, my awin sweit hart!
Now, duill fell me that wee twa man depart.

SENSUALITIE.

My Lord, howbeit this parting dois me paine,
I traist in God, we sal meit sone againe.

SPIRITUALITIE.

To cum againe, I pray yow, do your cure,
Want I yow twa, I may nocht lang indure.

[*Heir sal the Sergeants chase them away, and they sal gang to the seat of Sensualitie.*]

TEMPORALITIE.

My Lords, ye knaw The Thrie Estaits
For Common-weill suld mak debaits:
Let now, amang us, be devysit,
Sic Actis that with gude men be praysit, 2520
Conforming to the common law,
For of na man we sould stand aw:
And, for till saif us fra murmell,
Schone, Diligence fetch us Gude Counsell;
For quhy, he is ane man that knawis
Baith the Cannon, and Civill Lawis.

DILIGENCE.

Father, ye man incontinent
Pass to the Lordis of Parliament:
For quhy, thay ar determinat all,
To do na thing bot be your counsall.   2530

GUDE COUNSELL.

That sal I do within schort space;
Praying the Lord, to send us grace,
For till conclude, or wee depart;
That thay may profeit efterwart,
Baith to the Kirk, and to the King,
I sall desyre na uther thing.   [*Pausa.*

My Lords, God glaid the cumpanie!
Quhat is the caus, ye send for me?

MERCHAND.

Sit doun, and gif us your counsell,
How we sall slaik the greit murmell   2540
Of pure peopill, that is weill knawin,
And as the Common-weill hes schawin:
And als, we knaw, it is the Kingis will,
That gude remeid be put thairtill.
Sir Common-weill, keip ye the bar,
Let nane except yourself cum nar.

JOHNE.

That sall I do, as I best can,
I sall hauld out baith wyfe and man.
Ye man let this puir creature,

Support me, for till keip the dure: 2550
I knaw his name, full sickerly,
He will complaine, als weill as I.

GUDE COUNSELL.

My worthy Lords, sen ye have taine on hand,
Sum reformatioun to mak into this land:
And als ye knaw, it is the King's mynd,
Quha to the Common-weil hes ay bene kynd:
Thocht reif, and thift, wer stanchit weill aneuch,
Yit sumthing mair belangis to the pleuch.
Now, into peace, ye sould provyde for weirs,
And be sure of how mony thowsand speirs, 2560
The King may be, quhen he hes ocht ado;
For quhy, my Lords, this is my ressoun to:
The husband-men, and commons, thay war wont,
Go, in the battell, formest in the front,
Bot I have tint all my experience,
Without ye mak sum better diligence:
The Common-weill mon uther wayis be styllit,
Or, be my faith, the King will be begyllit.
Thir pure commouns, daylie, as ye may se,
Declynis doun till extreme povertie: 2570
For, sum ar hichtit sa into thair maill,
Thair winning will nocht find them water kaill.
How Prelats heichtis thair teinds, it is weill knawin,
That husband-men may not weill hald thair awin:
And, now begins ane plague, amang them new,
That gentill men thair steadings taks in few:
Thus man thay pay greit ferme, or lay thair steid,
And sum ar plainlie harlit out be the heid,
And ar distroyit, without God on thame rew.

PAUPER.

Sir, be God's breid, that taill is verie trew.   2580
It is weill kend, I had baith nolt, and hors;
Now, all my geir ye se upon my cors.

CORRECTIOUN.

Or I depairt, I think till mak ane ordour.

JOHNE.

I pray you, Sir, begin first at [the] Bordour:
For, how can we fend us aganis Ingland,
Quhen we can nocht, within our native land,
Destroy our awin Scots, common trator theifis,
Quha, to leill laborers, daylie dois mischeifis?
War I ane king, my Lord, be God's wounds,   [2590
Quha ever held common theifis within thir bounds,
Quhairthrow, that dayly leil men micht be wrangit,
Without remeid, thair chiftanis suld be hangit,
Quhidder he war ane Knicht, ane Lord, or Laird,
The Devill draw me to hell, and he war spaird.

TEMPORALITIE.

Quhat uther enemies hes thou, let us ken?

JOHNE.

Sir, I compleine upon the idill men:
For quhy, Sir, it is God's awin bidding,
All Christian men to wirk for thair living,
Sanct Paull, that pillar of the kirk,
Sayis to the wretchis, that will not wirk,   2600
And bene to vertews laith,

Qui non laborat, non manducet,
This is, in Inglische toung, or leit,
QUHA LABOURIS NOCHT HE SALL NOT EIT.
This bene against the strang beggers,
Fidlers, pypers, and pardoners ;
Thir jugglars, jestars, and idill cuitchours,
Thir carriers, and thir quintacensours ;
Thir babil-beirers and thir bairds,
Thir sweir swyngeours with lords, and lairds :   2610
Ma, than thair rents may susteine,
Or to thair profeit neidfull bene,
Quhilk bene ay blythest of discords,
And deidly feid amang thair lords :
For then, they sleutchers man be treatit,
Or els, thair querrels undebaitit.
This bene against thir great fat Freiris,
Augustenes, Carmleits, and Cordeleirs ;
And all uthers, that in cowls bene cled,
Quhilk labours nocht; and bene weill fed,   2620
I mein, nocht laborand spirituallie,
Nor, for thair living, corporallie :
Lyand, in dennis, lyke idill doggis,
I thame compair to weil-fed hoggis.
I think thay do thame selfis abuse,
Seing that thay the warld refuse :
Haifing profest sic povertie,
Syne fleis fast fra necessitie.
Quhat, gif thay povertie wald professe?
And do, as did Diogenes,   2630
That great famous philosophour ;
Seing, in earth, bot vaine labour,

Alutterlie, the warld refusit,
And, in ane tumbe, him self inclusit,
And leifit on herbs, and water cauld,
Of corporall fude, na mair he wald :
He trottit nocht, from toun to toun,
Beggand to fed his carioun :
Fra tyme that lyfe he did profes,
The warld of him was cummerles. 2640
Richt sa of Marie Magdalene,
And of Mary th' Egyptiane,
And of auld Paull, the first hermeit ;
All thir had povertie compleit.
Ane hundreth ma, I micht declair,
Bot, to my purpois I will fair ;
Concluding sleuthfull idilness,
Against the Common-weill expresse.

CORRECTIOUN.

Quhom upon ma, will ye compleine ?

JOHNE.

Marie ! on ma, and ma againe : 2650
For, the pure peopill cryis with cairis,
The infetching of Justice Airis,
Exercit mair, for covetice,
Than, for the punisching of vyce.
Ane peggrell theif, that steillis ane kow,
Is hangit ; bot he, that steillis ane bow,
With als meikill geir as he may turs,
That theif is hangit be the purs :
Sic pykand peggrall theifis ar hangit ;

Bot, he that all the warld hes wrangit, 2660
Ane cruell tyrane, ane strang transgressour,
Ane common publick plaine oppressour,
By buds may he obteine favours
Of Tresurers and Compositours,
Thocht he serve greit punitioun,
Gets easie compositioun:
And, throch laws Consistoriall,
Prolixt, corrupt, and perpetuall,
The common peopill ar put sa under,
Thocht thay be puir, it is na wonder. 2670

CORRECTIOUN.

Gude Johne, I grant, all that is trew,
Your infortoun full sair I rew:
Or I pairt aff this Natioun,
I sall mak reformatioun.
And als, my Lord Temporalitie,
I yow command, in tyme, that ye
Expell oppressioun aff your lands:
And als, I say to yow, Merchands,
Gif ever I find, be land, or sie,
Dissait be in your cumpanie, 2680
Quhilk ar to Common-weill contrair,
I vow to God, I sall nocht spair,
To put my sword to executioun,
And mak on yow extreme punitioun,
Mairover, my Lord Spiritualitie,
In gudelie haist, I will, that ye
Set into few your temporall lands,
To men that labours with thair hands;

Bot nocht to ane gearking gentill man,
That nether will he wirk, nor can : 2690
Quhairthroch the policy may incresse.

TEMPORALITIE.

I am content, Sir, be the Messe;
Swa, that the Spiritualitie
Sets thairs in few, als weill as wee.

CORRECTIOUN.

My Spirituall Lords, ar ye content?

SPIRITUALITIE.

Na, na! wee man tak advysement;
In sic maters, for to conclude
Ouir haistelie, wee think nocht gude.

CORRECTIOUN.

Conclude ye nocht with the Common-weill,
Ye salbe punischit, be Sanct Geill. 2700

[*Heir sall the Bischops cum with the Freir.*

SPIRITUALITIE.

Schir, we can schaw exemptioun,
Fra your temporall punitioun;
The quhilk we purpois till debait.

CORRECTIOUN.

Wa! than, ye think to stryve for stait.
My Lords, quhat say ye to this play?

TEMPORALITIE.

My soverane Lords, we will obay,
And tak your part, with hart and hand,
Quhat ever ye pleis us to command.

> [*Heir sal the Temporal Stait sit doun on thair kneis, and say:*

Bot, wee beseik yow, Soveraine!
Of all our cryms, that ar bygaine,   2710
To gif us ane remissioun;
And heir, wee mak to yow conditioun
The Common-weill for till defend,
From hence-forth, till our lives end.

CORRECTIOUN.

On that conditioun, I am content
Till pardon yow, sen ye repent,
The Common-weill tak be the hand,
And mak with him perpetuall band.

> [*Heir sall the Temporall Staitis, to wit, the Lords and Merchands, imbrasse Johne the Commonweill.*

Johne, haif ye ony ma debaits,
Aganis the Lords of Spirituall Staits?   2720

JOHNE.

Na, Sir, I dar nocht speik ane word;
To plaint on Preistis, it is na bourd.

CORRECTIOUN.

Flyt on thy fow fill I desyre thé;
Swa, that thou schaw bot the veritie.

JOHNE.

Grandmerces, then, I sall nocht spair,
First, to compleine on the Vickair:
The pure Cottar, lykand to die,
Haifand young infants, twa, or thrie;
And hes twa ky, but ony ma,
The Vickar must haif ane of thay,   2730
With the gray frugge, that covers the bed,
Howbeit, the wyfe be purelie cled,
And gif the wyfe die on the morne,
Thocht all the bairns sould be forlorne,
The uther kow, he cleiks away,
With the pure cot of raploch gray:
Wald God! this custome war put doun,
Quhilk never was foundit be ressoun.

TEMPORALITIE.

Ar all thay tails trew, that thou telles?

PAUPER.

Trew, Sir, the Divill stick me elles: 2740
For, be the Halie Trinitie,
That same was practeisit on me;
For our Vickar, God give him pyne,
Hes yit thrie tydie kye of myne:
Ane, for my father, and for my wyfe, ane uther,
And the thrid cow, he tuke, for Mald my mother.

JOHNE.

Our Persone, heir, he takis na uther pyne,
Bot, to ressave his teinds, and spend them syne:
Howbeit, he be obleist, be gude ressoun,
To preich the Evangell to his parochoun.   2750
Howbeit thay suld want preiching sevintin yeir,
Our Persoun will not want ane scheif of beir.

PAUPER.

Our Bischops, with thair lustie rokats quhyte,
Thay flow in riches, royallie, and delyte,
Lyke paradice, bene thair palices, and places,
And wants na plesour of the fairest faces.
Als, thir Prelates hes great prerogatyves;
For quhy, thay may depairt ay with thair wyves,
Without ony correctioun, or damnage;
Syne tak ane uther wantoner, but mariage.   2760
But doubt, I wald think it ane pleasant lyfe,
Ay on, quhen I list, to part with my lyfe;
Syne, tak ane uther of far greater bewtie:
Bot ever alace! my Lords, that may not be,
For I am bund, alace! in mariage;
Bot thay lyke rams, rudlie in thair rage,
Unpysalt, rinnis amang the sillie yowis,
Sa lang, as kynde of nature, in them growis.

PERSON.

Thou lies, fals huirson, raggit loun!
Thair is na preists, in all this toun,   2770
That ever usit sic vicious crafts.

JOHNE.

The Feind ressave thay flattrant chafts:
Sir Domine, I trowit, ye had be[ne] dum,
Quhair Devil, gat we this ill-fairde blaitie bum?

PERSON.

To speik of Priests be sure it is na bourds;
Thay will burne men, now, for rakles words,
And, all thay words ar herisie in deid.

JOHNE.

The mekil Feind resave the saul that leid;
All that I say is trew, thocht thou be greifit,
And that, I offer, on thy pallet, to preif it.   2780

SPIRITUALITIE.

My Lords, quhy do ye thoil that lurdun loun,
Of kirk-men, to speik sic detractioun:
I let yow wit, my Lords, it is na bourds,
Of Prelats, for till speik sic wantoun words.

[*Heir Spiritualitie fames and rages.*

You villaine puttis me out of charitie.

TEMPORALITIE.

Quhy, my Lord, sayis he ocht bot verity;
Ye can nocht stop ane pure man, for till pleinze,
Gif he hes faltit, summond him to your seinze.

SPIRITUALITIE.

Yea, that I sall, I mak greit God a vow!

He sall repent, that he spak of the kow ; 2790
I will nocht suffer sic words of yon villaine.

PAUPER.

Than, gar gif me my thrie fat ky againe.

SPIRITUALITIE.

Fals Carle, to speik to me, stands thou not aw ?

PAUPER.

The Feind resave them, that first devysit that law !
Within an houre, efter my dade was deid,
The vickar had my kow hard be the heid.

PERSON.

Fals huirson Carle ! I say that law is gude,
Becaus, it hes bene lang our consuetude.

PAUPER.

Quhen I am Paip, that law I sal put doun ;
It is ane sair law, for the pure commoun. 2800

SPIRITUALITIE.

I mak an vow, thay wordis thou sal repent.

GUDE COUNSELL.

I yow requyre, my Lords, be patient :
Wee came nocht heir, for disputatiouns ;
Wee came to mak gude reformatiouns.
Heirfoir, of this your propositioun,
Conclude, and put to executioun.

MERCHAND.

My Lords, conclud that al the Temporal lands
Be set, in few, to laboreris, with thair hands,
With sic restrictiouns as sall be devysit;
That thay may live, and nocht to be supprysit,　2810
With ane ressonabill augmentatioun:
And, quhen thay heir ane proclamatioun,
That the King's Grace dois mak him, for the weir,
That thay be reddie, with harneis, bow, and speir.
As for my self, my Lord, this I conclude.

GUDE COUNSELL.

Sa, say we all, your ressoun be sa gude:
To mak ane Act on this we ar content.

JOHNE.

On that, sir Scribe, I tak ane instrument:
Quhat do ye of the corspresent, and kow?

GUDE COUNSELL.

I wil conclude nathing of that, as now,　2820
Without my Lord of Spiritualitie
Thairto consent, with all this haill cleargie.
My Lord Bischop, will ye thairto consent?

SPIRITUALITIE.

Na, na! never, till the day of Judgement:
Wee will want nathing, that wee have in use,
Kirtil nor kow, teind lambe, teind gryse, nor guse.

TEMPORALITIE.

Forsuith, my Lord, I think we suld conclude ;
Seing this kow, ye have in consuetude :
We will decerne heir, that the King's grace
Sall wryte unto the Paipis Holines : 2830
With his consent, be proclamatioun,
Baith corspresent, and cow, wee sall cry doun.

SPIRITUALITIE.

To that, my Lords, wee plainlie disassent,
Noter, thairof I tak ane instrument.

TEMPORALITIE.

My Lord, be Him that al the warld hes wrocht,
Wee set nocht by, quhider ye consent, or nocht :
Ye ar bot ane Estait, and we ar twa,
Et ubi major pars, ibi tota.

JOHNE.

My Lords, ye haif richt prudentlie concludit ;
Tak tent, now, how the land is clein denudit, 2840
Of gould, and silver, quhilk daylie gais to Rome,
For buds, mair than the rest of Christindome.
War I ane king, Sir, be cok's passioun,
I sould gar mak ane proclamatioun,
That never ane penny sould go to Rome at all,
Na mair than did to Peter, nor to Paull.
Do ye nocht sa, heir, for conclusioun,
I gif yow all my braid black malesoun.

MERCHAND.

It is of treuth, Sirs, be my christindome,
That mekil of our money gais to Rome: 2850
For, we Merchants, I wait, within our bounds,
Hes furneist Preists ten hundreth thowsand pounds,
For thair finnance, nane knawis sa weill as wee :
Thairfoir, my Lords, devyse sum remedie ;
For throw thir playis, and thir promotioun,
Mair for denners, nor for devotioun,
Sir Symonie hes maid with them ane band,
The gould of weicht, thay leid out of the land ;
The Common-weill thairthroch bein sair opprest ;
Thairfoir, devyse remeid, as ye think best. 2860

GUDE COUNSELL.

It is schort tyme, sen ony benefice,
Was sped in Rome, except greit bischoprics.
Bot, now for ane unworthie vickarage,
Ane preist will rin to Rome, in pilgramage.
Ane cavell, quhilk was never at the scule,
Will rin to Rome, and keip ane bischop's mule ;
And syne cum hame, with mony colorit crack,
With ane buirdin of benefices on his back ;
Quhilk bene against the law, ane man alane,
For till posses ma benefices nor ane : 2870
Thir greit Commends, I say, withoutin faill,
Sould nocht be given, bot to the blude Royall :
Sa, I conclude, my Lords, and sayis for me,
Ye sould annull all this pluralitie.

SPIRITUALITIE.

The Paip hes given us dispensatiouns.

GUDE COUNSELL.

Yea, that is, be your fals narratiouns:
Thocht the Paip, for your pleasour, will dispence,
I trow, that can nocht cleir your conscience:
Advyse, my Lords, quhat ye think to conclude.

TEMPORALITIE.

Sir, be my faith, I think it verie gude,   2880
That, fra hence furth, na Preistis sall pas to Rome;
Becaus our substance thay do still consume,
For pleyis, and for thair profeit singulair,
Thay haif of money maid this realme bair:
And als, I think it best, be my advyse,
That ilk preist sall haif bot ane benefice:
And gif thay keip nocht that fundatioun,
It sall be caus of deprivatioun.

MERCHAND.

As ye haif said, my Lord, we wil consent:
Scribe, mak ane Act on this incontinent.   2890

GUDE COUNSELL.

My Lords, thair is ane thing yit unproponit;
How Prelats, and Preistis, aucht to be disponit:
This beand done, wee have the les ado;
Quhat say ye, Sirs? This is my counsall, lo!
That, or wee end this present Parliament,

Of this mater, to tak rype advysement.
Mark weill, my Lords, thair is na benefice,
Given to ane man, bot for ane gude office.
Quha taks office, and syne thay can nocht use it,
Giver and taker, I say, ar baith abusit.   2900
Ane bischop's office is for to be ane preichour,
And of the Law of God ane publick techour.
Richt sa, the Persone unto his parochoun,
Of the Evangell sould leir thame ane lessoun.
Thair sould na man desyre sic dignities,
Without he be abill for that office:
And for that caus, I say, without leising,
Thay have thair teinds, and for na uther thing.

SPIRITUALITIE.

Freind, quhair find ye, that we suld prechours be?

GUDE COUNSELL.

Luik quhat Sanct Paul wryts unto Timothie: 2910
Tak thair the Buik, let se, gif ye can spell.

SPIRITUALITIE.

I never red that, thairfoir reid it yoursell.

[*Gude Counsell sall read thir words on ane Buik:*

Fidelis sermo, Si quis Episcopatum desiderat, bonum opus desiderat. Oportet eum irreprehensibilem esse, unius uxoris virum, sobrium, prudentem, ornatum, pudicum, hospitalem, doctorem: Non vinolentum, non percussorem: sed modestum. That is:

"This is a true saying, If any man desire the office of a bishop, he desireth a worthie worke: A bishop therefore must be unreproveable, the husband of one wife," &c.

SPIRITUALITIE.

Ye temporall men, be Him that heryit hell,
Ye ar ovir peart, with sik maters to mell.

TEMPORALITIE.

Sit still, my Lord, ye neid not for til braull,
Thir ar the verie words of th' Apostill Paull.

SPIRITUALITIE.

Sum sayis, be Him that woare the croun of thorne,
It had bene gude that Paull had neir bene borne.

GUDE COUNSAL.

Bot ye may knaw, my Lord, Sanct Paul's intent,
Schir, red ye never the New Testament ? 2920

SPIRITUALITIE.

Na, Sir, be him that our Lord Jesus sauld,
I red never the New Testament, nor Auld ;
Nor ever thinks to do, Sir, be the Rude ;
I heir freiris say, that reiding dois na gude.

GUDE COUNSELL.

Till yow, to reid them, I think it is na lack,
For anis, I saw them baith, bund on your back :
That samin day, that ye was consecrat,

Schir, quhat meinis that?

SPIRITUALITIE.

The Feind stick them that wat.

MERCHANT.

Then, befoir God, how can ye be excusit?
To haif ane office, and waits not how to usit: 2930
Quhairfoir, war gifin yow all the temporal landis?
And all thir teinds, ye haif amang your hands:
Thay war givin yow, for uther causses, I weine,
Nor mummil matins and hald your clayis cleine.
Ye say till the Appostils that ye succeid,
Bot ye schaw nocht that, into word nor deid.
The law is plaine, our teinds suld furnisch teichours.

GUDE-COUNSELL.

Yea, that it sould, or susteine prudent preichours.

PAUPER.

Sir, God, nor I be stickit with ane knyfe,
Gif ever our Persoun preichit in all his lyfe.   2940

PARSON.

Quhat Devil raks thé of our preiching, undocht?

PAUPER.

Think ye, that ye suld haif the teinds, for nocht?

PARSON.

Trowis thou, to get remeid, Carle, of that thing?

PAUPER.

Yea, be God's breid, richt sone, war I ane King.

PARSON.

Wald thou, of Prelats mak deprivatioun?

PAUPER.

Na, I suld gar them keip thair fundatioun:
Quhat devill is this, quhom of sould kings stand aw?
To do the thing, that thay sould be the law.
War I ane King, be cok's deir passioun,
I sould richt sone mak reformatioun.   2950
Failzeand thairof, your grace sould richt sone finde,
That Preists sall leid yow, lyke ane bellic blinde.

JOHNE.

Quhat, gif King David war leivand in thir dayis?
The quhilk did found sa mony gay Abayis:
Or out of heavin, quhat gif he luikit doun?
And saw the great abominatioun,
Amang thir Abesses, and thir Nunries,
Thair publick huirdomes, and thair harlotries:
He wald repent, he narrowit sa his bounds,
Of yeirlie rent, thriescoir of thowsand pounds;   2960
His successours maks litill ruisse, I ges,
Of his devotioun, or of his holines.

ABBASSE.

How dar thou, Carle, presume, for to declair,
Or, for to mell thé, with sa heich a mater?

For, in Scotland, thair did yit never ring,
I let the wit, ane mair excellent King.
Of holines he was the verie plant,
And now, in heavin, he is ane michtfull Sanct;
Becaus, that fyftein Abbasies he did found;
Quhair throw, great riches hes ay done abound   2970
Into our Kirk, and daylie yit abunds,
Bot, kings now, I trow, few abbasies founds,
I dar weill say, thou art condempnit in hell,
That dois presume, with sic maters, to mell.
Fals hureson Carle, thou art ovir arrogant,
To juge the deids of sic ane halie Sanct.

JOHNE.

King James the first, roy of this regioun,
Said that he was ane sair Sanct to the croun.
I heir men say, that he was sumthing blind,
That gave away mair nor he left behind.   2980
His successours that halines did repent,
Quhilk gart thame do great inconvenient.

ABBASSE.

My Lord Bishop, I mervel how that ye
Suffer this Carle for to speik heresie.
For, be my faith, my Lord, will ye tak tent,
He servis for to be brunt incontinent.
Ye can nocht say, bot it is heresie,
To speik against our law and libertie.

SPIRITUALITIE.

Sancte Pater, I mak you supplicatioun,

Exame yon Carle, syne mak his dilatioun: 2990
I mak ane vow to God Omnipotent,
That bystour sal be brunt incontinent.
Venerabill Father, I sall do your command,
Gif he servis deid I sall sune understand.
                                                              [*Pausa.*

Fals huirsun Carle, schaw furth thy faith!

JOHNE.

Me think ye speik as ye war wraith.
To yow I will nathing declair;
For ye ar nocht my Ordinair.

FLATTERIE.

Quhom in trowis thou, fals monster mangit?

JOHNE.

I trow to God, to see thé hangit: 3000
War I ane King, be cok's passioun,
I sould gar mak ane congregatioun,
Of all the Freiris of the four Ordouris,
And mak yow vagers, on the Bordours.
Schir, will ye give me audience,
And I sal schaw your Excellence;
Sa that your grace will give me leife,
How into God that I beleife.

CORRECTIOUN.

Schaw furth your faith, and fenzie nocht.

JOHNE.

I beleife in God, that all hes wrocht, 3010

And creat everie thing of nocht,
And, in his Son, our Lord Jesu,
Incarnat of the Virgin trew;
Quha under Pilat tholit passioun,
And deit for our salvatioun;
And, on the thrid day, rais againe,
As halie scriptour schawis plane:
And als, my Lord, it is weill kend,
How he did to the heavin ascend;
And set him doun at the richt hand   3020
Of God the Father, I understand;
And sall cum judge on Dumisday:
Quhat will ye mair, Sir, that I say?

CORRECTIOUN.

Schaw furth the rest, this is na game.

JOHNE.

I trow *Sanctam Ecclesiam*,
Bot nocht in thir Bishops nor thir Freirs,
Quhilk will, for purging of thir neirs:
Sard up the ta raw, and doun the uther,
The mekill Devill resave the fidder.

CORRECTIOUN.

Say quhat ye will, Sirs, be Sanct Tan,   3030
Me think Johne ane gude Christian man.

TEMPORALITIE.

My Lordis, let be your disputatioun;
Conclude, with firme deliberatioun,

How Prelatis, fra thyne, sall be disponit.

MERCHAND.

I think, for me, evin as ye first proponit,
That the King's grace sall gif na benefice,
Bot till ane preichour, that can use that office:
The sillie sauls, that bene Christis scheip,
Sould nocht be givin to gormand wolfis to keip.
Quhat bene the caus of all the heresies,   3040
Bot the abusioun of the Prelacies?
Thay will correct, and will nocht be correctit:
Thinkand to na prince thay will be subjectit:
Quhairfoir, I can find na better remeid,
Bot that thir kings, man tak it in thair heid,
That thair be given to na man bishoprics,
Except thay preich out throch thair diosies;
And ilk persone preich in his parochon:
And this, I say, for finall conclusioun.

TEMPORALITIE.

Wee think your counsall is verie gude;   3050
As ye have said, wee all conclude.
Of this conclusioun, Noter, wee mak ane Act.

SCRYBE.

I wryte all day, bot gets never ane plack.

PAUPER.

Och! my Lords, for the Halie Trinitie,
Remember to reforme the Consistorie:
It hes mair neid of reformatioun,

Nor Ploutois court, Sir, by cok's passioun.

PERSON.

Quhat caus hes thou, fals pellour, for to pleinze,
Quhair was ye ever summond to thair senze?

PAUPER.

Marie! I lent my gossop my mear, to fetch hame coills,
And he hir drounit into the Querrell hollis: [3060
And I ran to the Consistorie, for to pleinze,
And thair I happinit amang ane greidie meinze.
Thay gave me first ane thing, thay call *Citandum*,
Within aucht dayis, I gat bot *Lybellandum*,
Within ane moneth, I gat *ad Opponendum*,
In half ane yeir, I gat *Interloquendum*,
And syne, I gat, how call ye it? *ad Replicandum*:
Bot, I could never ane word yit understand him;
And than, thay gart me cast out many plackis, 3070
And gart me pay for four-and-twentie actis:
Bot, or thay came half gait to *Concludendum*,
The Feind ane plack was left for to defend him:
Thus, thay postponit me twa yeir, with thair traine,
Syne, *Hodie ad octo*, bad me cum againe:
And than, thir ruiks, thay roupit wonder fast,
For sentence silver, thay cryit at the last.
Of *Pronunciandum*, thay maid me wonder faine;
Bot I got never my gude gray meir againe.

TEMPORALITIE.

My Lords, we man reforme thir Consistory lawis, 3080
Quhais great defame, above the heavins blawis.

I wist ane man, in persewing ane kow,
Or he had done, he spendit half ane bow :
Sa that the King's honour wee may avance ;
Wee will conclude, as thay have done in France,
Let Spirituall maters pas to Spritualitie,
And Temporall maters to Temporalitie.
Quha failzeis of this sall cost them of thair gude.
Scribe, mak ane Act, for sa wee will conclude.

SPIRITUALITIE.

That Act, my Lords, plainlie I will declair,   3090
It is againis our profeit singulair :
Wee will nocht want our profeit, be Sanct Geill.

TEMPORALITIE.

Your profeit is aganis the Common-weill.
It sal be done, my Lordis, as ye have wrocht,
We cure nocht, quhidder ye consent, or nocht :
Quhairfoir servis, then, all thir Temporall Judges?
Gif temporall maters sould seik, at yow, refuges,
My Lord, ye say that ye are Spirituall ;
Quhairfoir mell ye, than, with things temporall?
As we have done conclude, sa sall it stand.   3100
Scribe, put our Acts in ordour, evin fra hand.

SPIRITUALITIE.

Till all your Acts, plainlie, I disassent :
Notar, thairof, I tak ane instrument.

> [*Heir sall Veritie and Chastitie mak thair plaint at the bar.*

VERITIE.

My Soverane, I beseik your excellence,
   Use justice on Spiritualitie :
The quhilk to us hes done great violence ;
   Becaus we did rehers the veritie.
   Thay put us close into captivitie,
And sa remanit into subjectioun :
   Into great langour, and calamitie,   3110
Till we war fred be king Correctioun.

CHASTITIE.

My lord, I haif gret caus for to complaine,
   I could get na ludging intill this land ;
The Spirituall stait had me sa at disdane,
   With dame Sensuall, thay have maid sic ane band,
   Amang them all na freindschip, Sirs, I fand ;
And quhen I came the nobill innis amang,
   My lustie Ladie Priores, fra hand
Out of hir dortour, durlie, scho me dang.

VERITIE.

With the advyse, Sir, of the Parliament,   3120
   Hairtlie we mak yow supplicatioun :
Cause King Correctioun tak incontinent,
   Of all this sort examinatioun.
   Gif thay be digne of deprivatioun,
Ye have power for till correct sic cases :
   Chease the maist cunning Clerks of this natioun,
And put mair prudent Pastours in thair places.

My prudent Lords, I say, that pure craftsmen,
  Abufe sum Prelats, are mair for to commend :
Gar exame them, and sa ye sall sune ken   3130
  How thay, in vertew, Bischops dois transcend.

SCRYBE.

Thy life, and craft, mak to thir Kings kend :
Quhat craft hes thow, declair that to me plaine?

TAILZOUR.

Ane Tailzour, sir, that can baith mak and mend;
I wait nane better into Dumbartane.

SCRYBE.

Quhairfoir of Tailzeours beirs thou the styll?

TAILZOUR.

Becaus I wait is nane within ane myll
Can better use that craft, as I suppois :
For I can mak baith doublit, coat, and hois.

SCRYBE.

How cal thay you, sir, with the schaiping knife? 3140

SOWTAR,

Ane Sowtar, Sir, nane better in Fyfe.

SCRYBE.

Tel me, quhairfoir ane Sowtar ye are namit?

SOWTAR.

Of that surname I neid nocht be aschamit :

For I can mak schone, brotekins, and buittis:
Gif me the coppie of the King's cuittis,
And ye sall se, richt sune, quhat I can do:
Heir is my lasts, and weill wrocht ledder lo.

GUDE COUNSELL.

O Lord, my God, this is an mervelous thing,
How sic misordour in this realme sould ring.   3150
Sowtars and Tailzeours, thay ar far mair expert
In thair pure craft, and in thair handie art,
Nor ar our Prelatis in thair vocatioun:
I pray yow, Sirs, mak reformatioun.

VERITIE.

Alace! alace! quhat gars thir temporal kings
Into the kirk of Christ admit sic doings?
My Lords, for lufe of Christ's passioun,
Of thir ignorants, mak deprivatioun,
Quhilk, in the court, can do bot flatter and fleich,
And put into thair places that can preich:
Send furth, and seik sum devoit cunning Clarks, 3160
That can steir up the peopill to gude warks.

CORRECTIOUN.

As ye have done, Madame, I am content,
Hoaw! Diligence, pas hynd, incontinent,
And seik out throw all towns and cities;
And visie all the Universities.
Bring us sum Doctours of Divinitie,
With Licents, in the Law and Theologie,
With the maist cunning Clarks in all this land;

Speid sune your way, and bring them heir, fra hand.

DILIGENCE.

Quhat, gif I find sum halie Provinciall ? 3170
Or minister of the Gray Freiris all ?
Or ony Freir, that can preich prudentlie,
Sall I bring them with me in cumpanie ?

CORRECTIOUN.

Cair thou nocht quhat estait sa ever he be,
Sa thay can teich, and preich the veritie.
Maist cunning Clarks with us is best beluifit,
To dignitie thay sall be first promuifit ;
Quhidder thay be munk, channon, preist, or freir,
Sa thay can preich, faill nocht to bring them heir.

DILIGENCE.

Then fair-weill, Sir, for I am at the flicht, 3180
I pray the Lord to send yow all gude nicht.

[*Heir sall Diligence pas to the palzeoun.*

TEMPORALITIE.

Schir, we beseik your soverane celsitude,
  Of our dochtours to have compassioun ;
Quhom wee may na way marie, be the Rude,
  Without we mak sum alienatioun
  Of our land, for thair supportatioun ;
For quhy ? the markit raisit bene sa hie,
  That Prelats dochtours of this natioun
Ar maryit with sic superfluitie :

Thay will nocht spair to gif twa thowsand pound, 3190
   With thair dochtours, to ane nobill man :
In riches, sa thay do superabound :
   Bot we may nocht do sa, be Sanct Allane :
   Thir proud Prelats our dochters sair may ban ;
That thay remaine at hame sa lang unmaryit :
   Schir, let your barrouns do the best thay can,
Some of our dochtours, I dreid, sal be miscaryit.

CORRECTIOUN.

My Lord, your complaint is richt ressonabill,
And richt sa to our dochtours profitabill :
I think, or I pas aff this Natioun,   3200
Of this mater till mak reformatioun.

   [*Heir sall enter Commoun Thift.*

COMMOUN THIFT.

Ga by the gait, man, let me gang,
How Devill came I into this thrang ?
With sorrow I may sing ane sang,
   And I be taine :
For I have run baith nicht and day,
Throw speid of fut, I gat away :
Gif I be kend heir, wallaway !
   I will be slaine.

PAUPER.

Quhat is thy name, man, be thy thrift ?   3210

COMMOUN THIFT.

Huirson, thay call me Common Thift :

For quhy? I had na uther schift
    Sene I was borne:
In Ewisdaill was my dwelling place,
Mony ane wyfe gart I cry, Alace!
At my hand thay gat never grace,
    Bot aye forlorne.
Sum sayis ane King is cum amang us,
That purposis to head and hang us:
Thair is na grace, gif he may fang us,   3220
    Bot on ane pin.
Ring he, we theifis will get na gude,
I pray God, and the halie Rude,
He had bene smoird into his cude,
    And all his kin.
Get this curst King me in his grippis,
My craig will wit quhat weyis my hippis:
The Devill, I gif his toung and lippis,
    That of me tellis:
Adew! I dar na langer tarie;   3230
For be I kend, thay will me carie,
And put me in ane fierie farie,
    I se nocht ellis.
I raife, be Him that herryit hell,
I had almaist foryet my sell:
Will na gude fallow to me tell,
    Quhair I may finde
The Erle of Rothus best haiknay?
That was my earand, heir-away:
He is richt starck, as I heir say,   3240
    And swift as winde.
Heir is my brydill and my spurris,

To gar him lance ouir land and furris
Micht I him get to Ewis-durris,
 I tak na cuir.
Of that hors, micht I get ane sicht,
I haife na doubt, yit or midnicht,
That he and I sould tak the flicht
 Throch Dysert Mure.
Of cumpanarie, tell me, brother,   3250
Quhilk is the richt way to the Strother?
I wald be welcum to my mother,
 Gif I micht speid:
I wald gif baith my coat and bonet
To get my Lord Lindesayis broun jonet,
War he beyond the watter of Annet,
 We sould nocht dreid.

Quhat now, Oppressioun, my maister deir!
Quhat mekill devill hes brocht yow heir?
Maister, tell me the caus, perqueir,   3260
 Quhat is, that ye have done?

OPPRESSIOUN.

Forsuith, the King's majestie
Hes set me heir, as ye may se:
Micht I speik Temporalitie,
 He wald me releife sone.
I beseik yow, my brother deir,
Bot halfe ane houre for to sit heir;
Ye knaw, that I was never sweir
 Yow to defend;
Put in your leg in to my place,   3270
And heir, I sweir be God's grace,

Yow to reliefe within schort space,
   Syne let yow wend.

COMMOUN THIFT.

Than maister deir, gif me your hand,
And mak to me ane faithfull band,
That ye sall cum agane, fra hand,
   Withoutin faill.

OPPRESSIOUN.

Tak thair my hand, richt faithfullie,
Als I promit thé, verelie,
To gif to thé ane cuppill of kye,　　　　3280
   In Liddisdaill.

[*Heir sall Commoun Thift put his feit in the stokkis; and Oppressioun sall steill away and betray him.*

[Bruder, tak patience in thy pane,
For I sweir thé be Sanct Fillane,
We twa sall nevir meit agane,
   In land nor toun.

COMMOUN THIFT.

Maister, will ye not keip conditioun,
And put me furth of this suspitioun?

OPPRESSIOUN.

Na, nevir, quhill I get remissioun.
   Adew! my companyeoun;

I sall commend thé to thy dame. 3290

COMMOUN THIFT.

Adew! than, in the Devillis name!
For to be fals thinkis thow na schame?
   To leif me in this pane,
Thow art ane loun, and that ane liddir.

OPPRESSIOUN.

Bo, man! I will go to Balquhiddir;
It sall be Pasche, be Goddis moder,
   Or evir we meit agane.]
Haif I nocht maid ane honest schift,
That has betrasit Commoun Thift?
For thair is nocht under the lift, 3300
   Ane curster cors
I am richt sure, that he and I,
Within this half-yeir, craftely
Hes stolne ane thowsand scheip and ky,
   By meiris and hors.
Wald God! I war baith sound and haill
Now liftit into Liddisdaill,
The Mers sould find me beif and kaill,
   Quhat rak of bread:
War I thair liftit, with my lyfe, 3310
The Devill sould stick me with ane knyfe,
And ever I come againe to Fyfe,
   Quhyll I war dead.
Adew! I leife the Devill amang yow,
That in his fingers he may fang yow,
With all leill men that dois belang yow:

> For I may rew
> That ever I came into this land.
> For quhy? ye may weill understand,
> I gat na geir to turne my hand;   3320
> > Yit anis adew!

[Heir sall Diligence convoy the thrie Clarks.

DILIGENCE.

Schir, I have brocht unto your Excellence
Thir famous Clarks of greit intelligence:
For to the common peopill thay can preich,
And in the scuilis, in Latine toung, can teich.
This is ane Doctour of Divinitie,
And thir twa Licents, men of gravitie.
I heare men say, thair conversatioun
Is maist in Divine Contemplatioun.

DOCTOUR.

Grace, peace, and rest, from the hie Trinitie,   3330
Mot rest amang this godlie cumpanie;
Heir ar we cumde, as your obedients,
For to fulfill your just commandements.
Quhat evir it please your Grace us to command,
Sir, it sall be obeyit, evin fra hand.

REX.

Gude freinds, ye ar richt welcome to us all;
Sit doun all thrie, and geif us your counsall.

DIVYNE CORRECTIOUN.

Sir, I give yow baith counsal and command,

In your office, use exercitioun : [3340
First, that ye gar search out throch all your land,
  Quha can nocht put to executioun
  Thair office, efter the institutioun,
Of godlie lawis, conforme to thair vocatioun :
  Put in thair places men of gude conditioun,
And this ye do without dilatioun.

Ye ar the head, Sir, of this congregatioun,
  Preordinat be God Omnipotent ;
Quhilk hes me send, to mak yow supportatioun,
  Into the quhilk I salbe diligent :
  And quhasaever beis inobedient, 3350
And will nocht suffer for to be correctit,
  They sal be all deposit incontinent,
And from your presence thay sall be dejectit.

GUDE COUNSALL.

Begin first, at the Spiritualitie ;
  And tak of them examinatioun.
Gif they can use thair divyne dewetie,
  And, als, I mak yow supplicatioun,
All thay that hes thair offices misusit,
  Of them mak haistie deprivatioun :
Sa that the peopill be na mair abusit. 3360

DIVYNE CORRECTIOUN.

Ye ar ane Prince of Spiritualitie :
How have ye usit your office, now let se ?

SPIRITUALITIE.

My Lords, quhen was thair ony Prelatis wont

Of thair office till ony King mak count?
Bot of my office, gif ye wald have the feill,
I let yow wit, I have it usit weill:
For I tak in my count twyse in the yeir,
Wanting nocht of my teind ane boll of beir.
I gat gude payment of my Temporall lands,
My buttock-maill, my coattis, and my offrands, 3370
With all that dois perteine my benefice,
Consider now, my Lord, gif I be wyse.
I dar nocht marie, contrair the common law,
Ane thing thair is, my Lord, that ye may knaw.
Howbeit, I dar nocht plainlie spouse ane wyfe,
Yit concubeins I have had four or fyfe.
And to my sons I have givin rich rewairds,
And all my dochters maryit upon lairds.
I let yow wit, my Lord, I am na fuill,
For quhy? I ryde upon ane amland muill. 3380
Thare is na temporall lord, in all this land,
That maks sic cheir, I let yow understand.
And als, my Lord, I gif with gude intentioun,
To divers temporall lords ane yeirlie pensioun;
To that intent, that thay, with all thair hart,
In richt, and wrang, sal plainlie tak my part.
Now, have I tald yow, Sir, on my best ways,
How that I have exercit my office.

DIVYNE CORRECTIOUN.

I wein'd your office had bene for til preich,
And God's law to the peopill teich; 3390
Quhairfoir weir ye that mytour? ye me tell.

SPIRITUALITIE.

I wat nocht, man, be Him that herryit hell.

DIVYNE CORRECTIOUN.

That dois betakin, that ye, with gude intent,
Sould teich, and preich, the Auld and New Testament.

SPIRITUALITIE.

I have ane Freir to preiche into my place,
Of my office, ye heare na mair quhyll Pasche.

CHASTITIE.

My Lords, this Abbot, and this Priores,
  Thay scorne thair Gods, this is my reason quhy:
Thay beare ane habite of feinzeit halines,
  And in thair deid, thay do the contrary: 3400
  For to live chaist, thay vow solemnitly.
Bot, fra that thay be sikker of thair bowis,
  Thay live in huirdome, and in harlotry:
Examine them, Sir, how thay observe thair vowis.

DIVYNE CORRECTIOUN.

Sir Scribe, ye sall, at Chastitie's requeist,
Pas, and exame yon thrie, in gudlie haist.

SCRYBE.

Father Abbot, this Counsall bids me speir
How ye have usit your Abbay, thay wald heir:
And als, thir Kings hes given to me commissioun
Of your office, for to mak inquisitioun.   3410

ABBOT.

Tuiching my office, I say to yow plainlie,
My Monks and I, we leif richt easelie:
Thare is na monks, from Carrick to Carraill,
That fairs better, and drinks mair helsum aill.
My Prior is ane man of great devotioun:
Thairfor, daylie, he gets ane double portioun.

SCRYBE.

My Lords, how have ye keipt your thrie vows?

ABBOT.

Indeid richt weill, till I gat hame my bows,
In my Abbay, quhen I was sure professour,
Then did I leife, as did my predecessour.   3420
My paramours is baith als fat and fair,
As ony wench, intill the toun of Air.
I send my sons to Pareis, to the scuillis,
I traist in God that thay sall be na fuillis.
And all my douchters, I have weill provydit,
Now, judge ye, gif my office be weill gydit.

SCRYBE.

Maister Person, schaw us gif ye can preich?

PERSON.

Thocht I preich not, I can play at the caiche:
I wait thair is nocht ane amang yow all,
Mair ferilie can play at the fut-ball;   3430
And for the carts, the tabils, and the dyse,

Above all persouns, I may beir the pryse.
Our round bonats, we mak thame now four nuickit;
Of richt fyne stuiff, gif yow list, cum and luikit.
Of my office, I have declarit to thé;
Speir quhat ye pleis, ye get na mair of me.

SCRYBE.

Quhat say you now, my Ladie Priores?
How have ye usit your office, can ye ges?
Quhat was the caus ye refusit harbrie:
To this young, lustie, Ladie Chastitie? 3440

PRIORES.

I wald have harborit hir, with gude intent,
Bot, my complexioun thairto wald not assent:
I do my office, efter auld use and wount,
To your Parliament, I will mak na mair count.

VERITIE.

Now, caus sum of your cunning clarks,
Quhilk ar expert in heavinlie warkis,
And men fulfillit with charitie,
That can weill preiche the veritie,
My Lord, gif sum of them command,
Ane sermon for to mak, fra-hand. 3450

DIVYNE CORRECTIOUN.

As ye have said, I am content,
To gar sum preich incontinent.

[Pausa.

Magister Noster, I ken how ye can teiche,
  Into the scuillis, and that richt ornatlie:

I pray yow, now, that ye wald please to preiche,
　In Inglisch toung, land folk to edifie.

DOCTOUR.

Soverane, I sall obey yow humbillie,
With ane schort sermon, presentlie, in this place:
　And schaw the word of God unfeinzeitlie,
And sinceirlie, as God will give me grace.　　3460

　　[*Heir sall the Doctour pas to the pulpit, and say:*

　　Si vis ad vitam ingredi, serva mandata.

Devoit peopill, Sanct Paull, the preichour sayis,
　The fervent luife, and fatherlie pitie,
Quhilk God Almichtie hes schawin mony ways,
　To man, in his corrupt fragilitie,
　Exceids all luife, in earth, sa far, that we
May never to God mak recompence conding;
　As quha sa lists to reid the veritie,
In halie Scripture, he may find this thing:

　　Sic Deus dilexit mundum.

Tuiching nathing, the great prerogative,
　Quhilk God, to man, in his creatioun, lent:　　3470
How man, of nocht creat, superlative,
　Was to the image of God, Omnipotent:
　Let us consider that speciall luife ingent,
God had to man, quhen our foir father fell;
　Drawing us all, in his loynis immanent,
Captive from gloir, in thirlage to the hell.

Quhen angels fell, thair miserabil ruyne

Was never restorit, bot for our miserie,
The Sun of God, secund persone divyne,
   In ane pure Virgin tuke humanitie: 3480
    Syne, for our saik, great harmis suffered he,
In fasting, walking, in preiching, cauld and heit,
   And, at the last, ane schamefull death deit he,
Betwix twa theifis, on croce, he yeild the spreit:

And, quhair an drop of his maist precious blude
   Was recompence sufficient, and conding,
Ane thowsand warlds to ransoun, from that wod,
   Infernall feind, Sathan; nochtwithstanding,
    He luifit us sa, that for [our] ransoning,
He sched furth all the blude of his bodie,   3490
   Riven, rent, and sair woundit, quhair he did hing,
Naild on the croce, on the Mont Calvary:

     Et copiosa apud eum redemptio.

O cruell death, be thé, the venemous
   Dragon, the devill infernall, lost his pray:
Be thé, the stinkand, mirk, contageous,
   Deip pit of hell, mankynd escaipit fray:
   Be thé, the port of paradice alsway
Was patent maid unto the heavin sa hie:
   Opinnit to man and maid ane reddie way,
To gloir eternall, with th' haly Trinitie.   3500

And yit, for all this luife incomparabill,
   God askis na rewaird, fra us againe,
Bot, luife for luife, in his command, but fabill,
   Conteinit ar all haill the lawis ten;
    Baith ald, and new, and commandements ilk ane,

Luife bene the ledder, quhilk hes bot steppis twa:
　By quhilk, we may clim up to lyfe againe,
Out of this vaill of miserie, and wa.

　　*Diliges Dominum Deum tuum ex toto corde tuo,
　　　et proximum tuum sicut teipsum; in his
　　　　duobus mandatis, &c.*

The first step snithlie of this ledder is,
　To luife thy God, as the fontaine and well　　3510
Of luife, and grace; and the secund, I wis,
　To luife thy nichtbour as thou luiffis thy sell.
Quha tynis ane step of thir twa, gais to hell,
But he repent, and turne to Christ anone.
　Hald this na fabill, the halie Evangell
Bears, in effect, thir words, everie one:

　　Si vis ad vitam ingredi, serva mandata Dei.

Thay tyne thir steps, all thay quha ever did sin,
　In pryde, invy, in ire, and lecherie;
In covetice, or ony extreme win,
　Into sweirnes, or into gluttonye:　　3520
　Or quha dois nocht the deids of mercie,
Gif hungrie meit, and gif the naikit clayis.

PERSON.

Now, walloway! thinkis thou na schame to lie?
I trow, the devill a word is trew, thou sayis:

Thow sayis, thair is bot twa steppis to the hevin,
　Quha failzeis them man backwarts fall in hell:
I wait it is ten thowsand mylis, and sevin,
　Gif it be na mair, I do it upon thy sell.

Schort leggit men, I se, be Bryd's bell, [3530
Will nevir cum thair, thay steppis bene sa wyde:
  Gif thay be the words of the Evangell;
The Spirituall men hes mister of ane gyde.

ABBOT.

And I beleif, that cruikit men, and blinde,
  Sall never get up upon sa hich ane ledder:
By my gude faith, I dreid to ly behinde,
  Without, God draw me up into ane tedder;
Quhat and I fal, then I will break my bledder:
And I cum thair this day, the devill speid me;
  Except, God make me lichter, nor ane fedder,
Or send me doun gude widcok wingis to flie. 3540

PERSONE.

Cum doun, dastart, and gang sell draiff,
  I understand nocht quhat thow said;
Thy wordis war nather corne, nor caiff;
  I wald thy toung againe war laide.
Quhair, thou sayis pryde is deidlie sin:
  I say pryde is bot honestie,
And covetice of warldlie win
  Is bot wisdome, I say for me:
  Ire, hardines, and gluttonie,
Is nathing ellis, bot lyfis fude: 3550
  The naturall sin of lecherie
Is bot trew luife; all thir ar gude.

DOCTOUR.

God, and the Kirk, hes givin command,
  That all gude Christian men refuse them.

PERSONE.

Bot, war thay sin, I understand,
  We men of Kirk wald never use them.

DOCTOUR.

Brother, I pray the Trinitie,
  Your faith, and charitie, to support:
Causand yow knaw the veritie,
  That ye your subjects may comfort.   3560
To your prayers, peopill, I recommend,
  The rewlars of this nobill regioun:
That our Lord God his grace mot to them send,
  On trespassours, to mak punitioun:
Prayand to God, from feinds yow defend,
  And of your sins, to gif yow full remissioun:
I say na mair, to God, I yow commend!

    [*Heir Diligence spyis the Freir roundand to the
      Prelate.*

DILIGENCE.

My Lords, I persave, that the Sprituall Stait,
Be way of deid, purpois to mak debait:
For, be the counsall of yon flattrand Freir,   3570
Thay purpois, till mak all this toun on steir.

FIRST LICENTIATE.

Traist ye, that thay wil be inobedient,
To that, quhilk is decreitit in Parliament?

DILIGENCE.

Thay se the Paip, with awfull ordinance,
Makis weir aganis the michtie king of France :
Richt sa, thay think, that Prelats suld nocht sunzie,
Be way of deid, defend thair patrimonie.

FIRST LICENTIATE.

I pray thé, brother, gar me understand,
Quhair ever Christ possessit ane fut of land.

DILIGENCE.

Yea, that he did, Father, withoutin fail :   3580
For Christ Jesus was King of Israell.

FIRST LICENTIATE.

I grant that Christ was king abufe al kings :
Bot he mellit never with temporall things ;
As he hes plainlie done declair himsell,
As thou may reid, in his halie Evangell :
Birds hes thair nests, and tods hes thair den,
Bot Christ Jesus, the Saviour of men,
In all this warld, hes nocht ane penny braid,
Quhairon he may repois his heavinlie head.

DILIGENCE.

And is that trew ?

BATCHELOR.

                Yea, brother, be Alhallows :
Christ Jesus had na propertie but the gallows : [3590

And left not quhen he yeildit up the spreit,
To by himself ane simpill winding scheit.

DILIGENCE.

Christ's successours, I understand,
Thinks na schame to have temporall land.
Father, thay have na will, I yow assure,
In this warld, to be indigent, and pure:
Bot, Sir, sen ye ar callit sapient,
Declair to me the caus, with trew intent,
Quhy that my lustic ladie Veritie, 3600
Hes nocht bene weill treatit in this cuntrie?

BATCHELER.

Forsuith, quhair Prelats uses the counsall
  Of beggand Freirs, in monie regioun,
And thay Prelats, with Princes principall,
  The veritie, but doubt, is trampit doun;
  And Common-weill put to confusioun.
Gif this be trew, to yow, I me report:
  Tharfoir, My Lords, mak reformatioun
Or ye depairt, hartlie, I yow exhort.

Sirs, freirs wald never, I yow assure, 3610
  That ony prelats usit preiching:
And prelats tuke on them that cure,
  Freirs wald get nathing for thair fleiching.
    Thairfoir, I counsall yow fra hand,
    Banische yon Freir out of this land,
      And that incontinent:
    Do ye nocht sa, withoutin weir,

He will mak all this toun on steir,
    I knaw his fals intent.
Yon Priores, withoutin fabill,   3620
I think scho is nocht profitabill,
    For Christis regioun.
To begin reformatioun,
Mak of them deprivatioun,
    This is my opinioun.

FIRST SERGEANT.

Sir, pleis ye, that we twa invaid thame,
And ye sall se us sone degraid thame
    Of cowll, and skaplarie?

DIVYNE CORRECTIOUN.

Pas on, I am richt weill content;
Syne banische thame incontinent,   3630
    Out of this cuntrie.

FIRST SERGEANT.

Cum on, Sir Freir, and be nocht fleyit,
The King our maister mon be obeyit,
    Bot ye sall have na harme:
Gif ye wald travell, fra toun to toun,
I think this hude, and habbie goun,
    Will hald your wambe ouir warme.

FLATTRIE (the Freir).

Now, quhat is this, that thir monster meins?
I am exemptit fra Kings, and Queens,
    And fra all humane law.   3640

SECUND SERGEANT.

Tak ye the hude, and I the gown,
This limmer luiks als lyke ane lown,
   As any that ever I saw.

FIRST SERGEANT.

Thir Freiris, to chaip punitioun,
Haulds them at thair exemptioun,
   And na man will obey:
Thay ar exempt, I yow assure,
Baith fra Paip, King, and Empreour,
   And that maks all the pley.

SECUND SERGEANT.

On Dumisday, quhen Christ sall say,   3650
   Venite, Benedicti:
The Freirs will say, without delay,
   Nos sumus exempti.

  [*Heir sall thay spoilze Flattrie of the Freirs habite.*

GUDE COUNSALL.

Sir, be the Halie Trinitie,
This same is feinzeit Flattrie,
   I ken him, be his face:
Beleivand for to get promotioun,
He said that his name was Devotioun;
   And sa begylit your Grace.

FIRST SERGEANT.

Cum'on, my ladie Priores,   3660
    We sall leir yow to dance;
And that, within ane lytill space,
    Ane new pavin of France.

[*Heir sall thay spuilze the Priores, and scho sall
have ane kirtill of silk under hir habite.*

Now brother, be the Masse,
    Be my jugement, I think,
This halie Priores
    Is turnit in ane cowclink.

PRIORES.

I gif my freinds my malisoun,
That me compellit till be ane nun,
    And wald nocht let me marie: 3670
It was my freinds greadines,
That gart me be ane Priores,
    Now hartlie them I warie.
Howbeit, that nunnis sing nichts and dayis,
Thair hart waitis nocht quhat thair mouth sayis,
    The suith, I yow declair:
Makand yow intimatioun,
To Christis congregatioun,
    Nunnis are nocht necessair.
Bot I sall do the best I can,   3680
And marie sum gude honest man,
    And brew gude aill and tun:

Mariage, be my opinioun,
It is better religioun,
    As to be freir, or nun.

FLATTRIE (the Freir).

My Lords, for God's saik, let not hang me,
Howbeit, that widdiefows wald wrang me,
    I can mak na debait,
To win my meat, at pleuch, nor harrowis,
Bot, I sall help to hang my marrowis,   3690
    Baith Falset, and Dissait.

DIVYNE CORRECTIOUN.

Than pas thy way, and greath the gallowis,
Syne help for to hang up thy fellowis,
    Thou gets na uther grace.

FLATTRIE.

Of that office, I am content,
Bot our Prelatis, I dreid, repent,
    Be I fleimde from thair face.

[*Heir sall Flattrie pas to the stokkis, and sit besyd his marrowis.*

DISSAIT.

Now Flattrie, my auld companzeoun,
Quhat dois yon King Correctioun?
    Knawis thou nocht his intent?   3700
Declair to us of thy novellis.

[FLATTRIE.]

Ye'ile all be hangit, I se nocht ellis;
   And that incontinent.

DISSAIT.

Now, walloway! will ye gar hang us?
The Devill brocht yon curst King amang us,
   For mekill sturt and stryfe.

FLATTRIE.

I had bene put to deid amang yow,
War nocht I tuk on hand till hang yow;
   And sa I saifit my lyfe:
I heir them say, thay will cry doun   3710
All Freirs, and Nunnis, in this regioun,
   Sa far as I can feill:
Becaus, thay ar nocht necessair,
And als, thay think thay ar contrair,
   To Johne the Common-weill.

[*Heir sal the Kings and the Temporal Stait round togider.*]

DIVYNE CORRECTIOUN.

With the advice of King Humanitie,
  Heir I determine, with rype advysement,
That all thir Prelats sall deprivit be';
  And be decreit of this present Parliament,
   That thir thrie cunning Clarks sapient,   3720
Immediatlie thair places sall posses;

Becaus, that thay have bene sa negligent,
Suffring the word of God for till decres.

REX HUMANITAS.

As ye have said, but dout, it salbe done,
Pas to, and mak this interchainging sone.

[*The King's servants lay hands on the thrie Prelats and says:*]

WANTONNES.

My Lordis, we pray yow to be patient,
For, we will do the King's commandement.

SPIRITUALITIE.

I mak ane vow to God, and ye us handill,
Ye sallbe curst, and gragit, with buik and candill:
Syne, we sall pas unto the Paip, and pleinzie;   3730
And to the Devill of hell condemne this meinze:
For quhy? sic reformatioun, as I weine,
Into Scotland was never hard, nor seine.

[*Heir sal thay spuilze them with silence, and put
thair habite on the thrie Clarks.*]

MERCHAND.

We mervell of yow, paintit sepulturis,
That was sa bauld, for to accept sic cuiris.
With glorious habite, rydand upon your muillis,
Now men may se, ye ar bot verie fuillis.

SPIRITUALITIE.

We say, the Kings war greiter fuillis, nor we,
That us promovit to sa greit dignitie.

ABBOT.

Thair is ane thowsand, in the Kirk, but doubt, 3740
Sic fuillis as we, gif thay war weill socht out;
Now, brother, sen it may na better be,
Let us ga soup with Sensualitie.

    [*Heir sall thay pas to Sensualitie.*

SPIRITUALITIE.

Madame, I pray yow, mak us thrie gude cheir;
We care nocht to remaine with yow all yeir.

SENSUALITIE.

Pas fra us, fuillis, be Him that hes us wrocht,
Ye ludge nocht heir, becaus I knaw yow nocht.

SPIRITUALITIE.

Sir Covetice, will ye also misken me?
I wat richt weill, ye wil baith gif, and len me: [3750
Speid hand, my freind, spair nocht to break the lockis:
Gif me ane thowsand crouns out of my box.

COVETYCE.

Quhairfoir, Sir Fuill gif yow ane thowsand crownis?
Ga hence, ye seme to be thrie verie lowns.

SPIRITUALITIE.

I se nocht els, brother, withoutin faill,
Bot, this fals warld is turnit top ouir taill:
Sen, all is vaine, that is under the lift,
To win our meat, we man make uther schift.
With our labour, except we mak debait,
I dreid full sair, we want baith drink and meat.

PARSON.

Gif, with our labour, we man us defend,   3760
Then let us gang, quhair we war never kend.

SPIRITUALITIE.

I wyte thir Freirs, that I am thus abusit;
For, by thair counsall, I have bene confusit:
Thay gart me trow, it suffysit, allace!
To gar them plainlie preich, into my place.

ABBOT.

Allace! this reformatioun, I may warie;
For I have yit twa dochteris for to marie;
And thay ar baith contractit, be the Rude,
And waits nocht how to pay thair tocher-gude.

PARSON.

The Devill mak cair, for this unhappie chance,   3770
For I am young, and thinks to pas to France;
And tak wages, amang the men of weir,
And win my living, with my sword and speir.

[*The Bischop, Abbot, Persone, and Priores depairts altogidder.*]

GUDE COUNSALL.

Or ye depairt, Sir, aff this regioun,
Gif Johne the Common-weill ane gay garmoun;
Becaus, the Common-weill hes bene overluikit,
That is the caus, that Common-weill is cruikit.
With Singular Profeit, he hes bene sa supprysit,
That he is baith cauld, naikit, and disgysit.

DIVYNE CORRECTIOUN.

As ye have said, Father, I am content: 3780
Sergeants, gif Johne ane new abuilzement.
Of sating damais, or of the velvot fyne;
And gif him place in our Parliament syne.

[*Heir sal thay cleith Johne the Common-weill gorgeouslie, and set him doun amang them in the Parliament.*]

All verteous Peopil, now, may be rejoysit,
  Sen, Common-weill hes gotten ane gay garmoun:
And ignorants, out of the Kirk, deposit,
  Devoit Doctours, and Clarks of renoun,
  Now, in the Kirk, sall have dominioun:
And Gude Counsall, with ladie Veritie,
Ar profest with our King's Majestie. 3790

Blist is that realme, that hes ane prudent king,
  Quhilk dois delyte to heir the veritie;

Punisching thame, that plainlie dois maling,
 Contrair the common-weill, and equitie.
 Thair may na peopill have prosperitie,
Quhair ignorance hes the dominioun,
And Common-weill, be tirants, trampit doun.
                                        [*Pausa.*

Now Maisters ye sall heir incontinent,
 At great leysour, in your presence, proclamit
The nobill Acts of our Parliament;   3800
 Of quhilks, we neid nocht for to be aschamit.
Cum heir Trumpet, and sound your warning tone,
That every man may knaw quhat we have done.

 [*Heir sall Diligence with the Scribe and the Trumpet
  pas to the pulpit and proclame the actis.*

THE FIRST ACT.

It is devysit, be thir prudent Kings,
 Correctioun, and King Humanitie,
That thair leigis, induring all thair ringis,
 With the avyce of the Estaits Thrie,
 Sall manfullie defend and fortifie
The Kirk of Christ, and his religioun,
 Without dissimulance, or hypocrisie;   3810
Under the paine of thair punitioun.

 II. Als thay will, that the Acts honorabill,
  Maid be our prince, in the last parliament,
 Becaus thay ar baith gude, and profitabill;
  Thay will, that everie man be diligent
  Thame till observe, with unfenzeit intent:

Quha disobeyis, inobedientlye,
　Be thair lawis, but doubt, thay sall repent,
And painis conteinit thairin sall underly.

III. AND als the Common-weill, for til advance, 3820
　It is statute, that all the temporall landis,
Be set in few, efter the forme of France,
　Til verteous men, that labours, with thair hands;
　Resonabillie restrictit, with sic bands,
That thay do service, nevertheles,
　And to be subject ay under the wands;
That riches may, with policie, incres.

IV. ITEM, this prudent Parliament hes devysit,
　Gif lords halds under thair dominioun
Theifis, quhair throch puir pepil bein supprisit: 3830
　For them thay sall mak answeir to the croun,
　And to the pure mak restitutioun:
Without thay put them in the judges hands;
　For thair default to suffer punitioun;
Sa that na theifis remaine within thair lands.

V. To that intent, that justice sould incres,
　It is concludit, in this Parliament,
That into Elgin, or into Innernesse,
　Sall be ane sute of Clarks sapient,
　Togidder with ane prudent Precident; 3840
To do justice, in all the Norther airtis,
　Sa equallie, without impediment,
That thay neid nocht seik justice in thir pairts.

VI. With licence of the Kirks halines,
　　That justice may be done continuallie,
All the maters of Scotland, mair and les,
　　To thir twa famous saits, perpetuallie,
　　Salbe directit, becaus men seis plainlie,
Thir wantoun Nunnis ar na way necessair,
　　Till Common-weill, nor yit to the glorie　　3850
Of Christ's Kirk, thocht thay be fat and fair.

And als, that fragill ordour feminine
　　Will nocht be missit in Christ's religioun,
Thair rents usit till ane better fyne,
　　For Common-weill of all this regioun.
　　Ilk Senature, for that erectioun,
For the uphalding of thair gravitie,
　　Sall have fyve hundredth mark of pensioun.
And also bot twa sall thair nummer be.

Into the North, saxteine sall thair remaine,　　3860
　　Saxtein richt sa, in our maist famous Toun
Of Edinburgh, to serve our Soveraine;
　　Chosen without partiall affectioun
　　Of the maist cunning clarks of this regioun:
Thair Chancellar chosen of ane famous clark,
　　Ane cunning man of great perfectioun,
And for his pensioun have ane thowsand mark.

VII. It is devysit, in this Parliament,
　　From this day furth, na mater temporall,
Our new Prelats thairto hes done consent,　　3870
　　Cum befoir judges consistoriall,

Quhilk has bene sa prolixt, and partiall;
To the great hurt of the communitie:
   Let temporall men seik Judges temporall,
And spirituall men to spiritualitie.

VIII. Na benefice beis giffin, in tyme cumming,
   Bot to men of gude eruditioun;
Expert in the halie Scripture, and cunning,
   And that thay be of gude conditioun,
   Of publick vices but suspitioun;   3880
And qualifeit richt prudentlie to preich,
   To thair awin folk baith into land and toun,
Or ellis, in famous scuillis, for to teich.

IX. Als becaus of the great pluralitie
   Of ignorant Preists, ma than ane legioun,
Quhairthroch, of teicheouris the heich dignitie
   Is vilipendit, in ilk regioun:
   Thairfoir, our Court hes maid ane provisioun,
That na bischops mak teichours, in tyme cumming,
   Except men of gude eruditioun,   3890
And for preistheid qualifeit and cunning.

Siclyke as ye se, in the Borrows toun,
   Ane tailzeour is nocht sufferit to remaine,
Without he can mak doublet, coat, and gown,
   He man gang till his prenteischip againe:
   Bischops sould nocht ressave, me think certaine
Into the Kirk, except ane cunning Clark:
   Ane idiot preist, Esay compaireth, plaine,
Till ane dum dogge, that can nocht byte nor bark.

x. Fra this day furth, se na prelats pretend,   3900
  Under the paine of inobedience,
At Prince, or Paip, to purchase ane Commend
  Againe the kow, becaus it dois offence:
  Till ony preist, we think sufficience
Ane benefice, for to serve God withall;
  Twa prelacies sall na man have, from thence,
Without that he be of the blude royall.

xi. Item, this prudent counsall hes concludit,
  Sa that our haly vickars be nocht wraith,
From this day furth, thay salbe cleane denudit,   3910
  Baith of corspresent, cow, and unest claith,
  To pure commons, becaus it hath done skaith:
And mairover, we think it lytill force,
  Howbeit, the Barronns thairto will be laith,
From thine-furth, thay sall want thair hyrald hors.

xii. It is decreit, that in this Parliament,
  Ilk Bischop, Minister, Priour, and Persoun;
To the effect thay may tak better tent,
  To saulis, under thair dominioun,
  Efter the forme of thair foundatioun,   3920
Ilk Bischop, in his diosie sall remaine:
  And everilk Persoun, in his parochoun,
Teiching thair folk, from vices to refraine.

xiii. Becaus that Clarks our substance dois consume,
  For bils, and proces, of thair prelacies:
Thairfoir thair sall na money ga to Rome,
  From this day furth, or any benefice:

    Bot gif, it be for gret archbischopries;
As for the rest, na money gais at all :
    For the incressing of thair dignities,   3930
Na mair, nor did to Peter, nor to Paull.

XIV. CONSIDERING that our Preistis, for the maist
        part,
    Thay want the gift of chastitie, we se ;
Cupido hes sa perst thame throch the hart ;
    We grant them licence, and frie libertie,
That thay may have fair virgins to thair wyfis :
    And sa keip matrimoniall chastitie,
And nocht in huirdome, for to leid thair lyfis.

XV. THIS Parliament, richt sa, hes done conclude :
    From this day forth, our Barrouns temporall 3940
Sall na mair mix their nobil ancient blude
    With bastard bairns of stait Spirituall :
    Ilk stait amang thair awin selfis marie sall ;
Gif Nobils marie with the Spiritualitie,
    From thyne, subject thay sal be, and all
Sal be degraidit of thair Nobilitie.

And from amang the Nobils cancellit,
    Untill the tyme thay by thair lybertie,
Rehabilit, be the Civill magistrate :
    And sa sall marie the Spiritualitie ;   3950
    Bischops with bischops sall mak affinitie,
Abbots, and prioris, with the priores :
    As bischop Annas, in Scripture, we may se,
Maryit his dochter on bischop Caiphas.

Now, have ye heard the Acts honorabill,
  Devysit in this present Parliament,
To Common-weill we think agreabil :
  All faithfull folk sould heirof be content,
  Thame till observe, with hartlie trew intent;
I wait nane will against our acts rebell,   3960
  Nor till our law be inobedient,
Bot Plutois band, the potent Prince of hell.

  [*Heir sall Pauper cum befoir the King, and say:*

PAUPER.

I gif yow my braid bennesoun,
That hes givin Common-weill a goun :
I wald nocht, for ane pair of plackis,
Ye had nocht maid thir nobill Actis.
I pray to God ! and sweit Sanct Geill !
To gif yow grace to use them weill :
Wer thay weill keipit, I understand,
It war great honour to Scotland.   3970
It had bene als gude, ye had sleipit,
As to mak Acts, and be nocht keipit :
Bot, I beseik yow, for Alhallows,
To heid Dissait, and hang his fellows ;
And banische Flattrie aff the Toun,
For thair was never sic ane loun.
That beand done, I hauld it best,
That everie man ga to his rest.

DIVYNE CORRECTIOUN.

As thou hes said, it salbe done:

Suyith! Sergeants, hang yon swingeours sone.   3980

[*Heir sall the Sergeants lous the presoners out of
the stocks, and leid them to the gallows.*

FIRST SERGEANT.

Cum heir, Sir Theif, cum heir, cum heir:
Quhen war ye wont to be sa sweir?
To hunt cattell ye war ay speidie,
Thairfoir ye sall waive in ane widdie.

COMMOUN THIFT.

Man I be hangit? allace! allace!
Is thair nane heir, may get me grace?
Yit, or I die, gif me ane drink.

FIRST SERGEANT.

Fy! huirsun Carle, I feil ane stink.

COMMOUN THIFT.

Thocht I wald nocht, that it war wittin,
Sir, in gude faith, I am bedirtin: 3990
To wit the veritie, gif ye pleis,
Louse doun my hois, put in your neis.

FIRST SERGEANT.

Thou art ane limmer, I stand foir'd,
Slip in thy heid into this coird,
For thou had never ane meiter tippit.

COMMOUN THIFT.

Allace! this is ane fellon rippit.   [*Pausa.*

The widdifow Wairdanis tuke my geir,
And left me nether hors, nor meir;
Nor erthlie gude, that me belangit,
Now, walloway! I man be hangit.   4000
Repent your lyfis, ye plaine oppressouris,
All ye misdoars, and transgressours:
Or ellis, gar chuse yow gude confessours,
    And mak yow forde:
For gif ye tarie in this land,
And cum under Correctioun's hand:
Your grace salbe, I understand,
    Ane guid scharp coird.

Adew! my Bretheren, common theifis,
That helpit me, in my mischeifis: 4010
Adew! Grosars, Nicksons, and Bellis,
Oft have we run out-thoart the fellis.
Adew! Robsonis, Hansles, and Pylis,
That in our craft hes mony wyllis:
Lytils, Trumbels, and Armestrangs,
Adew! all theifis that me belangs;
Tailzeours, Eurwings, and Elwands,
Speidie of fut and wicht of hands.
The Scottis of Ewisdaill, and the Graimis,
I have na tyme, to tell your namis.   4020
With King Correctioun, and ye be fangit,
Beleif richt weill, ye wilbe hangit.

        FIRST SERGEANT.
Speid hand, man, with thy clitter clatter.

COMMOUN THIFT.

For God's saik, sir, let me mak watter;
Howbeit, I have bene cattel-gredie,
It schamis to pische into ane widdie.

[*Heir sal Commoun Thift be drawin up, or his figour.*

SECUND SERGEANT.

Cum heir, Dissait, my companzeoun,
Saw ever ane man, lyker ane loun,
    To hing upon ane gallows?

DISSAIT.

This is aneuch to mak me mangit,   4030
Duill fell me, that I man be hangit,
    Let me speik with my fallows.
I trow wan-fortune brocht me heir;
    Quhat mekill feind maid me sa speidie?
Sen it was said, it is sevin yeir,
    That I sould weave into ane widdie,
    I leirit my maisters to be gredie.
Adew! for I se na remeid:
    Luke quhat it is to be evil-deidie!

SECUND SERGEANT.

Now, in this halter slip thy heid.   4040
    Stand still, me think ye draw aback.

DISSAIT.

Allace! maister, ye hurt my crag.

SECUND SERGEANT.

It will hurt better, I woid ane plak,
Richt now, quhen ye hing on ane knag.

DISSAIT.

Adew ! my Maisters, merchant men,
I have yow servit, as ye ken,
   Truelie, baith air and lait :
I say to yow, for conclusioun,
I dreid, ye gang to confusioun,
   Fra tyme ye want Dissait.   4050
I leirit yow, merchants, mony ane wyle,
Upalands wyfis, for to begyle,
   Upon ane market day :
And gar them trow your stuffe was gude,
Quhen it was rottin, be the Rude,
   And sweir it was nocht sway.
I was ay roundand in your ear,
And leirit yow for to ban and sweir,
   Quhat your geir cost in France :
Howbeit, the devill ane word was trew,   4060
Your craft, gif King Correctioun knew,
   Wald turne yow to mischance.
I leirit yow wyllis monyfauld,
To mix the new wyne, and the auld,
   That faschioun was na follie :
To sell richt deir, and by gude-chaip,
And mix ry-meill amang the saip,
   And saiffrone with oyl-dolie.
Forzet nocht ocker, I counsall yow,

Mair than the Vicker dois the kow, 4070
    Or Lords thair doubill maill :
Howbeit, your elwand be too skant,
Or your pound wecht thrie unces want,
    Think that bot lytill faill.
Adew! the greit clan Jamesone,
The blude royal of Clappertoun,
    I was ay to yow trew :
Baith Andersone, and Patersone,
Above them all, Thome Williamsone,
    My absence ye will rew. 4080
Thome Williamsone, it is your pairt,
To pray for me, with all your hairt,
    And think upon my warks :
How I leirit yow ane gude lessoun,
For to begyle, in Edinburgh toun,
    The Bischop and his Clarks.
Ye young merchants may cry Allace,
For wanting of your wonted grace,
    Yon curst King ye may ban :
Had I leifit bot half ane yeir, 4090
I sould have leirit yow craftis, perqueir,
    To begyle wyfe, and man.
How may ye merchants mak debait ?
Fra tyme ye want your man, Dissait,
    For yow, I mak greit cair :
Without I ryse fra deid to lyfe,
I wait weill, ye will never thryfe,
    Farther nor the fourth air.

[*Heir sal Dissait be drawin up, or ellis his fygure.*

FIRST SERGEANT.

Cum heir, Falset, and mence the gallows,
Ye man hing up amang your fallows,   4100
    For your cankart conditioun :
Monie ane trew man have ye wrangit ;
Thairfoir, but dout, ye sal be hangit
    But mercie, or remissioun,

FALSET.

Allace! man I be hangit to?
Quhat mckill devill is this ado ;
    How came I to this cummer?
My gude maisters, ye Crafts men,
Want ye Falset, full weill I ken,
    Ye will all die for hunger.   4110
Ye men of craft may cry Allace !
Quhen ye want me, ye want your grace ;
    Thairfoir, put into wryte
My lessouns that I did yow leir,
Howbeit, the commons eyne ye bleir,
    Count ye nocht that ane myte.
Find me ane wobster, that is leill,
Or ane walker, that will nocht steill,
    Thair craftines, I ken :
Or ane millair, that is na falt,   4120
That will nather steill meall, nor malt ;
    Hald them for halie men.
At our fleschers tak ye na greife,
Thocht thay blaw leane mutton, and beife,
    That thay seime fat, and fair :

Thay think that practick bot ane mow,
Howbeit, the devill a thing it dow;
    To thame I leirit that lair.
I leirit tailzeours, in everie toun,
To schaip fyve quarters in ane goun,   4130
    In Angus, and in Fyfe:
To uplands tailzeours, I gave gude leife,
To steill ane sillie stump, or sleife,
    Unto Kittok, his wyfe.
My gude maister, Andro Fortoun,
Of tailzeours, that may weir the croun,
    For me, he will be mangit:
Tailzeour Baberage, my sone and air,
I wait for me, will rudlie rair,
    Fra tyme he se me hangit.   4140
The barfit deacon Jamie Ralfe,
Quha never yit bocht kow, nor calfe;
    Becaus he can nocht steall:
Willie Cadzeoch will mak na plead,
Howbeit, his wyfe want beife, and bread,
    Get he gude barmie aill.
To the brousters of Cowper toun,
I leife my braid black malesoun,
    Als hartlie, as I may:
To mak thinne aill, thay think na falt,   4150
Of mekill barme, and lytill malt,
    Agane the market day.
And thay can mak, withoutin doubt,
Ane kynde of aill, thay call Harns-out,
    Wait ye how thay mak that?
Ane curtill queine, ane laidlie lurdane,

Of strang wesche scho will tak ane jurdane,
    And settis in the gyle-fat:
Quha drinkis of that aill, man or page,
It will gar all his harnis rage: 4160
    That jurdane I may rew;
It gart my heid rin hiddie giddie,
Sirs, God! nor I die in ane widdie,
    Gif this taill be nocht trew.
Speir at the sowtar, Geordie Sillie,
Fra tyme that he had fil'd his bellie,
    With this unhelthsum aill:
Than all the baxters will I ban,
That mixes bread with dust and bran,
    And fyne flour with beir maill.   4170
Adew! my maisters, wrichts, and maissouns,
I have neid to leir yow few lessouns,
    Ye knaw my craft, perqueir:
Adew! blak-smythis, and lorimers,
Adew! ye craftie cordiners,
    That sellis the schone over deir.
Gold-smythis, fair-weill, abuve thame all!
Remember my memoriall,
    With mony ane sittill cast:
To mix, set ye nocht by twa preinis,   4180
Fyne ducat gold with hard gudlingis,
    Lyke as I leirnit yow last.
Quhen I was ludgit upaland,
The schiphirds maid with me ane band,
    Richt craftelie to steill:
Than, did I gif ane confirmatioun
To all the schiphirdis of this natioun,

That thay sould never be leill :
And ilk ane to reset ane uther,
I knaw fals schiphirds fyftie fidder, 4190
War thair carteleinis kend :
How thay mak, in thair conventiouns,
On montans, far fra ony touns,
God let them never mend.
Amang crafts men, it is ane wonder,
To find ten leill amang ane hunder,
The treuth I to yow tell :
Adew ! I may na langer tarie,
I man pass to the King of Farie,
Or ellis the rycht to hell. 4200

[*Heir sall he luke up to his fallows hingand, and say,*

Wais me ! for thee gude Common Thift,
Was never man maid ane mair honest schift,
His leifing for to win :
Thare was nocht ane, in all Liddisdaill,
That ky mair craftelie culd staill,
Quhair thou hings on that pin.
Sathan ressave thy saull, Dissait,
Thou was to me ane faithfull mait,
And als my father brother :
Duill fell the sillie merchant men, 4210
To mak thame service weill I ken,
Tha'ill never get sic ane uther.

[*Heir sall thay festin the cord to his neck, with ane dum countenance : thairefter he sall say :*

Gif any man list, for to be my mait,
Cum follow me, for I am at the gait :
Cum follow me all catyfe covetous kings,
Reavers, but richt, of uthers realmis, and rings ;
Togidder with all wrangous conquerours,
And bring with yow all publick oppressours ;
With Pharao, king of Egiptians,
With him, in hell, salbe your recompence, 4220
All cruell schedders of blude innocent,
Cum follow me, or ellis rin, and repent.
Prelats that hes ma benefeits nor thrie,
And will nocht teich, nor preiche, the veritie :
Without at God, in tyme, thay cry for grace,
In hiddeous hell, I sall prepair thair place.
Cum follow me all fals corruptit judges,
With Pontius Pilat, I sall prepair your ludges :
All ye officials, that parts men with thair wyfis,
Cum follow me, or els gang mend your lyfis : 4230
With all fals leiders of the Constrie law,
With wanton scribes, and clarks, intill ane raw ;
That to the puir, maks mony partiall traine,
Syne, *hodie ad octo* bids thame cum againe.
And ye, that taks rewairds at baith the hands,
Ye sall, with me, be bund in Baliel's bands.
Cum follow me all curst unhappie wyfis,
That, with your gudemen, dayly flytis, and stryfis,
And quyetlie with rybalds maks repair ;
And taks na cure to mak ane wrangous air : 4240
Ye sal in hell rewairdit be, I wein,
With Jesabell, of Israell the queine.
I have ane curst, unhappie wyfe my sell,

Wald God! scho war, befoir me, into hell:
That bismair, war scho thair, withoutin doubt,
Out of hell, the Devill scho wald ding out.
Ye maryit men, evin as ye luife your lyfis,
Let never preists be hamelie with your wyfis.
My wyfe, with preists, scho doith me greit unricht,
And maid me nine tymes cuckald, on ane nicht. 4250
Fairweill! for I am to the widdie wend,
For quhy, Falset maid never ane better end.

> [*Heir sal he be heisit up, and not his figure, and an Craw, or ane Ke, salbe castin up, as it war his saull.*]

FLATTRIE.

Have I nocht chaipit the widdie weill?
Yea, that I have, be sweit Sanct Geill;
   For I had nocht bene wrangit;
Becaus I servit, be Alhallows,
Till have bene merchellit amang my fallowis,
   And heich above them hangit.
I maid far ma faltis, nor my maits,
I begylde all The Thrie Estaits, 4260
   With my hypocrisie:
Quhen I had on my Freir's hude,
All men beleifit that I was gude;
   Now, judge ye gif I be.
Tak me, ane rackles rubiatour,
Ane theif, ane tyrane, or ane tratour,
   Of everie vyce the plant:
Gif him the habite of ane freir,

The wyfis will trow, withoutin weir,
    He be ane verie Saint.   4270
I knaw that cowle and skaplarie
Genners mair hait, nor charitie,
    Thocht thay be blak, or blew :
Quhat halines is thair within,
Ane wolfe cled in ane wedder's skin,
    Judge ye, gif this be trew.
Sen, I have chaipit this firie farie,
Adew ! I will na langer tarie,
    To cumber yow, with my clatter :
Bot, I will, with ane humbill spreit,   4280
Gang serve the Hermeit of Larcit :
    And leir him, for till flatter.

[AN INTERLUDE:

THE SERMON OF FOLY.]

[Heir sall enter Folie.

FOLIE.

Gude day, my Lords, and als God saine !
Dois na man bid, Gude day, againe ?
Quhen fuillis are fow, then are thay faine,
    Ken ye nocht me ?
How call thay me, can ye nocht tell ?
Now, be Him that herryit hell,
I wait nocht how thay call my sell.
    Bot gif I lie.   4290

DILIGENCE.

Quhat brybour is this, that maks sic beiris ?

FOLIE.

The Feind ressave that mouth, that speirs :
Gude man, ga play yow, with your feiris,
    With muck upon your mow.

DILIGENCE.

Fond Fuill, quhair hes thou bene sa lait ?

FOLIE.

Marie ! cummand throw the Schogait,

Bot, thair hes bene ane great debait,
    Betwix me, and ane sow.
The sow cryit guff, and I to ga,
Throw speid of fute, I gat awa,   4300
Bot, in the midst of the cawsa,
    I fell into ane midding:
Scho lap upon me, with ane bend,
Quha ever the middings sould amend,
God send them ane mischevous end!
    For, that is bot God's bidding.
As I was pudlit thair, God wait,
But with my club I maid debait;
Ise never cum againe that gait,
    I sweir yow, be Alhallows.   4310
I wald the officiars of the toun,
That suffers sic confusioun,
That thay war harbreit with Mahown,
    Or hangit on ane gallows.
Fy! fy! that sic ane fair cuntrie
Sould stand sa lang but policie:
I gif thame to the Devill, hartlie,
    That hes the wyte:
I wald the Provost wald tak in heid,
Of yon midding, to make remeid.   4320
Quhilk pat me and the sow at feid.
    Quhat may I do, bot flyte?

REX HUMANITAS.

Pas on my servant, Diligence,

And bring yon Fuill to our presence.

DILIGENCE.

That sall be done, but tarying :
Foly, ye man ga to the King.

FOLIE.

The King? quhat kynde of thing is that?
Is yon he, with the goldin hat?

DILIGENCE.

Yon same is he : cum on thy way.

FOLIE.

Gif ye be king, God [gif] yow gude day ! 4330
I have ane plaint, to make to yow.

REX HUMANITAS.

Quhom on, Folie?

FOLIE.

      Marie ! on ane sow.
Sir, scho hes sworne, that scho sall sla me,
Or ellis, byte baith my balloks fra me :
Gif ye be King, be Sanct Allan,
Ye sould do justice to ilk man.
Had I nocht keipit me with my club,
The sow had drawin me in ane dub.
I heir them say, thair is cum to the Toun,
Ane King, callit Correctioun : 4340
I pray yow, tell me, quhilk is he?

DILIGENCE.

Yon, with the wings ; may [thow] nocht se ?

FOLIE.

Now, wallie fall that weill-fairde mow,
Sir, I pray yow, correct yon sow :
Quhilk with hir teith, but sword or knyfe,
Had maist have reft me of my lyfe :
Gif ye will nocht mak correctioun,
Than gif me your protectioun,
Of all swyne for to be skaithles,
Betuix this Toun and Innernes. 4350

DILIGENCE.

Folie, hes thou ane wyfe, at hame ?

FOLIE.

Yea, that I have, God send hir schame !
I trow be this scho is neir deid,
I left ane wyfe bindand hir heid ;
To schaw hir seiknes, I think schame,
Scho hes sic rumbling in hir wambe,
That, all the nicht my hart overcasts,
With bocking, and with thunder-blasts.

DILIGENCE.

Peradventure, scho be with bairne.

FOLIE.

Allace ! I trow scho be forfairne, 4360

Scho sobbit, and scho fell in sown,
And than, thay rubbit hir up and doun :
Scho riftit, routit, and maid sic stends,
Scho yeild, and gaid, at baith the ends.
Till scho had castin ane cuppill of quarts,
Syne, all turnit to ane rickill of farts.
Scho blubert, bocket, and braikit still,
Hir arsse gaid evin lyke ane wind-mill.
Scho stumblit, and stutterit, with sic stends,
That scho recantit at baith the ends. 4370
Sic dismell drogs, fra hir scho schot,
Quhill scho maid all the fluir on flot :
Of hir hurdies scho had na hauld,
Quhyll scho had tumed hir monyfauld.

DILIGENCE.

Better bring hir, to the Leitches heir.

FOLIE.

Trittill, trattill ! scho may nocht steir,
Hir veric buttoks maks sic beir,
   It skars baith foill and fillie :
Scho bocks sic bagage fra hir breist,
He wants na bubbils that sittis hir neist, 4380
And ay scho cryis, A preist, a preist,
   With ilk a quhillie lillie.

DILIGENCE.

Recoverit scho nocht at the last ?

FOLIE.

Yea, bot wit ye weil, scho fartit fast ;

Bot, quhen scho sichis, my hart is sarie.

DILIGENCE.

Bot drinkis scho ocht?

FOLIE.

Yea, be Sanct Marie!
Ane quart at anis, it will nocht tarie,
 And leif the devill a drap:
Than sic flobbage, scho layis fra hir,
About the wallis, God wait sic wair,   4390
 Quhen it was drunkin, I gat to skair
 The lickings of the cap.

DILIGENCE.

Quhat is in that creill, I pray thé tell?

FOLIE.

Marie! I have Folie Hats, to sell.

DILIGENCE.

I pray thé, sell me ane, or tway.

FOLIE.

Na, tarie quhill the market day.
I will sit doun heir, be Sanct Clune,
And gif my babies thair disjune.
Cum heir gude Glaiks, my dochter deir,
Thou sal be maryit, within ane yeir,   4400
Upon ane freir of Tillilum;
Na, thou art nather deaf nor dum:

Cum hidder, Stult, my sone and air,
My joy, thou art baith gude and fair,
Now, sall I feud yow, as I may,
Thocht ye cry lyke ane Ke, all day.

> [*Heir sal the bairns cry Keck, lyke ane Ke, and
> he sal put meat in thair mouth.*

DILIGENCE.

Get up, Folie, but tarying,
And speid yow haistelie to the King;
Get up! me think, the Carle is dum.

FOLIE.

Now, bum, baleriebum, bum.   4410

DILIGENCE.

I trow the trucour lyis, in ane trance;
Get up, man, with ane mirrie mischance!
Or be Sanct Dyonis of France,
    Ise gar thé want thy wallet;
It's schame to se, man, how thow lyis.

FOLIE.

Wa, yit againe, now this is thryis:
The Devill wirrie me, and I ryse,
    Bot, I sall break thy pallet.
Me think, my pillok will nocht ly doun;
Hauld doun your head, ye lurdoun loun,   4420
Yon fair las, with the sating goun,
    Gars yow thus bek, and bend.

Tak thair ane neidill, for your cace :
Now, for all the hiding of your face,
Had I yow, in ane quyet place,
 Ye wald nocht waine to flend :
Thay bony armis, that's cled in silk,
Ar evin als wantoun as any wilk,
I wald forbeir baith bread and milk,
 To kis thy bony lippis :   4430
Suppois ye luke, as ye war wraith,
War ye at quyet, behind ane claith,
Ye wald not stick, to preife my graith,
 With hobling of your hippis.
[Be God, I ken ye weill anneuch ;
Ye are faine, thocht ye mak it tuich,
Think ye nocht, as into the sewch,
 Besyd the Quarrell hoillis,
Ye wan fra me baith hoiss and schone,
And gart me mak mowis to the mone, 4440
And ay lap on your course abone.

DILIGENCE.

 Thow man be dung with poillis !]
Suyith ! harlot, haist thee to the King,
And let allane thy trattilling.

Lo ! heir is Folie, Sir, alreadie,
Ane richt sweir swingeour, be our Ladie !

FOLIE.

Thou art nocht half sa sweir thy sell ;
Quhat meins this pulpit, I pray thé tell ?

DILIGENCE.

Our new Bischops hes maid ane preiching,
Bot thou heard never sic pleasant teiching :   4450
Yon Bischop will preich throch the coast.

FOLIE.

Than stryk ane hag into the poast,
For, I hard never, in all my lyfe,
Ane bischop cum to preich in Fyfe.
Gif Bischops to be preichours leiris,
Wallaway! quhat sall word of Freiris!
Gif prelats preich, in brugh, and land,
The sillie freirs, I understand,
Thay will get na mair meall, nor malt :
Sa I dreid freirs sall die for falt.   4460
Sen, sa is, that yon nobill King
Will mak men bischops for preiching :
Quhat say you, Sirs, hauld ye nocht best,
That I gang preich amang the rest?
Quhen, I have preichit on my best wyis,
Then, will I sell my merchandise,
To my bretherin, and tender maits,
That dwellis amang The Thrie Estaits :
For I have heir gude chaifery,
Till any Fuill that lists to by.   4470

[*Heir sall Folie hing up his Hattis on the pulpet,
and say:*

God sen, I had ane Doctours hude.

REX HUMANITAS.

Quhy, Folie, wald thou mak ane preiching?

FOLIE.

Yea, that I wald, Sir, be the Rude,
But eyther flattering, or fleiching.

REX HUMANITAS.

Now, brother, let us heir his teiching,
   To pas our tyme, and heir him raife.

DILIGENCE.

He war far meiter for the kitching,
   Amang the pottis, sa Christ me saife.
Fond Folie, sall I be thy Clark?
   And answeir thee ay, with Amen.   4480

FOLIE.

Now, at the beginning of my wark,
   The Feind ressave that graceles grim.

[*Heir sall Folie begin his Sermon, as followis:*

STULTORUM NUMERUS INFINITUS:

Salomon, the maist sapient king,
In Israell quhan he did ring,
Thir words, in effect, did write,
THE NUMBER OF FUILLIS AR INFINITE.
I think na schame, sa Christ me saife,
To be ane Fuill, amang the laife,

Howbeit, ane hundreth stands heir by,
Perventure, als great fuillis as I. 4490

Stultorum :

I have of my genelogie,
Dwelland in everie cuntrie,
Erles, Duiks, Kings, and Empriours,
With mony guckit conquerours :
Quhilk dois in folie perseveir,
And hes done sa this monie yeir ;
And seiks to warldlie dignities,
And sum to sensuall vanities :
Quhat vails all thir vaine honouris,
Nocht being sure to leife twa houris ? 4500
Sum greidie fuill dois fill ane box,
Ane uther fuill cummis, and breaks the lox ;
And spends that uther fuillis hes spair'd.
Quhilk never thocht on them to wairde.
Sum dois as thay sould never die,
Is nocht this Folie, quhat say ye ?

Sapientia hujus mundi, Stultitia est apud Deum.

Becaus thair is sa many Fuillis,
Rydand on hors, and sum on muillis :
Heir I have brocht gude chaffery,
Till ony fuill that listis to by ; 4510
And speciallie for The Thrie Estaits,
Quhair I have mony tender maits :
Quhilk causit them, as ye may se,

Gang backwart throw the haill cuntrie.
Gif with my merchandise, ye list to mell,
Heir I have Folie Hattis to sell.
Quhairfoir, is this Hat wald ye ken?
Marie, for insatiabill merchant men:
Quhen God hes send thame abundance,
Ar nocht content with sufficiance;   4520
Bot, saillis into the stormy blastis,
In winter, to get greater castis:
In mony terribill great torment,
Against the Acts of Parliament.
Sum tynis thair geir, and sum ar drounde,
With this, sic merchants sould be crounde.

DILIGENCE.

Quhom to, schaips thou to sell that Hude?
I trow, to sum great man of gude.

FOLIE.

This Hude to sell richt faine I wald,
To him that is baith auld, and cald: 4530
Reddie till pas to hell, or heavin,
And hes fair bairns sax, or seavin;
And is of age fourscoir of yeir,
And taks ane lasse to be his peir:
Quhilk is nocht fourteine yeir of age,
And joynis with hir in mariage:
Geifand hir traist, that scho nocht wald
Rycht haistelie mak him cuckald.
Quha maryes, beand sa neir thair dead,
Set on this Hat upon his head.   4540

DILIGENCE.

Quhat Hude is that, tell me I pray thé?

FOLIE.

This is ane halie Hude, I say thee;
This hude is ordanit, I thee assure,
For Spirituall Fuillis, that taks in cure,
The saullis of great Diosies,
And regiment of great Abesies,
For gredines of warldlie pelfe,
Than can nocht, justlie, gyde them selfe.
Uthers saullis to saife, it settis them weill,
Syne sell thair awin saullis to the Deuill.　　　4550
Quha ever dois sa, this I conclude,
Upon his heid set on this Hude.

DILIGENCE.

Folie, is thair ony sic men,
Now, in the Kirk, that thou can ken?
How sall I ken them?

FOLIE.

Na, keip that clois.

Ex operibus eorum cognoscetis eos:
And Fuillis speik of the Prelacie,
It will be hauldin for herisie.

REX HUMANITAS.

Speik on hardlie, I gif thé leife.

FOLIE.

Than, my remissioun is in my sleife. 4560
Will ye leife me to speik of Kings?

REX HUMANITAS.

Yea, hardlie speik of all kin things.

FOLIE.

Conforming to my first narratioun,
Ye ar all Fuillis, be cok's passioun!

DILIGENCE.

Thou leis, I trow, this Fuill be mangit.

FOLIE.

Gif I lie, God, nor thou be hangit:
For, I have heir, I to thé tell,
Ane nobill cap imperiell,
Quhilk is nocht ordanit, bot for doings
Of Empreours, of Duiks, and Kings, 4570
For princelie, and imperiall Fuillis,
Thay sould have luggis, als lang as muillis.
The pryde of princes, withoutin faill,
Gars all the warld rin top ouir taill.
To win thame warldlie gloir and gude,
Thay cure nocht schedding of saikles blude.
Quhat cummer have ye had in Scotland,
Be our auld enemies of Ingland?
Had nocht bene the support of France,
We had bene brocht to great mischance. 4580
Now, I heir tell the Empreour

Schaippis for till be ane conquerour,
And is muifing his ordinance,
Against the nobill King of France.
Bot, I knaw nocht his just querrell,
That he hes for till mak battell.
All the Princes of Almanie
Spainze, Flanders, and Italie,
This present yeir, ar in ane flocht :
Sum sall thair wages find deir bocht.   4590
The Paip, with bombard, speir, and scheild,
Hes send his armie to the feild.
Sanct Peter, Sanct Paull, nor Sanct Androw,
Raisit never sic ane oist, I trow.
Is this fraternall charitie,
Or furious folie, quhat say ye ?
Thay leirit nocht this at Christis scuillis :
Thairfoir, I think them verie fuillis.
I think it folie, be God's mother,
Ilk Christian prince to ding doun uther :   4600
Becaus, that this Hat sould belang them,
Gang thou and part it, evin amang them.

   The Prophesie, withouttin weir,
Of Merling beis compleit this yeir :
For my gudame, the Gyre Carling,
Leirnde me the Prophesie of Marling,
Quhairof I sall schaw the sentence,
Gif ye will gif me audience :

      Flan, fran, resurgent,
      Simul Hispan viribus urgent :   4610

Dani vastabunt,
Vallones valla parabunt :
Sic tibi nomen in a,
Mulier cacavit in olla :
Hoc epulum comedes.

DILIGENCE.

Marie ! that is ane ill savorit dische.

FOLIE.

Sa, be this Prophesie plainlie appeirs,
That mortall weirs sal be amang Freirs :
Thay sall nocht knaw weill, in thair closters,
To quhom thay sall say thair Pater Nosters.   4620
Wald thay fall to, and fecht with speir, and shield,
The feind mak cuir, quhilk of them win the feild.

Now, of my Sermon have I maid ane end,
To Gilly-Mowband I yow all commend :
And I yow als beseik, richt hartfullie,
Pray for the saull of gude Cacaphatie,
Quhilk laitlie drownit himself into Lochleavin,
That his sweit saull may be above the Heavin.

DILIGENCE.

Famous Pepill, hartlie, I yow requyre,
   This lytill sport to tak in patience;   4630
We traist to God, and we leif ane uther yeir,
   Quhair we have failit, we sall do diligence,
   With mair plesure, to mak yow recompence;
Becaus we have bene sum part tedious,
   With mater rude, denude of eloquence,
Likewyse, perchance, to sum men odious.

[Adew, we will mak no langar tary,
   Prayand to Jesu Chryst, oure Salviour,
That be the requeist of his moder Mary,
   He do preserve this famous Auditour,   4640
   Withowt that grittar materis do ineure,
For your plesour we sall devyce ane sport,
   Plesand tyll every gentill creatour,
To raiss your spreitis to plesour and confort.]

     Now, let ilk man his way avance,
     Let sum ga drink, and sum ga dance:
     Menstrell, blaw up ane brawll of France,
        Let sé quha hobbils best:
     For, I will rin incontinent,
     To the tavern, or ever I stent: 4650
     And pray to God Omnipotent,
        To send yow all gude rest.

Rex sapiens æterne Deus genitorque benigne,
   Sit Tibi perpetuo gloria, laus, et honor.

ANE DIALOG BETUIX
EXPERIENCE AND ANE COURTEOUR.

ANE DIALOG

BETUIX EXPERIENCE AND ANE COURTEOUR OF THE MISERABYLL ESTAIT OF THE WORLD.

Absit Gloriari, nisi in Cruce Domini nostri Jesu Christi.

THE EPISTIL TO THE REDAR.

Thou lytill Quair, of mater miserabyll,
Weil auchtest thou coverit to be with sabyll,
   Renunceand grene, the purpur, reid, and quhit:
To delicat men thou art nocht delectabyll,
Nor yit tyll amorous folkis amiabyll:
   To reid on thee thai wyl haif no delite;
   Warldlye peple wyll have at thee dispyte,
Quhilk fyxit hes thare hart and hole intentis
On sensuall luste, on dignitie, and rentis.

We have no Kyng thee to present, allace!   10
· Quhilk to this countrie bene ane cairfull cace;
   And als our Quene, of Scotland Heretour,
Sche dwellith in France: I pray God saif hir Grace.
It war too lang for thee to ryn that race,

And far langar or that young tender Flour
  Bryng home tyll us ane Kyng and Governour.
Allace, tharefor, we may with sorrow syng,
Quhilk muste so long remane without one Kyng.

I nott quhome to thy simpylnes to sende :   [20
With cunnyng men, from tyme that thou be kende,
  Thy vaniteis no waye thay wyll advance,
Thynkand thee proude sic thyngis to pretende ;
Nochtwithstanding, the straucht way sal thou wende
  To thame quhilk hes the realme in governance :
  Declare thy mynde to thame with circumstance.
Go first tyll James, our Prince and Protectour,
And his Brother, our Spirituall Governour,

And Prince of Priestis in this Natioun :
Efter reverend recommendatioun,
  Under thare feit thow lawlye thee submyt,   30
And mak thame humyll supplicatioun,
Geve thay in thee fynd wrang narratioun,
  That thay wald pleis thy faltis to remyt :
  And of thare grace geve thay do thee admyt,
Than go thy waye quhare ever thow plesis best ;
Be thay content, mak reverence to the rest :

To faithfull prudent Pastouris Spirituall,
To nobyll Erlis, and Lordis Temporall,
  Obedientlye tyll thame thow thee addres,
Declaryng thame this schort memoriall,   40
Quhow Mankynd bene to miserie maid thrall.
  At lenth to thame the cause plainlie confesse,

Beseikand thame all lawis to suppresse
Inventit be mennis traditioun,
Contrar to Christis institutioun :

And cause them cleirlye for tyll understand
That, for the brekyng of the Lordis command,
   His thrynfald wande of flagellatioun
Hes scurgit this pure Realme of Scotland,
Be mortall weris baith be sey and land,   50
   With mony terrabyll trybulatioun.   Re. xxiiii.
   Tharefor, mak to thame trew narratioun,   and The. ii.
That all thir weiris, this derth, hunger, and pest,
Was nocht bot for our synnis manifest.   1 Cor. lii.

Declare to thame quhow, in the tyme of Noye,   Gene. vii.
Alluterlye God did the Warld destroye,
   As Holy Scripture maketh mentioun ;
Sodom, Gomor, with thare regioun and roye ;   Gene. xix.
God sparit nother man, woman, nor boye ;
   But all were brynt for thare offensioun.   60
   Jherusalem, that moste tryumphant town,   Matthew
Distroyit was for thare iniquity,   xxxiii.
As in the Scripture planelye thay may se.   Luc. xiii.

Declare to thame, this mortall miserie,
Be sweird and fyre, derth, pest, and povertie,
   Procedis of syn, gyf I can rycht discryve,   Jere. xv.
For laik of faith, and for idolatrye,
For fornicatioun, and for adultrye,
   Of Princis, Prelatis, with mony ane man and wyve,
   Expell the cause, than the effect belyve   70

Sall cease: quhen that the peple doith repent,
Than God sall slak his bow, quhilk yit is bent.

Mak thame requeist quhilk hes the Governance
The sinceir word of God for tyll avance
   Conforme to Christis institutioun.
Without hypocrisie or dissimulance:
Causyng Justice hauld evinlye the ballance;
   On Publicanis making punyssioun;
   Commendyng thame of gude conditioun.
That beyng done, I dout nocht bot the Lorde   80
Sall of this countrie have misericorde.

Thocht God with mony terrabyll effrayis
Hes done this countrie scurge by divers wayis;
   Be juste jugement, for our grevous offence,
Declare to thame they sall have mery dayis,
Efter this trubyll, as the Propheit sayis,
   Quhen God sall se our humyll repentance:
   Tyll strange pepyll thocht he hes gevin lycence
To be our scurge induryng his desyre,
Wyll, quhen he lyste, that scurge cast in the fyre.   90

Pray thame that thay putt nocht thare esperance
In mortall men onelye, thame tyll advance,
   Bot principallye in God Omnipotent:
Than neid thai not to charge the realme of France
With gounnis, galayis, nor uther ordinance,
   So that thay be to God obedient;
   In thir premyssis be thay nocht negligent,

Psalme cxvii.

Displayand Christis banar hie on heycht,
Thare ennimeis of thame sall have no mycht.

Go hence, pure Buke, quhilk I have done indyte 100
In rurall ryme, in maner of dispyte,
   Contrar the Warldis variatioun:
Of Rethorick heir I proclame thee quyte.
Idolatouris, I feir, sall with thee flyte,
   Because of thame thow makis narratioun:
   Bot cure thow nocht the indignatioun
Of Hypocritis, and fals Pharisience,
Quhowbeit on thee thay cry ane lowde vengence.

Requeist the Gentyll Redar that thee redis,
Thocht ornat termes in to thy park not spredis, 110
   As thay in thee may have experience:
Thocht barran feildis beris nocht bot weidis,
Yit brutall beistis sweitlye on thame feidis:
   Desyre of thame none uther recompance
   Bot that thay wald reid thee with pacience:
And, geve thay be in ony way offendit,
Declare to thame, it salbe weill amendit.

HEIR ENDIS THE EPISTIL AND FOLLOWIS THE PROLOG.

THE PROLOG

OF THE MISERABILL ESTAIT OF THIS WARLD.

Musing and marvelling on the miserie
    Frome day to day in erth quhilk dois incres,
And of ilk stait the instabilitie   120
    Proceding of the restless besynes
    Quhare on the most part doith thair mynd addres
Inordinatlie, on houngrye covatyce,
Vaine glore, dissait, and uther sensuall vyce:

Bot tumlyng in my bed I mycht nocht lye;
    Quharefore I fuir furth, in ane Maye mornyng,
Conforte to gett of my malancolye,
    Sumquhat affore fresche Phebus uprysing,
    Quhare I mycht heir the birdis sweitlie syng:
In tyll ane park I past, for my plesure   130
Decorit weill be craft of dame Nature.

Quhow I ressavit confort naturall
    For tyll discryve at lenth it war too lang;
Smelling the holsum herbis medicinall,
    Quhare on the dulce and balmy dew down dang,
    Lyke aurient peirles on the twistis hang;
Or quhow that the aromatik odouris
Did proceid frome the tender fragrant flouris;

Or quhow Phebus, that king etheriall,
    Swyftlie sprang up in to the Orient,   140
Ascending in his throne imperiall,

Quhose brycht and beriall bemes resplendent
　Illumynit all on to the Occident,
Confortand everye corporall creature
　Quhilk formit war, in erth, be dame Nature;

Quhose donke impurpurit vestiment nocturnall,
　With his imbroudit mantyll matutyne,
He lefte in tyll his regioun aurorall,
　Quhilk on hym waitit quhen he did declyne
　Towarte his Occident palyce vespertyne,　　　150
And rose in habyte gaye and glorious,
Brychtar nor gold or stonis precious.

Bot Synthea, the hornit nychtis quene,
　Scho loste hir lychte and lede ane lawar saill,
Frome tyme hir soverane lorde that scho had sene,
　And in his presens waxit dirk and paill,
　And ouer hir visage kest ane mistye vaill;
So did Venus, the goddès amorous,
With Jupiter, Mars, and Mercurius.

Rycht so the auld intoxicat Saturne,　　　160
　Persaving Phebus powir, his beymes brycht,
Abufe the Erth than maid he no sudgeourne,
　Bot suddandlye did lose his borrowit lycht,
　Quhilk he durst never schaw bot on the nycht.
The Pole Artick, Ursis, and Sterris all
Quhilk situate ar in the Septentrionall,

Tyll errand schyppis quhilks ar the souer gyde,
　Convoyand thame upone the stormye nycht,

Within thare frostic circle, did thame hyde.
    Howbeit that sterris have none uthir lycht   170
    Bot the reflex of Phebus bemes brycht,
That day durst none in to the hevin appeir,
Till he had circuit all our Hemispheir.

Me thocht it was ane sycht celestiall,
    To sene Phebus so angellyke ascend
In till his fyrie chariot triumphall,
    Quhose bewtie brychte I culd nocht comprehend.
    All warldlie cure anone did fro me wend,
Quhen fresche Flora spred furth hir tapestrie,
Wrocht be dame Nature, quent and curiouslie   180

Depaynt with mony hundreth hevinlie hewis;
    Glaid of the rysing of thare royall Roye,
With blomes breckand on the tender bewis,
    Quhilk did provoke myne hart tyl natural joye.
    Neptune, that day, and Eoll held thame coye,
That men on far mycht heir the birdis sounde,
Quhose noyis did to the sterrye hevin redounde.

The plesand powne prunyeand his feddrem fair;
    The myrthfull maves maid gret melodie;
The lustye lark ascending in the air,   190
    Numerand his naturall notis craftilye;
    The gay goldspink; the merll rycht myrralye;
The noyis of the nobyll nychtingalis;
Redoundit throuch the montans, meids, and valis.

Contempling this melodious armonye,
    Quhow everilke bird drest thame for tyl advance,

To saluss Nature with thare melodye,
  That I stude gasing, halflingis in ane trance,
  To heir thame mak thare naturall observance,
So royallie, that all the roches rang,   200
Throuch repercussioun of thare suggurit sang.

I lose my tyme, allace! for to rehers
  Sic unfruitful and vaine discriptioun,
Or wrytt, in to my raggit rurall vers,
  Mater without edificatioun;
  Consydering quhow that myne intentioun
Bene tyll deplore the mortall misereis,
With continuall cairfull calamiteis,

Consisting in this wracheit vaill of sorrow:
  Bot sad sentence sulde have ane sad indyte;   210
So termes brycht I lyste nocht for to borrow.
  Of murnyng mater men hes no delyte:
  With roustye termes, tharefor, wyl I wryte,
With sorrowful seychis, ascending from the splene,
And bitter teris distellyng from myne eine;

Withoute ony vaine invocatioun
  To Minerva, or to Melpominee:
Nor yitt wyll I mak supplicatioun
  For help to Cleo nor Calliopee:
  Sic marde Musis may mak me no supplee.   220
Proserpyne I refuse, and Apollo,
And rycht so Ewterp, Jupiter, and Juno,

Quhilkis bene to pleasand Poetis conforting:

Quharefor, because I am nocht one of tho,
I do desyre of thame no supporting.
　For I did never sleip on Pernasso,
As did the Poetis of lang tyme ago,
And, speciallie, the ornate Ennius;
Nor drank I never with Hysiodus,

Of Grece the perfyte poet soverane,　　　　230
　Of Hylicon, the sors of eloquence,
Of that mellifluous, famous, fresche fontane:
　Quharefor I awe to thame no reverence.
I purpose nocht to mak obedience
To sic mischeand Musis nor Malmontrye
Afore tyme usit in to Poetrye.

Raveand Rhamnusia, goddés of dispyte,
　Mycht be to me ane Muse rycht convenabyll,
Gyff I desyrit sic help for tyll indyte
　This murnyng mater, mad and miserabyll.　　240
　I mon go seik ane Muse more comfortabyll,
And sic vaine superstitioun to refuse,
Beseikand the gret God to be my Muse;

Gen. i.　　Be quhose wysdome al maner of thing bene wrocht,
　The heych hevinnis, with all thair ornamentis;
And without mater maid all thing of nocht:
　Hell in myd centir of the Elementis.
iii. Re. iii.　　That hevinlye Muse to seik my hole intent is,
Psalme lxxxix.　The quhilk gaif sapience to king Salomone,
Juges iii.　To David grace, strenth to the strang Sampsone,　250

And of pure Peter maid ane prudent precheour ; Mat. iiii.
   And, be the power of his Deitee,
Of creuell Paule he maid ane cunnyng techeour. Actis. ix.
   I mon beseik, rycht lawly on my knee,
   His heych superexcellent Majestie,
That with his hevinlye spreit he may inspyre
To wrytt no thyng contrarye his desyre.

Beseikand als his Soverane Sonne, Jesu, Luc. 1.
   Quhilk wes consavit be the Holy Spreit,
Incarnat of the purifyit Virgin trew,   260
   In to the quhome the Prophicie was compleit,
   That Prince of peace, moist humyll and mansweit,
Quhilk onder Pylate sufferit passioun, Luc. xxiii.
Upone the Croce, for our salvatioun.

And be that creuell deith intollerabyll
   Lowsit we wer frome bandis of Belyall ;
And mairattour, it wes so proffitabyll
   That to this hour come nevir man, nor sall,
   To the tryumphant joye imperiall Hebr. ix.
Of lyfe, quhowbeit that thay war nevar sa gude, 270
Bot be the vertew of that precious blude.

Quharefor, in steid of the Mont Pernaso,
   Swyftlie I sall go seik my Soverane,
To Mont Calvarie the straucht waye mon I go,
   To gett ane taist of that moist fresche fontane.
   That sors to seik my hart may nocht refrane
Of Hylicone, quhilk wes boith deip and wyde,
That Longeous did grave in tyll his syde. Jho. xix.

From that fresche fontane sprang a famous flude,
 Quhilk redolent rever throuch the warld yit
  rynnis,   280
As christall cleir, and mixit bene with blude;
 Quhose sound abufe the heyest hevinnis dinnis,
 All faithfull pepil purgeing frome thare sinnis,
Quharefor I sall besoik his Excellence
To grant me grace, wysedome, and eloquence;

And baythe me with those dulce and balmy strandis
 Quhilk on the Croce did spedalie out spryng
Frome his moste tender feit and hevinly handis;
 And grant me grace to wrytt nor dyte no thyng
 Bot tyll his heich honour and loude lovyng; 290
But quhose support thare may na gud be wrocht
Tyll his plesure, gude workis, word, nor thocht.

Tharefor, O Lorde, 1 pray thy Majestie,
 As thow did schaw thy heych power Divyne,
First plainlie in the Cane of Galelee,
Jhon. ii. Quhare thow convertit cauld watter in wyne,
 Convoye my mater tyll ane fructuous fyne,
And save my sayingis baith frome schame and syn :—
Tak tent, for now I purpose to begyn.

HEIR ENDIS THE PROLOG AND BEGINNIS
THE MATER.

ANE DIALOG

BETUIX EXPERIENCE AND ANE COURTEOUR:

THE FIRST BUKE.

In to that Park I sawe appeir 300
One ageit Man, quhilk drew me neir,
Quhose beird wes weill thre quarter lang;
His hair doun ouer his schulders hang,
The quhilk as ony snaw wes quhyte;
Quhome to behald I thocht delyte;
His habitt Angellyke of hew,
Of culloure lyke the sapheir blew.
Onder ane hollyng he reposit,
Of quhose presens I was rejosit.
I did hym saluss reverendlye; 310
Sa did he me, rycht courteslye.
To sitt down he requeistit me,
Onder the schaddow of that tre,
To saif me frome the sonnis heit,
Amangis the flowris softe and sweit;
For I wes werye for walking.
Than we began to fall in talking:
   I sperit his name, with reverence?
   I am, said he, EXPERIENCE.

COURTEOUR.

   Than, Schir, said I, ye can nocht faill 320
To gyff ane desolate man counsaill.

Ye do appeir ane man of fame;
And, sen Experience bene your name,
I praye yow, Father venerabyll,
Geve me sum counsell confortabyll.

EXPERIENCE.

Quhat bene, quod he, thy vocatioun,
Makand sic supplycatioun?

COURTEOUR.

I haif, quod I, bene to this hour,
Sen I could ryde, ane Courteour;
Bot now, Father, I thynk it best,   330
With your counsell, to leif in rest,
And frome thyne furth to tak myne cais,
And quyetlie my God to pleais,
And renunce curiositie,
Levyng the Court, and lerne to dé.
Oft have I sailit ouer the strandis,
And travalit throuch divers landis,
Boith South, and North, and Est, and West;
Yitt can I never fynd quhare Rest
Doith mak his habitatioun,   340
Withoute your supportatioun.
Quhen I belief to be best easit,
Most suddantlye I am displeasit;
Frome trubbyll quhen I fastest fle,
Than fynd I most adversatie.
Schaw me, I pray you hartfullye,
Quhow I may leif most pleasandlie,
To serve my God, of kyngis Kyng,

Sen I am tyrit for travellyng;
And lerne me for to be content 350
Of quyet lyfe, and sobir rent,
That I may thank the Kyng of Glore,
As thocht I had ane mylyeoun more.
Sen everilk Court bene variant,
Full of invy, and inconstant:
Mycht I, but trubbyll, leif in rest
Now in my aige, I thynk it best.

EXPERIENCE.

Thow art ane gret fuill, Sonne, said he,
Thyng to desyre quhilk may nocht be,
Yarnyng to have prerogatyve 360
Above all Creature on lyfe.
Sen Father Adam creat bene
In to the campe of Damascene,
Mycht no man say, on to this hour,
That ever he fand perfyte plesour,
Nor never sall, tyll that he se
God in his Divyne Majestie:
Quharefore prepair thee for travell,
Sen mennis lyfe bene bot battell. Job. vii.
All men begynnis for tyll de 370
The day of thare Nativitie;
And journelly thay do proceid,
Tyll Atrops cut the fatell threid;
And, in the breif tyme that thay have
Betuix thare byrth on to thare grave;
Thow seis quhat mutabiliteis,
Quhat miserabyll calamiteis;

Quhat trubbyll, travell, and debait
Seis thow in everie mortall stait!
Begyn at pure lawe Creaturis,   380
Ascending, syne, to Senaturis,
To gret Princis and Potestatis,
Thow sall nocht fynd, in non estatis,
Sen the begynning, generallie,
Nor in our tyme now, speciallie,
Bot teddious, restles besynes
But ony maner of sickernes.

COURTEOUR.

  Prudent Father, quod I, allace!
Ye tell to me one cairfull cace;
Ye say, that no man, to this hour,   390
Ies found in erth perfyte plesour,
Without infortunat variance:
Sen we bene thrall to sic myschance,
Quhy do we set so our intentis
On ryches, dignitie, and rentis?
Sen in the Erth bene no man sure
One day but trubbyll tyll indure;
And, werst of all, quhen we leist wene,
The creuell deith we mon sustene,
Geve I your Fatherheid durst demand,   400
The cause I wald faine understand:
And als, Father, I yow implore,
Schaw me sum trubbyll gone afore;
That, heryng utheris indigence,
I may the more haif patience.
Marrowis in trybulatioun
Bene wracheis consolatioun.

EXPERIENCE.

Quod he, Efter my small cunnyng
To thee I sall mak answeryng.
Bot, ordourlie for to begyn,   410
This misarie procedis of syn.
Bot it wer lang for to defyn it
Quhow all men ar to syn inclynit.
Quhen syn aboundantlye doith ryng,
Justly God makith punyssing:
Quharefore gret God in to his handis,
To dant the warld, hes divers wandis;
Efter our evyll conditioun
He makis on us punytioun,
With hunger, darth, and indigens;   420
Sum tyme gret plagis, and pestilens,
And sum tyme with his bludy wand,
Throw creuell weir be sey and land:
Concludyng, all our misarie
Proceidis of syn, alluterlie.

COURTEOUR.

Father, quod I, declare to me
The cause of this fragyllitie,
That we bene all to syn inclynde,
In werk, in word, and in our mynde.
I wald the veritie wer schawin,   430
Quho hes this seid amang us sawin?
And quhy we ar condampnit to dede?
And quhow that we may get remede?

EXPERIENCE.

<small>Gen. iii.</small>

Quod he, The Scripture hes concludit
Men frome felicitie wer denudit
Be Adam, our progenitour,
Umquhyle of Paradyse possessour;
Be quhose most wylfull arrogance
Wes Mankynd brocht to this myschance;
Quhen he wes inobedient,　　　　　　　440
In breking Godis commandiment.
Be solystatioun of his wyfe
He loste that hevinlye plesand lyfe;
Etand of the forbiddin tre,
Thare began all our miserie.
So Adam wes cause radicall

<small>Rom. v.</small>

That we bene fragyll synnaris all.
Adam brocht in this natioun
Syn, Deith, and als dampnatioun.

<small>1 Joh. i.</small>

Quho wyll say he is no synnar,　　　　450
Christ sayis, he is ane gret lear.
Mankynde sprang furth of Adamis loynis,
And tuke of hym flesche, blude, and bonis;
And so, efter his qualytie
All ar inclynit synnaris to be.
Bot yit, my Sonne, dispare thow nocht;
For God, that all the warld hes wrocht,
Hes maid ane Soverane remede,
To saif us boith frome syn and dede,
And frome etarne dampnatioun:　　　　460
Tharefore tak consolatioun.
For God, as Scripture doith recorde,

Haveyng of man misericorde,
Send doun his onelye Sonne, Jesu,
Quhilk lychtit in one Virgin trew,
And cled his heych Divynitie
With our pure vyle Humanytie;
Syne frome our synnis, to conclude,
He wysche us with his precious blude.   Apoca. ii.
Quhowbeit throw Adam we mon dee,   470   Rom. v.
Throuch that Lord we sall rasit bee;   Hebre. x
And everilk man he sall releve
Quhilk in his blude doith ferme beleve;
And bryng us all unto his glore
The quhilk throw Adam bene forlore;
Without that we, throw laik of faith,
Of his Godheid incur the wraith:
Bot quho in Christ fermely belevis   Joh. iii. 5.
Sall be relevit frome all myschevis.

COURTEOUR.

Quhat Faith is that that ye call ferme?   480
Schir, gar me understand that terme.

EXPERIENCE.

Faith without Hope and Charitie   Hebre. xi.
Avalit nocht, my Sonne, said he.

COURTEOUR.

Quhat Charitie bene, that wald I knaw.

EXPERIENCE.

Quod he, My Sonne, that sall I schaw:

First, lufe thy God above all thyng,
And thy nychtbour but fenzeyng; *1 Cor. xiii.*
Do none injure nor villanie,
Bot as thow wald wer done to thee:
Quyk faith but cheritabyll werkis   490 *Jaco. ii.*
Can never be, as wryttis Clerkis,
More than the fyre, in tyll his mycht,
Can be but heit, nor Sonne but lycht;
Geve Charitie into thee failis,
Thy Faith nor Hope no thyng availis.
The Devyll hes Faith, and trymlis for dreid;
Bot he wantis Hope and Lufe in deid.
Do all the gude that may be wrocht,
But Charitie, all availis nocht.
Quharefore pray to the Trinitie   500
For tyll support thy Charitie.

 Now have I schawin thee as I can,
Quhow Father Adam, the first man,
Brocht in the warld boith Syn and Dede,
And quhow Christ Jesu maid remede,
Quhilk, on the day of Jugement,
Sall us delyver frome torment,
And bryng us to his lestyng glore,
Quhilk sall indure for ever more.
Bot in this warld thow gettis no rest,   510
I mak it to thee manifest;
Tharefore, my Sonne, be diligent,
And lerne for to be patient;
And in to God sett all thy traist:
All thyng sall than cum for the best.

COURTEOUR.

Father, I thank yow hartfullye
Of your conforte and cumpanye,
And hevinlye consolatioun;
Makand yow supplicatioun,
Geve I durst put yow to sic pyne, 520
That ye wald pleis for to defyne,
And gar me cleirlye understand,
Quhow Adam brak the Lordis command;
And quhow, throw his transgressioun,
Wer punyst his successioun.

EXPERIENCE.

My Sonne, quod he, wald thow tak cure
To luke on the Divyne Scripture,
In to the Buke of Genesis
That storye thare thow sall nocht mis.
And alswa syndrie cunnyng Clerkis 530
Hes done rehers, in to thare werkis,
Of Adamis fall, full ornatly,
Ane thousand tymes better nor I
Can wrytt of that unhappy man.
Bot I sall do the best I can
Schortlie to schaw that cairfull cace,
With the support of Goddis grace.

ANE EXCLAMATIOUN TO THE REDAR, TWYCHEYNG THE WRYTTING OF VULGARE AND MATERNALL LANGUAGE.

Gentyl Redar, haif at me non dispyte,
   Thynkand that I presumptuously pretend,
In vulgair toung so heych mater to writ;   540
   Bot quhair I mys I pray ye tyll amend.
    Tyll unlernit I wald the caus were kend
Of our most miserabyll travell and torment,
And quhow, in erth, no place bene permanent.

Quhowbeit that divers devote cunnyng Clerkis
   In Latyne toung hes wryttin syndrie bukis,
Our unlernit knawis lytill of thare werkis,
   More than thay do the ravyng of the rukis.
    Quharefore to colyearis, cairtaris, and to cukis,
To Jok and Thome, my rhyme sall be directit,   550
With cunnyng men quhowbeit it wylbe lackit.

Thocht every Commoun may nocht be one Clerk,
   Nor hes no leid except thare toung maternall,
Quhy suld of God the marvellous hevinly werk
   Be hid from thame? I thynk it nocht fraternall.
    The Father of Hevin, quhilk wes and is Eternall,
To Moyses gaif the Law, on Mont Senay,
Nocht in to Greik nor Latyne, I heir say.

He wrait the Law, in Tablis hard of stone,
   In thare awin vulgare language of Hebrew,   560
That all the bairnis of Israell, every one,
   Mycht knaw the Law, and so the same ensew.
   Had he done wryt in Latyne or in Grew,
It had to thame bene bot ane sawrles jest:
Ye may weill wytt God wrocht all for the best.

Arristotyll nor Plato, I heir sane,
   Wrait nocht thare hie Philosophie naturall
In Duche, nor Dence, nor toung Italiane,
   Bot in thare most ornate toung maternall,
   Quhose fame and name doith ryng perpetuall.   570
Famous Virgill, the Prince of Poetrie,
Nor Cicero, the flour of Oratrie,

Wrait nocht in Caldye language, nor in Grew,
   Nor yit into the language Sarazene,
Nor in the naturall language of Hebrew,
   Bot in the Romane toung, as may be sene,
   Quhilk wes thair proper language, as I wene.
Quhen Romanis rang dominatoris in deid,
The ornat Latyne wes thare propir leid.

In the mene tyme, quhen that thir bauld Romanes,
   Over all the warld had the dominioun,   [580
Maid Latyne scolis thare glore for tyll avance,
   That thair language mycht be over all commoun:
   To that intent, be my opinioun,
Traisting that thare Impyre sulde ay indure:
Bot of fortune alway thay wer nocht sure.

Gene. xi.
Of Languagis the first diversytie
  Wes maid be Goddis maledictioun.
Quhen Babilone wes beildit in Calde,
  Those beildaris gat none uther afflictioun :   590
  Affore the tyme of that punyssioun
Wes bot one toung, quhilk Adam spak hym self,
  Quhare now of toungis thare bene thre score and twelf.

Nochtwithstandyng, I thynk it gret plesour,
  Quhare cunnyng men hes languagis anew,
That, in thare youth, be deligent laubour,
  Hes leirnit Latyne, Greik, and ald Hebrew :
  That I am nocht of that sorte sore I rew ;
Quharefore I wald all bukis necessare
For our faith were in tyll our toung Vulgare.   600

Acts ii.
Christ, efter his glorious Ascentioun,
  Tyll his Disciplis send the Holy Spreit,
In toungis of fyre, to that intentioun,
  Thay, beand of all languagis repleit,
  Throuch all the warld, with wordis fair and sweit,
Tyll every man the faith thay suld furth schaw
In thare awin leid, delyverand thame the Law.

Tharefore I thynk one gret dirisioun,
  To heir thir Nunnis and Systeris nycht and day
Syngand and sayand Psalmes and Orisoun,   610
  Nocht understandyng quhat thay syng nor say,
  Bot lyke one Stirlyng or ane Papingay,
Quhilk leirnit ar to speik be lang usage :
Thame I compair to byrdis in ane cage.

Rycht so childreyng and ladyis of honouris
   Prayis in Latyne, to thame ane uncuth leid,
Mumland thair Matynis, Evinsang, and thair Houris,
   Thare Pater Noster, Ave, and thare Creid.
   It wer als plesand to thare spreit, in deid,
God have mercy on me, for to say thus,   620
As to say, *Miserere mei Deus.*

Sanct Jerome in his propir toung Romane
   The Law of God he trewlie did translait,
Out of Hebrew and Greik, in Latyne plane,
   Quhilk hes bene hid from us lang tyme, God wait,
   Onto this tyme: bot, efter myne consait,
Had Sanct Jerome bene borne in tyll Argyle,
In to Yrische toung his bukis had done compyle.

Prudent Sanct Paull doith mak narratioun   1 Cor. xiiii.
   Twycheyng the divers leid of every land,   630
Sayand, thare bene more edificatioun
   In fyve wordis that folk doith understand,
   Nor to pronounce of wordis ten thousand
In strange langage, sine wait not quhat it menis:
I thynk sic pattryng is not worth twa prenis.

Unlernit peple, on the holy day,
   Solemnitlye thay heir the Evangell sung,
Nocht knawyng quhat the Preist dois sing nor say,
   Bot as ane bell quhen that thay heir it rung:
   Yit, wald the Preistis in to thare mother toung
Pas to the pulpitt and that doctryne declare   [640
Tyll lawid pepyll, it wer more necessare.

I wald Prelattis and Doctouris of the Law
    With us lawid peple wer nocht discontent,
Thocht we in to our vulgare toung did knaw
    Of Christ Jesu the lyfe and Testament
    And quhow that we sulde keip commandiment;
Bot in our language lat us pray and reid
Our Pater Noster, Ave, and our Creid.

I wald sum Prince of gret discretioun   650
    In vulgare language planelye gart translait
The neidfull Lawis of this Regioun:
    Than wald thare nocht be half so gret debait
    Amang us peple of the law estait.
Geve every man the verytie did knaw,
We nedit nocht to treit thir Men of law.

Tyll do our nychtbour wrang we wald be war,
    Gyf we did feir the lawis punysment:
Thare wald nocht be sic brawlyng at the bar,
    Nor Men of law loup to sic royall rent.   660
    To keip the law gyf all men war content,
And ilk man do as he wald be done to,
The Jugis wald get lytill thyng ado.

The Propheit David, Kyng of Israell,
    Compyld the plesand Psalmes of the Psaltair
In his awin propir toung, as I heir tell;
    And Salamone, quhilk wes his sone and air,
    Did mak his buke in tyll his toung Vulgare.
Quhy suld nocht thare saying be tyll us schawin
In our language? I wald the caus wer knawin.   670

Lat Doctoris wrytt thare curious questionis,
   Aud argumentis sawin full of sophistrye,
Thare Logick, and thare heych opinionis,
   Thare dirk jugementis of Astronomye,
   Thare Medecyne, and thare Philosophye ;
Latt Poetis schaw thare glorious ingyne,
As ever thay pleis, in Greik or in Latyne ;

Bot lat us haif the Bukis necessare
   To Commoun weill and our Salvatioun
Justlyc translatit in our toung Vulgare.   680
   And als I mak thee Supplicatioun
   O gentyll Redar, haif none indignatioun,
Thynkand I mell me with so hie matair.
Now to my purpose fordwart wyll I fair.

FINIS.

HEIR FOLLOWIS THE CREATIOUN OF ADAM AND EVE.

<small>Gene. i.</small>

Quhen God had maid the hevinis brycht,
The Sone and Mone for to geve lycht,
The Sterry Hevin and Christellyne,
And, be his Sapience Divyne,
The Planetis, in thair circlis round
Quhirling about with merie sound,   690
Of quhome Phebus was principall,
Juste in his lyne Eclipticall;
And gave, be Divyne Sapience,
Tyll every Ster thare influence,
With motioun continuall,
Quhilk doith indure perpetuall;
And, farrest frome the Hevin impyre,
The Erth, the Walter, Air, and Fyre:
He cled the Erth with herbis and treis;
All kynd of fysches in the seis,   700
All kynd of beist, he did prepair,
With fowlis fleying in the air.
Thus, be his word all thyng was wrocht
Without materiall, maid of nocht:
So, be His wysedome infinyte
All wes maid plesand and perfyte.

    Quhen Hevin and Erth, and thare contentis,
Wer endit, with thare ornamentis,
Than, last of all, the Lord began

Of most vyle erth to mak the Man. 710
Nocht of the lillie, nor the rose,
Nor syper tre, as I suppose,
Nother of gold, nor precious stonis;
Of erth he maid flesche, blude, and bonis.
To that intent God maid hym thus,
That man sulde nocht be glorious,
Nor in hym selfe no thyng suld se
Bot matere of humylitie.
Quhen Man wes maid, as I have tald,
God in his face did hym behald, 720
Breithand in hym ane lyflie spreit.   Gene. ii.
Quhen all thir werkis wer compleit,
He maid Man, to his simylitude,
Precelland in to pulchritude,
Dotit with giftis of Nature
Above all erthlye creature;
Syne plesandlye did hym convoye
To ane regioun repleit with joye,
Of all plesour quhilk bair the pryce.
And callit Erthly Paradyce; 730
And brocht, be Divyne providence,
All beistis and byrdis tyll his presence.
Adam did craftelye impone
Ane speciall name tyll every one,
And to all thyngis materiall,
He namyt thame in speciall:
Quhow he thame namyt yitt bene kend,
And salbe to the warldis end.
In to that Gardyng of plesance
Two treis grew most tyll avance, 740

Above all uther quhilk bair the pryce,
In myddis of that Paradyce.
The one wes callit the Tre of lyfe;
The uther tre began our stryfe,
The tre to knaw boith gude and evyll,
Quhilk, be perswatioun of the Devyll,
Began our misarie and wo.
Bot lat us to our purpose go.
    Quhow God gave Adam strait commande
That tre to twyche nocht with his hand :   750
All uther fructis of Paradyce
He bad him eit at his devyce;
Sayand, Gyf thow eit of this tre,
With dowbyll deith than sall thow dee :
Tharefor I thé command, be war,
And frome this tree thow stand afar.
Yitt Father Adam wes allone,
But cumpanye of ony one :
Than thocht the Lord it necessare
Tyll hym to creat ane helpare.   760
    God putt in Adam sic sapour
That for to sleip he tuke plesour,
And laid hym down apone the grounde;
And quhen Adam wes slepand sounde,
He tuke ane rib furth of his syde,
Syne fyld it up with flesche and hyde,
And maid ane Woman of that bone :
Fairar of forme wes never none.
Than tyll Adam incontinent
That fair Ladye he did present,   770
Quhilk schortlye said, for to conclude,

Thow art my flesche, my bonis, and blude;
And Virago he callit hir, than,
Quhilk is, interpreit, maid of man,
Quhilk Eva efterwart was namyt,
Quhen, for hir falt, sche was diffamyt.
Than did the Lord thame sanctyfie,
Saying, Incres and multiplie.
Be this men suld leif all thair kyn,
And with thare Wyffis mak dwellyn,   780
And, for thare saik, leif Father and Mother,
And lufe thame best above all uther:
For God has ordanit thame, trewlye,
To be two saulis in one bodye.
 My wytt is waik for tyll indyte
Thaire heavinlye plesouris infinyte,
Wes never none erthlye creature
Sen syne had sic perfyte plesoure.
Thay had puyssance imperiall
Above all thyng materiall.   790
Als cunnyng Clerkis dois conclude,
Adam preceld in pulchritude
Most naturall, and the farest Man
That evir wes, sen the warld began,
Except Christ Jesu, Goddis Sonne,
To quhome wes no comparisone;
And Eva, the fairest Creature
That ever wes formit be nature.
Thocht thay wer naikit as thay wer maid,
No schame ather of uther haid: 800
Quhat plesour mycht ane man haif more
Nor haif his Lady hym before,

So lustye, plesand, and perfyte,
Reddy to serve his appetyte?
Thay had none uther cure, I wys,
Bot past thare tyme with joye and blys.
Wyld beistis did to thame repair;
So did the fowlis of the air,
With noyis most angelycall
Makand thame myrthis musicall;   810
The fyschis soumand in the strandis
Wer holelye at thair commandis:
All Creaturis, with ane accorde,
Obeyit hym as thare soverane Lorde.
Thay sufferit nother heit nor cald,
With every plesour that thay wald.
Als, to the deith thay wer nocht thrall;
And rychtso suld we have bene all:
For he and all his successouris
Suld have possedit those plesouris,   820
Syne frome that joye materiall
Gone to the glore imperiall.
Thay had, geve I can rycht discryve,
Gret joy in all thare wyttis fyve,
In heiryng, seying, gustyng, smellyng,
Induryng thare delytesum dwellyng:
Heiryng the byrdis armoneis,
Taistyng the fructis of divers treis,
Smellyng the balmye dulce odouris
Quhilk did proceid frome fragrant flowris,   830
Seying so mony hevinlye hewis
Of blomes brekyng on the bewis;
Of twycheyng, als thay had delyte

Of utheris bodeis soft and quhyte;
But doute, induryng that plesour,
Thay luffit uther Paramour;
No marvell bene thocht swa suld be,
Consyderyng thare gret bewte.
Als, God gave thame command expres
To multyplie and tyll incres, 840
That thare seid and successioun
Mycht pleneis every Natioun.

   I lyst nocht tary tyll declare
All properteis of that place preclare;
Quhow herbis and treis grew ay grene,
Nor of the temperat air serene;
Quhow fructis indeficient,
Ay alyke rype and redolent;
Nor of the fontane, nor the fludis,
Nor of the flowris pulchritudis. 850
That mater Clerkis dois declare;
Quharfore I speik of thame na mare.
The Scripture makis no mentioun
Quhow lang thay rang in that Regioun;
Bot I beleve the tyme wes schorte,
As divers Doctouris dois reporte.

FINIS.

OF THE MISERABYLL TRANSGRESSIOUN
OF ADAM.

COURTEOUR.

Father, How happinit that mischance?
Quod I; schaw me the circumstance,
Declaryng me that carefull cace,
Quhow Adam lost that plesand place   860
Frome hym and his successioun.
Quhow did proceid that transgressioun?

EXPERIENCE.

  Quod he, Efter my rude ingyne
I sall rehers thee that rewyne.
  Quhen God, the Plasmatour of all,
In to the Hevin imperiall
Did creat all the Angellis brycht,
He maid one Angell most of mycht,
To quhome he gave preheminence,
Above thame all, in sapience.   870
Because all uther he did prefer,
Namit he wes brycht Lucifer.
He wes so plesand and so fair
He thocht hymself without compair,
And grew so gay and glorious
He gan to be presumptuous,
And thocht that he wald sett his sait
In to the North, and mak debait
Agane the Majestic Divyne;
Quhilk wes the cause of his rewyne.   880

For he incurrit Goddis ire,
And banyst frome the Hevin impyre,
With Angellis mony one legioun,
Quhilkis wer of his opinioun,
Innumerabyll with hym thare fell:
Sum lychtit in the lawest Hell,
Sum in the Sey did mak repair,
Sum in the Erth, sum in the Air,
  That most unhappy cumpanye
At Father Adam had invye,   890
Parsaveyng Adam and his seid
In to thare places to succeid.
The Serpent wes the subtellest   Gene. iii.
Above all beistis, and craftyest.
Than Sathan, with ane fals intent,
Did enter in to that Serpent;
Imagenyng sum craftye wyle,
Quhow he mycht Adam best begyle,
And gar hym brek commandiment.
Bot to the Woman first he went;   900
Traistyng the better to prevaill,
Full subtellye did hir assaill.
With facund wordis, fals and fair,
He grew with hir familiair,
That he his purpose mycht avance;
Belevand in hir inconstance.
  Quhat is the cause, Madame, said he,
That ye forbeir yone plesand tre,
Quhilk bene, but peir, most pretious,
Quhose fruct bene moste delytious?   910
  I nyll, quod sche, thare to accord:

We ar forbyddin be the Lord,
The quhilk hes given us lybertie
Tyll eit of every fruct and tre
Quhilk growis in to Paradyse;
Brek we command, we ar nocht wyse.
He gave tyll us ane strait command
That tre to twyche nocht with our hand;
Eit we of it, without remede,
He said, but dout, we sulde be dede. 920
    Beleve nocht that, said the Serpent:
Eit ye of it, incontinent
Repleit ye sall be with science,
And haif perfyte intelligence,
Lyke God hym self, of evyll and gude.
    Than, haistellye for to conclude,
Heiryng of this prerogatyve,
Sche pullit doun the fruct belyve,
Throw counsall of the fals Serpent,
And eit of it to that intent, 930
And patt hir Husband in beleve,
That plesand fruct gyf he wald preve,
That he suld be als sapient
As the gret God Omnipotent.
Thynk ye nocht that ane plesand thyng,
That we, lyke God, suld ever ryng?
    He, herand this narratioun,
And be hir solistatioun,
Movit be prydefull ambitioun,
He eit, on that conditioun. 940
The principall poyntis of this offence
War pryde and inobedience,

Desyring for to be equall
To God, the Creatour of all.
 Allace! Adam, quhy did thow so?
Quhy causit thow this mortall wo?
Had thow bene constant, firme, and stabyll,
Thy glore had bene incomparabyll.
Quhare wes thy consyderatioun,
Quhilk had the dominatioun   950
Of every levying creature
That God had formit be Nature,
Tyll use thame at thy awin devyse?
Wes thow nocht prince of Paradyse?
Wes never man, sen syne, on lyve
That God gave sic prerogatyve:
He gaif thee strenth above Sampsone,
And sapience more than Salomone;
Young Absolone, in his tyme moste fair,
To thy bewtie wes no compair;   960
Arestotyll thow did precell
In to phylosophie naturell;
Virgill, in tyll his poetrye,
Nor Cicero, in tyll oratrye,
War never half so eloquent.
Quhy brak thow Goddis commandiment?
Quhare wes thy wytt, that wald nocht flee
Far frome the presens of that tree?
Gaif nocht thy Maker thee free wyll
To take the gude and leif the evyll?   970
Quhow mycht thy forfalt be excusit,
That Goddis commandiment refusit,
Throuch thy wyffis perswasioun?

Quhilk hes bene the occasioun,
Sen syne, that mony nobyll men,
Be the evyll counsall of wemen,
Alluterlye distroyit bene,
As in the Storeis may be sene,
Quhilk now we neid nocht tyll declair,
Bot fordwart tyll our purpose fair. 980
    Quhen thay had eaitin of the frute,
Of joye than wer thay destitute.
Than gan thay boith for to thynk schame,
And to be naikit thocht defame,
And maid thame breikis of levis grene,
That thair secreitis suld nocht be sene.
Bot in the stait of Innocence
Thay had none sic experience;
Bot, quhen thay war to Syn subjectit,
To schame and dreid thay war coactit. 990
And in ane busk thay hid thame clois,
Aschamit of the Lordis voice,
Quhilk callit Adam be his name.
    Quod he, My Lord, I thynk gret schame
Naikit to cum to thy presence.
Thow had none sic experience,
Quod God, quhen thow wes innocent:
Quhy brake thow my commandiment?
Allace! quod Adam to the Lorde,
The veritie I sall recorde; 1000
This Woman that thow gaif to me
Gart me eit of yone plesand tre.
Rycht so the Woman hir excusit,
And said, The Serpent me abusit.

Than to the Serpent God said thus,
O thow Dissaver venimous,
Because the Woman thow begylit,
Frome thynefurth sall thow be exylit:
Curst and waryit sall thow be,
So sall thy seid be, efter thee: 1010
Cauld erth salbe thy fude, also,
And creipand on thy breist sall go:
Als, I sall putt inamitie
Betuix the woman ever and thee:
Betuix thy seid and womanis seid
Salbe continuall mortall feid.
Quhowbeit thow hes wrocht thir myschevis,
It sall nocht be as thow belevis:
Sic seid salbe in woman sawin,
That thy power salbe doun thrawin; 1020
Treddyng thy heid that thow may feill,
And thow sall tred hym on the heill.
This was his promys and menyng,
That the Immaculat Virgyng
Sulde beir the Prince Omnipotent,
Quhilk suld tred doun that fals Serpent,
Sathan, and all his companye,
And thame confunde alluterlye.

COURTEOUR.

Quod I, Geve Sathan, prince of Hell,
Spak in the Serpent, as ye tell, 1030
And beistis can no way syn at all,
Quhy wes the Serpent maid so thrall?
I heir men say, affore that hour

The Serpent had ane fair figour,
And yeid straucht up upone his feit,
And had his membris all compleit,
As utheris beistis upone the bent.

EXPERIENCE.

Quod he, For he wes instrument
To Sathan, in this miserie,
Puneist he wes, as ye may se ;   1040
As, be experience, thow may knaw,
Expres in to the Commoun Law,
Ane man convickit for bewgrye,
The beist is brynt, als weill as he,
Quhowbeit the beist be innocent:
And so befell of the Serpent.
It was the Feynd, full of dispyte,
Of Adamis fall quhilk had the wyte,
As he hes had of mony mo :
Bot tyll our purpose lat us go.   1050
Than to the Woman, for hir offence,
God did pronunce this sore sentence,
All plesour that thow had afforrow
Sall cheangit be in lestyng sorrow :
Quhare that thow suld with myrth and joy
Have borne thy byrth, but pane or noy,
Now all thy bairnis sall thow bair
With dolour and continuall cair ;
And thow salbe, for oucht thow can,
Ever subjectit to the Man.   1060
Be this sentence, God did conclude
Wemen frome lybertie denude,

Quhilk, be experience, ye may se,
Quhow Quenis of moste hie degre
Ar under moste subjectioun,
And sufferis moste correctioun;
For thay, lyke byrdis in tyll ane cage,
Ar keipit ay under thirlage:
So all wemen, in thare degre,
Suld to thare men subjectit be.   1070
Quhowbeit sum yit wyll stryve for stait,
And for the maistrye mak debait,
Quhilk gyf thay want, boith ewin and morrow
Thare men wyll suffer mekle sorrow.
Of Eve thay tak that qualitie,
To desyre Soveranitie.

   And than tyll Adam, said the Lord,
Because that thow hes done accord
Thy wyll, and harknit to thy wyfe,
Now sall thow lose this plesand lyfe: 1080
Thow wes tyll hir obedient,
Bot thow brake my commandiment;
Curste and barren the erth salbe,
Quhare ever thow gois, tyll that thow de:
But labour, it sall beir no corne,
Bot thrisyll, nettyll, breir, and thorne:
For fude thow gettis none uther beild,
Bot cait the herbis upone the feild:
Sore laubouryng, tyll thy browis sweit,
Frome thyne furth sall thow wyn thy meit: 1090
I maid thee of the erth, certane,
And thow in erth sall turne agane.
Than maid he thame abilzement,

Of skynnis ane raggit rayment,
Thame to preserve frome heit and cauld :
Than grew thare dolour mony fauld.
Now, Adam, are ye lyke tyll us,
With your gay garment glorious ?
To thame thir wordis said the Lorde.
Then cryit thay boith Misericorde,   1100
  Quhen frome that Garth, with hartis sore,
Baneist thay wer, for ever more,
On to this wracheit vaill of sorrow,
With daylie laubour, evin and morrow.
Efter quhose dolorous departyng,
The Lorde gave Paradyce in kepying
Tyll ane Angell of Cherubin,
That none suld have entres thare in ;
Att the quhilk entres he did stand,
With flammand fyrie sweird in hand,   1110
To keip that Adam and his wyfe
Sulde nocht taist of the tre of lyfe :
For, geve thay of that tre had previt,
Perpetuallye thay mycht have levit.
So Adam and his Successioun
Of Paradyce tynt possessioun ;
And be this syn Originall
War men to miserie maid thrall.
  My Sonne, now may thow cleirly se,
This Warld began with miserie ;   1120
With miserie it doith proceid,
Quhose fyne sall dolour be and dreid.

COURTEOUR.

Father, quod I, quhat kynd of lyfe

Led Adam, with his lustye wyfe,
Efter thare bailfull banesyng?

EXPERIENCE.

Quod he, Continuall womentyng:
My hart hes yitt compassioun,
Quhow thay went wandryng up and doun,
Weipyng, with mony lowde Allace!   Gene. iiii.
That thay had lost that plesand place;   1130
In wyldernes to be exilde,
Quhare thay fand nocht bot beistis wylde,
Manesyng thame for tyll devore,
Quhilkis all obedient war affore.

COURTEOUR.

Father, quod I, in quhat countrie
Did leif Adam, efter that he
Was banesit from that delyte?

EXPERIENCE.

Clerkis, quod he, hes put in wryte
Quhow Adam dwelt, with mekle baill,
In Mamber, in that lusty vaill,   1140
Quhilk efter was the Jowis land;
Quhare yit his Sepulture dois stand.
I lyste nocht tary tyll discryve
The wo of Adam nor his Wyve;
Nor tell quhen thay had sonnis two,
Cayn and Abell, and no mo;
Nor quhow curst Cayn, for invy,
Did slay his Brother creuelly:

Nor of thare murnyng, nor thare mone,
Quhen thay, but sonnis, wer left allone,   1150
Abell lay slane upone the ground,
Curst Cayn flemit and vagabound;
Nor quhow God, of his speciall grace,
Send thame the thrid sonne, fair of face,
Most lyke Adam of flesche and blude,
Seth was his name, gratious and gude;
Nor quhow blynd Lameth raikleslye
Did slay Cayn, unhappelye.

   Adam, as Clerkis dois discrive,
Begat with Eve, his wofull wyve,   1160
Of men childryng thretty and two,
And of dochteris alyke also.
Be this thow may weill understand
That Adam saw mony ane thowsand
That of his body did descend,
Or he out of the warld did wend.

   Adam leifit in erth, but weir,

Gene. v.   Compleit nyne hundreth and thretty yeir;
And all his dayis war bot sorrow,
Rememberyng, boith evin and morrow,   1170
Of Paradyce the prosperitie,
Syne of his gret miseritie:
His hart mycht never be rejosit,
Remembryng quhow the hevin wes closit
Frome hym and his successioun,
And that, be his transgressioun.
Efter his deith, as I heir tell,
His Saul descendit to the hell,
And thare remanit presoneir,

In that dungeoun, thre thousand yeir   1180
And more, so did boith evyll and gude,
Tyll Christ for thame had sched his blude :
Than, be that most precious ransoun,
Thay wer delyverit of presoun.
  I have declarit now, as I can,
  The miserie of the first man.

HEIR FOLLOWIS QUHOW GOD DISTROYIT ALL
LEVEAND CREATURE IN ERTH, FOR SYN,
AND DROWNIT THAME BE ANE
TERRIBYLL FLUDE, IN THE
TYME OF NOYE.

COURTEOUR.

Prudent Father Experience,
Declare to me, or ye go hence,
Quhat wes the cause God did destroye
All Creature, in the tyme of Noye.   1190

EXPERIENCE.

  Quod he, I trymmyll for to tell
That infortune, quhow it befell ;
The cause bene so abhominabyll,
And the mater so miserabyll.
Bot, for to schaw the circumstance,
Manefestlye, of that myschance,
First I mon gar thee understand
Quhow Adam gaif expresse command

Gene. vi.

That those quhilkis come of Sethis blude,
Because thay wer gratious and gude,   1200
Suld nocht contract with Caynis kyn,
Quhilkis wer inclynit all to syn.
Tyll observe that commandiment,
Cayn past in the Orient,
With his wyfe, callit Calmana,
Quhilk was his awin syster alswa,
Quhare his ofspryng did lang remane,
Besyde the Montane of Tarbane.
And Seth did lang tyme leid his lyfe;
With Delbora, his prudent wyfe,   1210
Quhilk wes his syster, gude and fair,
In Damascene maid thare repair:
In that countrie of Sethis clan
Descendit mony holy man.
So lang as Adam was leveand,
The peple did observe command;
Quhen he wes dede, and laid in ground,
And peple greitly did abound,
And Cayn slane, as I have schawin,
And Sethis dayis all ouer blawin,   1220
The sonnis, than, of Sethis blude,
Seand the plesand pulchritude
Of the ladyis of Caynis kyn,
Quhowbeit thay knew weill it wes syn,
Opprest with sensuall lustis rage,
Did tak thame into mariage:
And so corruptit wes that blude,
The gude with evyll, and evyll with gude.
Than, as the peple did incres,

Thay did abound in wickitnes,   1230
As Holy Scripture dois rehers :
Quhilk I abhor to put in vers,
Or tell with toung I am nocht abyll ;
The suthe bene so abhominabyll,
Quhow men and women schamefullye
Abusit thameselfis unnaturallye ;
Quhose foull abhominatioun
And uncouthe fornicatioun
I thynk gret schame to put in wryte :
All that Paull Orose doith indyte ;   1240
Quhilk gyf I wald at lenth declair,
It wer yneuch to fyill the air.
Gret Clerkis of Antiquiteis
Hes wryttin mony trew storeis,
Quhilkis ar worthy to be commendit,
Quhowbeit thay be nocht comprehendit
At lenth in the Divyne Scripture :
Bot I sall do my besye cure
To tak the best, as I suppose,
That moste pertenis my purpose ;   1250
And, with support of Christ, our Kyng,
I purpose to confirme no thyng
Of the auld Historicience
Contrarious tyll his excellence.
Quhowbeit, sum mennis traditionis,
Contrar Chrystis institutionis,
Of thame thocht sum thyng I declair,
Now latt us proceid forthermair,
And, with ane language lamentabyll,
Declare this mater miserabyll.   1260

COURTEOUR.

Father, the causis wald I knaw
Quhy thay of Nature brak the Law?

EXPERIENCE.

I traist, quod he, that wyckitnes
Generith, throw sleuthfull ydilnes.
The Devyll, with all the craft he can,
Quhen he persavis ane ydill man,
Or woman gevin tyll ydilnes,
He gettis eisalye entres;
And so, be this occasioun,
And be the Feindis perswasioun,   1270
The hole warld, universalye,
Corruptit was alluterlye.

COURTEOUR.

Quhat wes the cause thay ydill ware?
That cace, quod I, to me declare.

EXPERIENCE.

Quod he, Be my imaginatioun,
For laik of vertuous occupatioun:
For of craftis thay had small usage,
Of marchandyce, nor laborage.
The Erth, than, wes so plentuous
Of fruct and spyce delicious;   1280
The herbis wer so comfortabyll,
Delytesum, and medicinabyll;
The fontannis, fresche and redolent;

To labouryng thay tuke lytill tent.
All maner of beistis, at thare plesour,
Did multyplie, without laubour.
The tyme betuix Adam and Noye,
To se the erth it wes gret joye,
Plantit with precious treis of pryce.
Four famous Fludis of Paradyce   1290
Ran throw the erth, in syndrie partis,
Spreddyng thare branchis in all airtis;
The watter was so strang and fyne,
Thay wald nocht laubour to mak wyne;
The fruct and herbis wer so gude,
Thay maid no cair for uther fude:
And so the peple tuke no cure
Bot past thare tyme at thare plesure,
Ay fyndand new inventiounis
To fulfyll thare intentiounis: 1300
So that the Lord Omnipotent
That he maid Man did Hym repent,
And schew ontyll his servand Noye
That he wald all the Warld destroye,
Except hym self and his meinye.

 Allace! quod Noye, quhen sall that be?
Than said the Lord, Sen thow so speris,
I sall prolong sax score of yeris,
Tarying upon thare repentance,
Or I fulfyll my just sentence.   1310
In the mene tyme, fall thow to warke
Incontinent, and beild ane Arke.
Quhilk Noye began, obedientlye,
And wrocht on it continuallye;

VOL. II.   S

And to the peple daylie precheit;
To cry for grace he to thame techeit,
And to thame planelye did declair
That God his wand no more wald spair,
Bot on thame he wald wyrk vengence.
To Noye yit gave thay no credence; 1320
And so thay wer incounsolabyll,
Usyng thare luste abominabyll:
And tuke his precheyng in dispyte,
Ay following thare foull delyte,
More and more, tyll that dulefull day
Quhilk all the Warld pat in affray.

COURTEOUR.

Father, ye gart me understand,
Quhen Adam brak the Lordis command,
Tyll augment his afflictioun,
God gave his maledictioun 1330
Onto the Erth, quhilk wes so fair,
That it suld barren be, and bair,
And without laubour beir no corne,
Nor fruct, bot thrissyll, breir, and thorne.
Now, say ye, in the tyme of Noye
To se the erth it was gret joye,
Plantit with fructis gude and fair;
The suthe of this to me declair:
Thir sayingis two gar me consydder,
Quhow ye mak thame agree togydder. 1340

EXPERIENCE.

God maid that promys sickerlye,

Quhowbeit, it come nocht instantlye,
Quod he, as Clerkis dois conclude;
Bot efter, quhen the furious Flude
Distroyit the Erth alluterlye,
Than come that promys sickerlye.
Evin siclyke as God gave command
Adam to twyche nocht with his hand,
Nor eit of the forbidden Tree;
Geve he did so, that he sulde dee: 1350
Quhowbeit, he deit nocht, but weir,
Efter that day nyne hundreth yeir.
Rycht so, the Propheit Esayas,
Speikand of Christ, the gret Messias,   Esay ix.
Sayand, The Bairne is tyll us borne,
To saif mankynd, quhilk is forlorne,
As he had bene borne instantlye;
Yit wes he nocht borne veralye,
Efter that saying, mony one yeir,
As in the Scripture thow may heir: 1360
Ane thousand yeir, quho reknyth rycht,
Is bot one hour in Goddis sycht.   ii. Pet. ii.
Exemplis mony I mycht tell,
Wer it nocht tedious for to dwell.

  Tyll our purpose latt us proceid,
Schawand the heycht, and lenth, and breid,
And qualitie of Noyis Arke;
Quhilk wes ane rycht excellent warke,
Of pyne tre maid, bound weill about;
Laid ouer with pik, within and out, 1370
Junit full close with nalis strong,
And wes thre hundreth cubittis long,

Fifty in breid, thretty in heycht;
Thre chalmeris, junit weill and wycht,
And everilk loft above ane uther;
Withouttin anker, air, or ruther:
Ane rycht cubeit, as I heir tell,
Of mesour now mycht be ane ell.
In the myd syde ane dur thare wes,
For beistis ane easy entres. 1380
This Ark, quhilk was boith lang and lairge,
Maid in the bodum lyke one bairge,
Coverit with burdis weill abufe,
Moste lyke ane house with sett-on rufe,
Quhose riggyng wes ane cubeit braid,
Quharein thare wes ane wyndo maid,
Sum sayis, weill closit with christall cleir,
Quharethrouch the day lycht mycht appeir.
This work the more wes to be prysit,
Because be God it was devysit. 1390
The makyng of this Ark, but weir,
Indurit weill ane hundreth yeir.

Gen. vii.

Quhen Noye had done compleit this wark,
God did hym close within the Ark;
With hym his Wyfe, and Sonnis thre,
With thare thre Wyfis, but mo menyé:
And of all foulis of the air
Of everilk kynd enterit ane pair;
Rycht so, two beistis of everilk kynde;
For quhy it wes the Lordis mynde 1400
That generatioun suld nocht faill:
Quharefor of fameill and of maill

Of everilk kynd wer keipit two.
Bot to rehers myne hart is wo
The dolent lamentatioun,
That tyme of everilk Natioun,
Sayand Allace! ane thousand syis,
Quhen wynd and rane began to ryis:
The roikis with rerd began to ryve,
Quhen uglie cluddis did ouerdryve,   1410
And dirkynnit so the Hevinnis brycht
That Sonne nor Mone mycht schaw no lycht:
The terrabyll trymling of erthquaik
Gart biggyngis bow, and cieteis schaik;
The thounder raif the cluddis sabyll,
With horrabyll sound appoventabyll;
The fyreflauchtis flew ouerthorte the fellis;
Than wes thare nocht bot yowtis and yellis.
 Quhen thay persavit without remede
All Creature to suffer dede: 1420
All fontanis frome the Erth up sprang,
And frome the Hevin the rane doun dang
Fourty dayis and fourty nychtis,
Than ran the peple to the heychtis;
Sum clam in cragis, sum in treis,
And sum to heychast montanis fleis,
With more terrour than I can tell,
Bot all for nocht: the fludis fell,
And wynd did rowt with sic ane reird
That everilk wycht waryit his weird,   1430
Cryand, Allace! that they wer borne,
Into that flude to be forlorne.
Men mycht no help mak to thare wyfis,

Nor yit support thare bairnis lyfis.
The Fludis rose with so gret mychtis
That thay ouer coverit all the heychtis:
Thay mycht no more thare lyvis lenth,
Bot swame so lang as thay had strenth,
And so, with cryis lamentabyll,
Endit thare lyvis miserabyll.   1440
 Above montainis that wer moste hie
Fifty cubeitis rose the See.
Men may imagyne, in thare mynd,
All Creature, in to thare kynd,
Boith beistis and foulis in the air,
In thare maneir maid mekle cair.
The fyschis thocht thame evyll begyld,
Quhen thay swame through the woddis wyld;
Quhalis tumbland amang the treis,
Wyld beistis swomand in the seis.   1450
Byrdis, with mony pietuous pew,
Affeiritlye in the air thay flew
So lang as thay had strenth to flee,
Syne swatterit doun in to the sea.
No thyng on erth wes left on lyve,
Beistis nor foulis, man nor wyve:
God hailelye did thame distroye,
Except thame in the Ark, with Noye,
The quhilk lay fleittand on the flude:
Welterand amang the stremes wode,   1460
With mony terrabyll affrayis,
Remanit ane hundreth and fyfty dayis,
In gret langour and hevynes,
Or wynd or rane began to ceis;

Sumtyme effectuouslye prayand,
Sumtyme the beistis vesiand:
For, be the Lordis commandiment,
He maid provisioun sufficient.
   For Noye dwelt in that Ark, but dout,
Ane yeir compleit, or he come out;   1470
Quhow, at more lenth in Holy wryte
This dulefull storye bene indyte,   Gen. viii.
And quhow that Noye gan to rejose,
Quhen conductis of the Hevin did close,
So that the rane no more discendit,
Nor the flude no more ascendit.
Quhen he persavit the Hevinnis cleir,
He send furth Corbie messingeir
In to the air, for to espy
Geve he saw ony montanis dry.   1480
Sum sayis the Ravin did furth remane,
And come nocht to the Ark agane.
Furth flew the Dow, at Noyis command,
And, quhen scho did persave dry land,
Of ane olyve scho brak ane branche,
That Noye mycht know the watter stanche;
And thare no more scho did sudjorne,
Bot with the branche scho did returne,
That Noye mycht cleirly understand
That felloun Flude was decressand: 1490
And so it did, tyll at the last
The Ark upone the ground stak fast,
On the tope of ane montane hye,
Into the land of Armanye.

And quhen that Noye had done espye
Quhow that the Erth began to drye,
Than dang he doun the durris all,
And lowsit thame the quhilk wes thrall;
The Foulis flew furth in the air,
And all the beistis, peir and pair,   1500
Past furth to seik thare pasturages:
Thare wes than, bot aucht personages,
Noye, his thre Sonnis, and thare Wyvis,
On Erth that left was with thare lyvis;
Quhome God did blys and sanctyfie,
Sayand, Incres and multiplie.
 God wait geve Noye wes blyith and glaid,
 Quhen of that presoun he wes fraid.

Quhen Noye had maid his sacrifyce,
Thankand God of his benefyce,   1510
He standand on Mont Armanye
Quhare he the countrie mycht espye;
Ye may beleve his hart was sore,
Seying the Erth, quhilk wes affore
The feilde so plesand and perfyte,
Quhilk to behald wes gret delyte,
That now was barren maid, and bair,
Afore quhilk fructuous was and fair;
The plesand treis beryng fructis
Wer lyand revin up be the rutis;   1520
The holsum herbis and fragrant flouris
Had tynt boith vertew and cullouris;
The feildis grene, and fluryst meidis,

Wer spulyeit of thare plesand weidis.
The Erth, quhilk first wes so fair formit,
Wes, be that furious Flude, deformit;
Quhare umquhyle wer the plesand planis,
Wer holkit glennis, and hie montanis:
Frome clattryng cragis, gret and gray,
The erth wes weschin quyte away.   1530
   Bot Noye had gretast displesouris,
Behauldand the dede creatouris,
Quhilk wes ane sycht rycht lamentabyll;
Men, women, beistis, innumerabyll,
Seying thame ly upone the landis,
And sum wer fleityng on the strandis:
Quhalis and monstouris of the seis
Stickit on stobbis, amang the treis;
And, quhen the Flude was decressand,
Thay wer left welteryng on the land.   1540
Affore the Flude duryng that space,
The Sey wes all in to ane place;
Rycht so the Erth, as bene desydit,
In syndrie partis wes nocht devydit,
As bene Europe and Asia
Devydit ar frome Africa.
Ye se now, divers famous Ilis
Stand frome the maine-land mony mylis:
All thir gret Ilis, I understand,
War than equall with the ferme land.   1550
Thare wes none Sey Mediterrane,
Bot onely the gret Occeane,
Quhilk did nocht spred sic bulryng strandis
As it dois now ouirthort the landis.

Than, be the ragyng of that Flude,
The Erth of vertew wes denude,
The quhilk affore wes to be prysit,
Quhose bewtie than wes dissagysit.
Than wes the maledictioun knawin
Quhilk wes be God tyll Adam schawin. 1560
   I reid quhow Clerkis dois conclude,
Induryng that moste furious Flude
With quhilk the Erth wes so supprest,
The wynd blew furth of the South-west ;
As may be sene, be experience,
Quhow, throw the watteris violence,
The heych montanis, in every Art,
As bair forgane the South-west part :
As the Montanis of Pyraneis,
The Alpis, and rochis in the seis ; 1570
Rycht so, the rochis, gret and gray,
Quhilk standis into Narroway.
The heychast hyllis, in every art,
And in Scotland, for the moste part,
Throuch weltryng of that furious flude,
The cragis of erth war maid denude :
Travellyng men may consydder best
The montanis bair nyxt the South-west.

COURTEOUR.

Declare, quod I, or ye conclude,
Quhow lang levit Noye efter the flude. 1580

EXPERIENCE.

Quod he, In Genesis thow may heir

Quhow that Noye wes sax hundreth yeir,
The tyme of this gret punysment,   Gene. ix.
And aye to God obedient;
And wes the best of Sethis blude;
And als, he levit efter the Flude
Thre hundreth and fyfty yeris,
As the same Scripture wytnes beris,
And wes, or he randerit the spreit,
Nyne hundreth and fyfty yeris compleit.   1590
   To schaw this storie miserabyll
At lenth my wyttis ar nocht abyll:
And als, my Sonne, as I suppose,
It langis nocht tyll our purpose
To schaw quhow Noyis sonnis thre
Gan to incres and multyplie;
Nor quhow that Noye plantit the wyne,
And drank tyll he wes dronkin syne,
And sleipit with his memberis bair;
And quhow Cham maid for hym no cair,   1600
Bot leuch to se his Father so,
Quhowbeit his Brether wer rycht wo;
Nor quhow Noye, but restrictioun,
Gave Cham his maledictioun,
And put hym under servytude
To Sem and Japhet, that war gude;
Nor quhow God maid ane covenent
With Noye, to mak no punysment,
Nor be no Flude the peple droun:
In signe of that conditioun,   1610
His rane-bow sett in to the air,
Of divers hevinlye colouris fair,

For to be ane perpetuall sing
Be Flude to mak no punyssing.

This Story geve thow lyste to knaw,
At lenth the Bibyll sall thee schaw.

HEIR ENDIS THE FIRST PART.

NOTES AND VARIOUS READINGS.

NOTES AND VARIOUS READINGS.

SATYRE OF THE THRIE ESTAITIS.—Page 1.

So far as can be discovered, Lyndsay's Satyre, or Play, exists only in two forms: the one, in the Manuscript collections of George Bannatyne, written in the year 1568; the other, in the old printed edition, at Edinburgh, by Robert Charteris, 1602. In the former, the Play is subdivided into a series of eight Interludes, by omitting large portions, or, to use the transcriber's own words, "levand the grave matter tharcof, becaus the samyne abuse is weill reformit in Scotland, praysit be God." The text of the printed edition was adopted by Chalmers; and, indeed, there could be no alternative, in order to exhibit the progress of the Play in its regular course. Pinkerton, in his "Scotish Poems, reprinted from Scarce Editions," had previously given these Interludes from an inaccurate transcript of Bannatyne's MS.; but before that collection was published, in 1792, he obtained the use of a printed copy, and subjoined the additional passages, rendering the whole a strange piece of patchwork. Sibbald, in his "Chronicle of Scottish Poetry, 1802," also included most of these Interludes, while at the same time he printed a limited impression of the Satyre in a separate form, ostensibly from Bannatyne's MS., but interpolating large portions from the old printed text, and altering or attempting to disguise the coarse, objectionable words and phrases which unfortunately disfigure this most remarkable production.

Chalmers is very severe on these editions by Pinkerton and Sibbald. He himself adhered slavishly to the old printed copy, and makes no use of the earlier text of Bannatyne's MS., which commences with the preliminary Interlude of "THE AULD MAN AND HIS WYF." It is not contained in the edition of 1602, and was rejected by Chalmers as spurious, not on account of its indelicacy, but upon very inconclusive reasoning, " that the play had been acted many years before this Interlude was written by whatever hand."* No doubt it contains allusions to events in the year 1547; but Mr. Chalmers might have remembered that the Play was represented on different occasions, that the Interludes were varied, and other changes made, which we have no means of ascertaining; while the coarse broad humour which this Interlude exhibits, affords but too unequivocal marks of Lyndsay's hand, to leave any doubt in regard to its authorship.

While, however, in the Satyre I have given various lines from the MS., which were omitted in the old printed copy, including several of the stage directions, which serve to render some of the scenes more intelligible, I thought it preferable to subjoin the Interlude in question as an Appendix to the present volume, distinct by itself, rather than to connect it with the Play itself.

On the opposite page is an exact copy of the title-page of the old edition of 1602. Chalmers asserts in the most positive terms the existence of two editions by Charteris, in 1602 and 1604. After a careful examination and comparison of all the accessible copies, I have come to a different conclusion. In particular, I have compared the identical copies which he mentions, that of 1602, which was

* Works, vol. i. p. 65.

ANE SATYRE OF THE THRIE ESTAITS,

in commendation of vertew
in vituperation of vyce.
Maid be Sir Dauid Lindesay of the
Mont, alias, Lyon King
of Armes.

At Edinbvrgh
Printed Be ROBERT
CHARTERIS.
1602.
Cvm Privilegio Regis.

in his own collection, and the other called 1604, which belonged to Mr. Caley. Both these are now in the Library at Britwell House. The second copy wants the title, (of which a facsimile is given on the preceding page,) in place of which it has a detached title-page, intended for a re-issue of Lyndsay's Works in 1604. Both copies have the same colophon, dated 1602, as follows :—

Printed at Edinburgh be Robert Charteris.

AN. DO. MDCII.

And are to be fauld in his Buith on the North-fide of the Gait, at the West-fide of the auld Prouofts Closhead.

Upon collating the two copies referred to, Mr. Chalmers discovered some variations, and pointed out eight instances, "five of which, he says, are right in what he calls the 1602 edition, and wrong in that of 1604; while three are wrong in the first, but right in the second." I shall quote these instances, on which he has laid so much stress, to show that they are mere typographical mistakes, corrected in some copies while the work was at press; that which he quotes as 1604 being, if I mistake not, the earlier issue of the two.

It is not indeed a matter of any great importance to settle this point; but as Chalmers is so dogmatic, I endeavoured, by careful examination, to ascertain the fact that only one edition actually exists. First, as to the variations which he points out to make it demonstrable that there were two editions. "Thus (he says) the edition of 1602 is wrong sometimes, when the edition of 1604 is right:

Edit. 1602.	Edit. 1604.		
Knw.	Knaw,	. . Page	126
Except.	Expect,	. . ,,	130
By.	But,	. . . ,,	87
And.	Am,	. . . ,,	39
Thair.	Your,	. . ,,	39

" The edition of 1604 is wrong, when the edit. 1602 is right:

Edit. 1604.	Edit. 1602.		
Da.	Do,	. . . Page	97
Trael.	Travel,	. . ,,	129
Habbie.	Heavie,	. . ,,	129

"It is only in an instance or two that the expression is changed, as (line 2727) *being like to die*, in edit. 1602; *lykand to die*, in edit. 1604, at p. 94." Mr. Chalmers adds, "After so decisive a collation, scepticism cannot doubt, whether there were one or two editions of Lyndsay's Play."

There needs be no "scepticism" in this matter, as any one accustomed to the mysteries of printing, upon comparing the two alleged impressions, would say, it was an utter impossibility (had such an attempt been made) to have reproduced the book so exactly in the use and position of letters, and arrangement of the lines and pages to the most minute particulars. If actually reprinted, while correcting the above trivial typographical mistakes, or others of a similar kind, the printer surely would not have slavishly copied palpable blunders which occur in both these copies, such as the following:

Line 490, *wthin* for *within*.
,, 522, *bis rago* for *his rage*.

Line 553, *Quistand*, for *Quhisland* (whistling).
,, 826, *Fyteine*, for *Fyfteine*.
,, 894, *Philsophie* for *Philosophie*.
,, 912, *Costorphine*, for *Corstorphine*.
,, 1060, *Lo leid* for *To leid*.
,, 1226, *Lustie Lastie* for *Lustie Ladie*.
,, 1281, *To harbie* for *To harbrie*.
,, 1333, *Ane ledder*, for *Ane tedder*.
,, 1843, *Live to sing*, for *Leave to sing*.
,, 2342, *Thay will be he heir*, for *Thay will be heir*
,, 3302, *Within the habzeir*, for *Within the half yeir*.
,, 3816, *Thay willl*, for *Thay will*, &c.

In printing off additional copies, other corrections were easily made, without altering the pages, such as in

Line 1029, *Smioks* in some copies corrected to *smaiks*.
,, 1512, *For filence* to *For silence*.
,, 1597, *Correcioun* to *Correctioun*.
,, 1603, *And toc anse*, to *And to cause*.
,, 1617, *Weir in and pouertie*, to *In weir and pouertie*.
,, 1627, *Weill conteht*, to *Weill content*.
,, 3248, *Dysetr* to *Dysert*.
,, 3255, *Amet* to *Annet*.
,, 3335, *Ferinds* to *Freinds*, &c.

In all the copies I have examined, the last leaf has the same colophon dated 1602, as above, p. 290. Why should this date have been retained, if reprinted in 1604?

The following introductory notice to Lyndsay's Play, by Mr. CHALMERS, may be quoted without abridgement:—

" Obscure as the origin of the drama is in England, as well as in Scotland, inquiry will find that their dramatic exhibitions were derived from the same source; as the progenitors of the people of both were the same. In England, perhaps in all the Gothic countries of Europe, the *Mysteries* were the first productions of the dramatic muse, representing usually the most mysterious parts of Scripture story. If they were originally little better than dumb show, with the intermixture of some speeches, they became at length somewhat improved by the formation of regular dialogues, which were divided of course into acts and scenes. The first drama in Scotland whereof we have any satisfactory evidence, was a *Mystery*, called the *Haliblude*, which was acted on the Windmill-hill at Aberdeen in 1445, as we know from the city records. Such representations of mysterious stories continued to be performed on festivals and rejoicings in the principal towns, till the age of Lyndsay: In 1540 the queen rode to Aberdeen, which received her with pageants, *verses*, and *playes;* as we learn from Holinshed. John Bale is supposed to have written the last of the *Mysteries* about the year 1538. Soon after the Reformation, the Church of Scotland prohibited the representation of Scripture stories. These representations, in which the Bible was burlesqued, and religion was profaned, from motives of piety, as the historian of the English poetry remarks, were followed by *Moralities*, a sort of natural succession, which, as they were not devoid of invention, exhibit the outlines of the dramatic art, as doctor Percy has observed. Under the severe reign of Henry VIII. appeared *moral plays*, which almost approached to tragedies and comedies. In 1503, at the marriage of James IV. with Margaret, the daughter of Henry VII., a *Moralitie* was played after *dynar* by some English actors, who had accompanied the queen from Wyndsor. But it was reserved for Lyndsay to exhibit a *Morality* which was intended by the poet as *ane Satyre of the Three Estaitis*, in *commendatioun* of *vertew* and in *vituperatioun* of *vyce*. None of the earliest English dramatists, Parfre, Bale, or Heywood, would have been permitted to go the length of ridiculing every order in the state; yet in England the reformers and their opponents were brought upon the stage by their several partisans: And Heath, the archbishop of York, in opposing the act of uniformity in 1559, complained in parliament of the stage plays, which had been made in mockery of the catholick religion. The Satyre of Lyndsay was acted at Coupar in Fife in 1535; at Linlithgow in 1539; and at Edinburgh in 1554. Whether the matter or the manner of this drama be considered, it must be allowed to be a very singular performance; and to have carried away the palm of dramatic composition from the contemporary *moralities* of England, till the epoch of the first tragedy in *Gorboduc*, and of the first comedy in *Gammer Gurton's Needle*: Lyndsay's play has certainly as much *moral* as *Gorboduc*, and as much wit as *Gammer Gurton's Needle*. The earliest dramas of both these countries were defiled with extraordinary grossness, as they were represented before a rude people. 'To talk of the grossness and absurdity of such manners,' says Warton, 'is little to the purpose; the poet is only concerned in the justness and faithfulness of the representation.' Such must be the apology of Lyndsay, whose picture is faithful, though it represents vulgar manners in *vulgar* language. We may learn, from the length of the perusal of Lyndsay's Satyre of the Three Estates, that its representation must have consumed 'the live-long day with patient expectation.' It began about nine in the morning, and continued during nine hours with little intermission, as we are told by Henry Charteris, the bookseller, who saw 'this play playit besyde Edinburgh in 1554, in presence of the Quene regent; lestand fra nyne houris afoir none till sex houris at evin.' But what is this length of representation to the length of the English mysteries, during the persevering curiosity of antient times? In 1391, as we learn from honest Stow, 'a play was playde by the parish clerks of London, which continued three days together, the king, queene, and nobles of the realme being present: And another was plaide in 1409, which lasted eight days, and was of matter from the creation of the worlde, whereat was present most of the nobilitie and gentrie of England.' That the king in 1540, and much more, that the queen, who was a woman of elegance and a sovereign of policy, should have allowed Lyndsay's *Satyre of the Three Estates* to be acted in such a country during a period of perturbation, is quite wonderful; of them it can be said that,

> They had a sharp *foresight*, and working wit,
> That never idle was, ne once could rest a whit.

What Lyndsay's intentions were, more than the gratification of his present humour, it is not easy to discover. Like other great reformers, he probably did not foresee that, when he had prompted a passion for novelty with a contempt for order,

> The hearts of all his people should revolt from him.
> And kiss the lips of unacquainted change.

From every intimation it is apparent that this *moralitie*, which cannot be equalled in the English drama during that age, must have been written towards the end of the year 1535."

Mr. CHALMERS, in the previous part of his edition, "On the Chronology of Lyndsay's Poems," says, in regard to "The Play, or SATYRE ON THE THREE ESTATES:"

"This remarkable Drama of a rude age was undoubtedly presented at Epiphany 1539-40, before the King and Queen, the court, and country, on the Playfield, near Linlithgow. It must necessarily have been written some years before. The King is everywhere spoken of as still unmarried; but he changed his unmarried state in 1537, so that this Play must have been written before that year both of joy and of sorrow. Among the many fools whom Lyndsay satirizes, he ranks the insatiable merchantmen:

> Quhen God has send them abundance
> Ar nocht content with sufficiance;
> Bot, sailis into the stormy blastis
> In *winter*, to get greater castis
> In mony terribill great torment
> *Against the Acts of Parliament.*

"The satirist alludes both generally and specially to the noble acts of parliament; to the acts honorabill made by our prince in *the last* parliament, because they are baith gude and profitabill. The whole context of this singular Drama evinces, then, that it was originally written or at least finished in 1535. It was first acted on the Playfield at Coupar in Fife during the year 1535; and indeed much of the scene is laid in Fife, where several men and things are mentioned which must have been very familiar to the people of that shire. It was acted at Linlithgow by the express command of the King, on the day of Epiphany 1539-40. And it was a third time presented *beside* Edinburgh in presence of the Queen regent, a great part of the nobility, and an exceeding great number of people, 'fra ix hours afore none till vi hours at even;' as we learn from Henry Charteris, the bookseller, who was present, no doubt. It is to be remarked, however, that the *Satyre on the three Estates*, like *the Rehearsal*, when acted by Garrick and Cibber, admitted of recent retrospection and temporary allusions. An accurate eye, adverting to the dates, may trace Lyndsay's interpolations for the purpose of alluding to late events, in order to *elevate and surprise* the unpractised auditors."

At page 4 of the present volume I have already remarked that no evidence can be produced to show that the Play, as Chalmers asserts, was first represented at Cupar in Fife in 1535; and that any supposed allusions to the personal character of James the Fifth in the play, are quite unwarranted or inconclusive. But I shall have occasion in the Memoir to consider these points more carefully.

The Interludes in Bannatyne's MS. begin on folio 164, and end on folio 210. In printing these from the MS., Mr Pinkerton says, "The preceding pages were printed before any copy of David Lyndsay's Satyre, or Play, came to the hands of the editor, that piece being extremely scarce. Having at length been so fortunate as to procure the loan of the edition printed at Edinburgh in 1602, 4to, the following variations have appeared between the play and the interludes here published:

"The Play presents one continued succession of action, undivided into Interludes. The order is also different, as will appear by the following statement, comparing these Interludes with the printed text of the Play."

I have partly copied Pinkerton's statement, with special references to the pages of the MS., as well as to the lines in the present edition.

Interlude I. THE AULD MAN AND HIS WIFE is wanting in the printed copy of 1602; but from the Prologue it palpably formed part of the Play on the occasion of its representation at Cupar in Fife.—See Appendix to the present volume.

After the Proclamation and this first Interlude (fol. 168) is written, "Heir begynnis Schir Dauid Lyndsay[is] Play maid in the Grenesyd besyd Edinburgh, quhilk I [haif] writtin bot schortly be Interludis, levand the grave mater therof, becaws the samyne abuse is weill reformit in Scotland, praysit be God; quhairthrow I omittit that principall mater, and writtin only Sertane mirry Interludis thairof, verry plesand, begynning at the first part of the Play."

In another part (fol. 177) he writes, "Heir followis certane mirry and sportsum Interludis, contenit in the Play maid be Schir Dauid Lyndsay of the Month, knycht, in the Playfeild of Edinbur^t, to the mocking of abusionis usit in the cuntré be diverse sortis of Estait." And, at the beginning of another Interlude (fol. 196^b.), "I tak heir bot certane schort pairtis out of the speichis, becauss of lang proces of the Play."

Interlude II. HUMANITIE AND SENSUALITIE begins the Play (Edit. 1602, pp. 1-20), Lines 1 to 620, concluding with the SOUTAR AND HIS WIFE, Lines 1288 to 1411.

MS. fol. 168.

Interlude III. THE PUIR MAN AND THE PARDONER. This begins the second part of the Play (Edit. 1602., pp. 64-80), Lines 1932 to 2297. MS. fol. 177.

Interlude IV. THE SERMON OF FOLLY. This concludes the Play (pp. 144-155). Lines 4283 to 4628. MS. fol. 182.

Interlude V. FLATTERY, DECEIT, AND FALSEHOOD MISLEAD KING HUMANITY (Edit. 1602, pp. 20-38). Lines 603 to 938.

MS. fol. 187.

Interlude VI. THE THREE VICES OVERCOME TRUTH AND CHASTITY (Edit. 1602, pp. 39-63), Lines 939 to 1018, 1077 to 1183, 1200 to 1215, 1412 to 1481. MS. fol. 192.

Interlude VII. THE PARLIAMENT OF CORRECTION (Edit. 1602, pp. 83-109), Lines 1908 to 1931, 1482 to 1579, 1620 to 1881, 2395 to 3103 (with numerous passages omitted).

MS. fol. 195.

Interlude VIII. THE PUNISHMENT OF THE VICES (Edit. 1602, pp. 109-145), but with still larger omissions). Lines 3202 to 3321, 3614 to 3715, 3973 to 4282, 3774 to 3797, and 4629 to 4652. MS. fol. 203.

"Heir endis the schort Interludis of Sr Dauid Lyndsayis Play, maid in the Grenesyd besyd Edinburt, in anno 155[4] zeiris" (fol. 210).

Line 32—*Be Him that Judas sauld.* Mr. Chalmers says, "The one half of conversation in that age, both in England and in Scotland, was made up by *swearing*. The following is a list of the most fashionable Oaths which have been gleaned from this Play:

Be Cokis passion; Be Gods passion; Be Cokis deir passion.
Be Coks tois; Be Gods wounds.
Be Gods Croce.
Be Gods Mother.
Be Gods Breid, *i.e.* the altar.
Be Gods goun.
Be God himsell.
Be greit God that all has wrocht.
Be him that all the Warld has wrocht.
Be him that the Warld wrocht.
Be him that has us wrocht.
Be him that made the Mone.
Be him that wore the Croun of thorn.
Be him that bure the cruel Croun of thorn.
Be him that herryit Hell.
Be him that Judas sauld.
Be the gude Lord.
Be the Rude, *i.e.* the Cross.
Be the Trinity; be the haly Trinity.
Be the Sacrament; be the haly Sacrament.
Be the Messe; the Mass.
Be him that our Lord Jesus sauld.
Be him that deir Jesus sauld.
Be our Ladie; be Sanct Mary; be sweit Sanct Mary; be Mary bricht.

Be Alhallows.
Be Sanct James.
Be Sanct Michell.
Be Sanct Ann.
Be Sanct Bryde; be Brydes bell.
Be Sanct Geill; be sweit Sanct Geill.
Be Sanct Blais.
Be Sanct Blane.
Be Sanct Clone; be Sanct Clune.
Be Sanct Allan.
Be Sanct Fillane.
Be Sanct Tan.
Be Sanct Dyonis of France.
Be Sanct Mavene.
Be the gude Lady that me bare.
Be my Saul.
Be my Thrift.
Be my Christendom.
Be this Day.

"The Parliament at length interposed; and by an act 'Anent them that swearis abhominable aithes,' 5 parl. Mary [1551], ch. 16, this odious practice, which continued, notwithstanding *frequent preachings*, was prohibited under severe penalties. A similar practice came down from the old moralities to the dramas of England, till it was prohibited by one of the first statutes of king James."—CHALMERS.

Line 52.—*And se the Burgessis spair not for expence.*— "This is a satiric stroke of Lyndsay at the representatives of the burghs, who then considered their duty, in parliament, as a burden, and expected to be paid their expenses."—CHALMERS.

Line 105.—*And pas tyme, with pleasure.* See note on line 417.

Line 106.—*Als lang leifis the mirrie man*
As the sorie for ocht he can.

In a ballad, "quod FLEMYNG," in Bannatyne's MS., and printed in various collections, beginning *Be mirrie, Brethrene, ane and all,* are the similar lines:—

> For als lang leivis the mirry man
> As dois the wrech, for ocht he can.

Chalmers says, "This appears to have become a common saw in Lyndsay's time; but whether he was the original author is not certain. I do not observe that this *saw* is among the *Adagia Scotica*." Kelly gives the proverb, "*As long lives the mirry man as the sad, and a night longer.* A cheerful temper is no enemy to health and long life, but rather a friend," p. 48.

Line 132.—*The beriall of all bewtie,* means the *brightest* of all beauty: So in Candlemas-day. Hawkins O. P. v. 1. 24: "Brighter than *berall* outhir clere crystal." In Dunbar's *Golden Terge:* "The ruby skyis kest *berial* bemis on emerant bewis grene." Dunbar speaks of Aberdeen as, "Blyth Aberdene, thou *beriall* of all towns." The root is in *beryl* (Gr.), an Indian green stone, of great brightness.—Coles."
—CHALMERS.

Line 147.—*Sing the tribill part,* so in Bannatyne's MS. The edit. 1602 has troubill.

Line 156—*I may sing, Peblis on the Greine.* "The allusion is to some popular song, quite different from the ludicrous poem of *Peblis at the Play.*"—CHALMERS.

Line 161.—*The Bowis.* This may have been a local allusion to the Nether-bow, and to the Upper or West-bow of Edinburgh.

Line 261.—*The Monks of Bamirrinoch.* "Balmirinoch, a well-known monastery in Fife, whence the Elphinstons in 1604 derived an unfortunate title. The satire is sly and severe."—CHALMERS.

Line 269—*The buik sayis, Omnia probate.* This is rather a perversion of the Scripture injunction, "Prove all things: hold fast that which is good." (Omnia autem probate: quod bonum est tenete.)   1 Thessal. v. 21.

Line 349.—*Be cokis passioun.* "So in Shakspeare: 'Cocks passion! silence, I hear my master.' Such oaths are common in the old poets."—CHALMERS.

Line 417.—*Pastyme with pleasance,* the name of an old English song, beginning *Passetyme with good companye,* called "The Kynges Ballade," and attributed both words and music to Henry the Eighth, is printed by Dr. Rimbault in "A Little Book of Songs and Ballads, gathered from Ancient Music Books," p. 37. Lond. 1851, 8vo.

Line 468.—*Hay as ane brydlit cat I brank.* "Hey! as a bridled cat I prance: To '*brank* like a bridled cat,' is still a common expression.—CHALMERS." "We sall gar brank yow (or restrain you), occurs in that singular poem in 'The Gude and Godly Ballates,' p. 181,—*The Paip, that Pagane fwll of pryde.*"—Edit. 1568.

Line 478.—*Be Him that herryit Hell.* "This was a common oath among the old poets; as in Chaucer:
'Say what thou wolt, I shal it never telle,
To child, ne word, *by him that harrwed helle.*'"
—CHALMERS.

Lines 480, 490, &c., to 600.—In numbering these lines a mistake is made in placing 480, 490, &c., each of them one line too high, that is, opposite to 479, 489, &c.

Line 531.—*Nor the lamber.* " Sweeter than the amber. Before the days of Shakespeare, *amber* was highly prized as a *perfume.* Milton alludes to the *fragrance* of *amber:* " An *amber scent* of *odorous perfume.*"—CHALMERS.

Lines 539 and 540, are evidently the words of Hameliness, although not so marked either in the old printed copy or in Chalmers.

Lines 580; 581.—*That garris, &c.* " That makes our guiders, or rulers, all want *grace,* the effect of God's influence." *Die befoir thair day:* " The allusion is to the Scotish kings, who mostly all died prematurely."—CHALMERS.

Lines 602, 604.—This speech of Flattery, as Chalmers remarks, has a close resemblance to a passage in " The Droichis part of the Play," attributed to Dunbar.—(See Dunbar's Poems, vol. ii. p. 59); but which Sibbald imagined might have been written by Lyndsay.

Line 611.—*Beyond the May,* or the Isle of May, an island lying at the mouth of the Firth of Forth, on the side nearest the coast of Fife. There was at an early period a religious establishment here, dedicated to All-Saints, and resorted to, even after the Reformation, on account of its reputation for curing barrenness of women. In the reign of Charles the First, a beacon light was erected on the island, which is now uninhabited, except by the keepers of the present light-house, so well known to mariners.

Line 618.—*On steirburd.* "On the *Tempest* of Shakespeare, Johnson remarks that it furnishes the *first* example of *seamen's language* on the English stage: But we thus see that Lyndsay gave specimens of *schipmen's* speech, and

described a tempest, long before Shakespeare was born."—
CHALMERS.

Line 635.—*Wa sair.* In the old printed copies, the word is very indistinct, Chalmers made the exclamation *Wa fair the Devill,* for woe befal the Devil. In Bannatyne's MS., the word is written *serve.*

Line 642.—*Quhen freindis meits, harts warms.* This proverbial saying in Kelly's Scottish Proverbs (p. 340), *When friends meet, Hearts warm,* and quotes the line (from Horace Serm. i. v. 44),—

Nil ego contulerim jucundo sanus amico.

Line 643.—*That frelie fude.* Hearty fellow: *Frelie* is free, liberal, worthy, from A.-Sax. *freolie:* and *fude, fode,* is a person, man, woman, or child. So, in Rhymour's Prophecy, "With him cummis mony *frelie fude:*" Again, "Defouled is mony doughtie *fude.*" The romance of the Kyng of Tars, describing the battle, says, the Soudan,

Feolde the Cristene to the ground,
Mony a *freoly feode.*

Minot calls king Edward a "*frely fode;*" and so Wyntown terms queen Mald:

Syne Saxon and the Scottis blude,
Togidder is in yhon *frely fude.*"—CHALMERS.

Line 660.—*I say, Koks bons!* In the old printed copies first issued, the words *Aisy! Coks bons!* were corrected to *I say.* Mr Chalmers, overlooking this, adds as a note, "*Aisay! Coks bons!* Easy! God's bones! So '*Cockes bones,*' in Chaucer. Cocks bones, Cocks wounds, Cocks passion, and others, were common exclamations and oaths, from the time of Chaucer to that of Lyndsay and Shakespeare. *God's 'ounds* is now the representative of the whole."

Line 671.—*Katie unsell was my mother.* In a former note Mr Chalmers says, "*Kaity* is the familiar name of Catherine; and is also applied to any wanton girl." Here he adds, "*Katie unsell; unsel,* is bad, naughty, wicked, from the Saxon, *un-sel,* and it is here properly made the name of Deceit's mother. Montgomerie, in his Flyting with Polwart, uses the term for a bad or wicked creature: 'There an elf, on an ape, an *unsell* begat.'"

Line 695—*Pray you,* should read, *I pray you: I* was accidentally omitted.

Line 698—*That samin hors is my awin mair,* a Scottish proverb, says Chalmers, denoting sameness of object.

Lines 763 and 4401—*Tullilum.* The third order of the Carmelites or Begging Friars of the order of the Blessed Mary of Mount Carmel. They obtained the name of White Friars from the colour of their outward garment. Their convent of Tullilum, situated a little to the west of the city of Perth, was founded in the reign of Alexander III. in the year 1262. Upon the dissolution of Religious houses, at the period of the Reformation, the lands and rents of this convent instead of being granted to some courtier or neighbouring proprietor, were fortunately annexed to the Hospital of king James VI. at Perth. Some of the Charters of Tullilum are printed in a volume called "The Book of Perth, by John Parker Lawson," Edinb. 1847, 8vo.

Line 848—*Now the Vycis cumis:* These are "the *old vice,*" mentioned in the *What you Will* of Shakespeare. *The vice* was *the fool* of the old *Moralities,* saith Johnson, who holds that *Punch* is the legitimate successor of *the old vice.*

But the *vycis* of Lyndsay's *Satyre* were more *knaves* than *fools*. This character was always acted in a *mask*, and probably had its name, saith Steevens, from the old French word *vis*, for which they now use *visage*."—CHALMERS.

Line 860—This line, omitted in the old printed text, is supplied from Bannatyne's MS. It is not noticed by Chalmers.

Line 912—*And all Christendome*. "We have here a sequence of witticisms, consisting of alliterations and comparisons of small things with great: Danskin with Denmark; Spittelfeild with Spaine; Renfrew, a small shire, with the realm of France; Ruglan, a little town in Lanarkshire, with Rome; Corstorphine, a small parish, with Christendome."—CHALMERS.

Line 980—*Ruglen*. Ruglen (in common pronunciation) or Rutherglen, is a small town on the south bank of the Clyde, in Lanarkshire, about three miles S.E. from Glasgow. It was erected, in early times, into a Royal borough, and to increase its importance, it could boast of a Castle, which was demolished after the battle of Langsyde, in 1569.

Line 982—*Never so teuch*. "*Teuch;* difficult, strange, as in Chaucer: 'And made it neither *tough* ne queint.' And in the Murning Maiden : 'Albeit ye mak it never sa *teuch*.' —Maitland Poems, p. 209."—CHALMERS.

Lines 997 to 1020—*And mak betwix us sikker bands*. "It is curious to remark that almost the whole of this *counsel* of the *Vyces*, with a slight variation or two, is copied from Lyndsay's *Complaynt*."—CHALMERS. See vol. i. p. 50, line 1871.

Line 1031—*Better go revell, &c.* This and the next three lines "are almost literally copied from our poet's

Complaynt (vol. i., p. 49), where he describes the courtiers managing the young King:

> Sum gart him *revel at the racket,*
> Sum harlit him to the *hurlie hacket;*
> And sum to *schaw thair courtlie corses,*
> Wald ryde to Leith and *ryn thair horses.*
> —CHALMERS.

Line 1153—*This is the New Testament, in English toung, and printit in England.* This of course refers to Tyndale's translation. It was first printed abroad in 1525, but all the attempts to suppress it, only encouraged the appearance of numerous impressions, which found their way into this country, and were extensively circulated before Henry the Eighth granted permission to have copies printed in England in the year 1537.

Line 1288—The old printed text affords no authority for giving what follows, on to line 1411, as a separate INTERLUDE. But the emendation was required, as this Interlude interrupts the progress of the Play—and it was evidently intended to amuse the lower classes of the auditors.

Line 1393—*Go East about the Nether mill.* In the Interlude in Bannatyne's MS. this is changed to *I will go by the Castill hill,* which as Pinkerton, p. 260, suggested, was probably a variation between the representations at Cupar and Edinburgh, Chalmers referring to this, says, "the elision here is very harsh. The Sowtar's wife means to say, that she will not run the risque of drowning herself; *but*, will go east about, by the nether mill. In the mutilated abstract of Lyndsay's drama, which is published by Mr. Pinkerton, the scene is laid at Edinburgh, and not at Cupar, or Linlithgow, where there are considerable streams, the Sowtar's wife says, "I will go by *the Castle-hill.*"—CHALMERS.

The local allusions, however, in this Interlude clearly refer to Cupar-Fife. In Bannatyne's MS., no doubt, it reads the Castel-hill, but this does not necessarily refer to Edinburgh. In fact, so far as Edinburgh is concerned, it has no meaning. In early times a Castle which belonged to the family of Macduff, the Thanes of Fyfe, was erected in Cupar, and its site, a small eminence at the east end of the town, still retains the name. In the small Plan or sketch of Cupar by James Gordon, minister of Rothiemay, dated 1642, we find both the Castell, and the Mill port, or gate, at the bridge crossing the Eden into which falls the rivulet known as Our Lady's Burn, and which may have been the water to be crossed in order to get from the Playfeild to the Town.

Line 1578—*Salbe worth.*—"The old printed text was *Thy feit sal be with fourtie handis:* this seems not to be sense: if we might suppose, that Lyndsay wrote *worth*, for *with*, this would make some sense; by making Deceit say,—"If you run fast enough to catch me, thy feet shall be *worth* to thee forty hands."—CHALMERS.

In Bannatyne's MS., we have, *Sall be wirth*, which confirms the above emendation.

Line 1636—The name of the speaker, CORRECTIOUN, on pages 86 to 95, is so in the old copy; it should rather have been DIVYNE CORRECTIOUN, as in line 1597, he says, I am callit Divyne Correction.

Line 1640.—*Thay play Bo-keik.* Or Bo-peip, a child's game, Chalmers says, "to play at bo-peip is to look out, and draw back, as if frighted."

Line 1702.—*Be suir that meir belangis to the pleuch.* See note to line 2557.

Line 1704—*The king Sardanapall.* "Sardanapalus, the Assyrian King, who was famous for his effeminacy, and died about 767 years before the birth of Christ."—CHALMERS.

Line 1812.—*The teind mussellis of the Ferrie myre.* "This is ironically offered as a thing of no value; and alluded probably to the shoals near the Queen's-ferry."—CHALMERS.

Line 1817.—*In the colpots of Tranent.* Meaning, says Chalmers, "the coalpits of Tranent, in Haddingtonshire, which are very ancient." Tranent, in the county of Haddington, about nine miles from Edinburgh, had long been memorable for the coal-pits in that neighbourhood. Chalmers, in his Caledonia, refers to a grant by Seyer de Quency, Lord of the manor of Tranent, in the year 1202, in favour of the monks of Newbattle, of a coal-pit and quarry on the lands of Preston. This charter is printed in the Chartulary of Newbattle, p. 53 No. 66. The words used are *carbonarium et quarrarium.* Other early charters might be quoted. (See Chalmers's Caledonia, vol. ii., p. 400. New Statistical Account, Haddington, p. 285. Editor's Preface to the Chartulary of Newbattle, p. xxxiv., Edin. 1849, Bannatyne Club.) The working of the collieries in that district, at the present time is still carried on very extensively.

Lines 1819-1822.—By some awkward mistake of the printer, two of these lines have been transposed. They should have stood thus:—

> All nicht I had sa mekill drouth,
>   I micht nocht sleip a wink :
> Or I proclame ocht with my mouth
>   But doubt I man haif drink.

Line 1972—*At Session, na Senzie.* "The present Court of Session, was established, in May 1532. The word *senzie* is supposed to mean the *assizes*, MS. Glos. It is, however, certain, that it meant the *consistory*; the purpose of the poet being to satirize both the civil and the ecclesiastical courts. The Pauper afterwards says to the Pardoner; 'Or to the bishop, I sall pass and plenzie, in Sanct Androis; and summon yow to the *senzie*.' Again, the Temporal Estate says to the spirituality : 'Gif he has faltit, summon him to *your senzie*.' The *senzie* was plainly, then, an ecclesiastical court. The synod, in the modern sense, did not exist in that age."—CHALMERS.

Line 1982—*Ane meir that carryit salt and coill.* "We here see (says Chalmers) that coals were brought to towns on mare's backs." The invariable practice of carrying coals, &c., in paniers, on horse's backs, continued till about the middle of the last century. See New Statistical Account, Haddingtonshire, p. 287.

Line 1985—*The town of Air.* "The town of Air, is here brought in merely for the rhyme. The poor man lived at Tranent, a place of ancient colliery; and to carry coals to Edinburgh, on his mare, was a natural circumstance; but the town of Air had no connection with the man and his mare. What a *quibble* was to Shakespeare, according to Johnson, a *rhyme* was to Lyndsay, the fatal Cleopatra, for whom he lost the world, and was content to lose it. Yet, is the story well, and ably, and artfully told."—CHALMERS.

Line 1991—*Hyryeild.* The fine paid to the landlord, on the death of his vassal or tenant.—CHALMERS. See note to line 3915.

Line 2049—*Ane Pardoner . . admitted by the Pape.*

"*Pardoners* were well known characters, at the epoch of the Reformation, who retailed the Pope's indulgences, for profit, in every Christian country. Chaucer exposed them to ridicule in England. Luther raised the indignation of Germany against them; and Lyndsay now tried to make the pardoner contemptible in Scotland. The impositions of the pardoners, on the credulity of the people, were checked by several councils. See Du Cange in v. *Quæstuarii*, and *Quæstionarius*. By the stat. 22 Henry VIII. c. 12. all *Proctors*, and *Pardoners*, going about in any country, without sufficient authority, are to be treated as vagabonds."—CHALMERS.

Line 2091—*Of Fine Macoull the richt chaft blaid.* "Of Fyn-Mac-Coul the proper jaw-bone. The allusion is obviously pointed to *Fin-Mac-Coull*, the famous Fingal, the son of Comhall. Fin-Mac-Coull is a personage, who, with the other heroes of Ossian, was very familiar to the historians and poets of Scotland, during the age of Lyndsay, and during some centuries before. They were mentioned by Barber, in 1375; by Holland in his *Howlat*, 1453; by bishop Douglas, in his *Palice of Honour;* by the historians, Boece and Lesley; and even by Colvill, in his *Whigs Supplication*, 1681. From all those premisses, it follows, that neither of the contending parties, about the genuineness of *Ossian*, are altogether right. The chronology of Hanmer, Macpherson, and their followers, is most egregiously erroneous, On the other hand, those who insist on the forgery of Ossian's Poems by Macpherson, and on the recentness of Ossian, argue against facts which cannot be contradicted. Gawin Douglas, in his *Palice of Honour*, mentions

> Gret Gow Mac Morne, and Fin MacCowl, and how
> They suld be goddis, in Ireland, as they say.

Gow MacMorne is *Gaul*, the son of Morni; *Gow* being the Scoto-Saxon pronunciation of *Gaul.*"

After mentioning the connexion of Ossian and his heroes with the arrival of the Danes in Ireland, at the beginning of the ninth century, Mr Chalmers concludes his long note, as follows:—

"Of consequence, in fair discussion, the story of Ossian and his heroes, cannot be carried back beyond the *ninth* century: neither can poems, which are chiefly founded on that story, be older than the events which compose that story. But we find, in fact, that several of the heroes of Ossian were mentioned by our historians and poets for centuries before Macpherson was born; and Ossian, and his heroes, are to this day interwoven into the *topography* of Scotland, and the traditions of the country."—CHALMERS.

In repudiating the claims of Macpherson's Ossian, both in regard to their epic form, as exhibited in his Fingal and Temora, and to the remote antiquity of these compositions (even in a fragmentary state) there is yet no reason to call in question the fact, that heroic ballads, or what is styled Ossianic poetry, existed at an early period among the Celtic population both of Scotland and Ireland. Such an admission, indeed, will by no means satisfy a true Highlander. Nevertheless, although no Gaelic poetry in writing has been discovered earlier than the Dean of Lismore's collection (1512-1529); a single leaf of the Dean's MS., would, I think, be sufficient to overturn the theories of Malcolm Laing and others, who have alleged that the Poems published under the name of Ossian were forgeries, or the invention of Macpherson.

The "Fragments of Ancient Poetry collected in the Highlands of Scotland, and translated from the Gaelic or Erse language," which Macpherson published in 1760, were no doubt genuine compositions of the Highland bards, and these he skilfully worked up into his Epic poems. He himself seems to have had no dislike to be considered the reputed author of Ossian.

"The Dean of Lismore's Book, a selection of Ancient Gaelic Poetry," &c., has now been edited with a translation and notes by the Rev. T. M'Lauchlan. Edinb. 1862, 8vo.

Line 2095—*Balquhidder.* "A parish in the west of Perthshire: the MacConnals were a powerful clan in Lyndsay's age: but they lived chiefly in Kintyre."—CHALMERS.

Line 2097—*Johne the Armistrang.* "Johnny Armstrong, the well-known border freebooter, who, by a great effort of justice, was hanged, in June 1529, near Carlenrig, in Teviotdale."—CHALMERS.

Line 2175—*Ilk ane of yow, &c.* Chalmers notices that a similar punishment is presented in the curious and well-known English play "Gammer Gurton's Needle."
This shows that such coarseness was not peculiar to one country. See Hawkins, vol. i., p. 238.

Line 2231—*At the horne.* "A person is said, in the Scotish law, to be *at the horn*, when he is proclaimed a rebel, and outlawed by three blasts of a horn."—CHALMERS.
To put to the horn, is a forensic phrase, signifying, to denounce as a rebel or outlaw.

Line 2298—This title is not found in the old printed copies, and has been supplied.

Line 2393—*Dempster.* "The executive officer who pronounces the *dome*, or judgment of the court."—CHALMERS.

Line 2394—*And fence the Court.* "To proclaim the sitting of the court. When the courts of justice sat in the open air, it became necessary to fence the court; for keeping off the multitude."—CHALMERS.
To fence a court is explained in Dr Jamieson's dictionary, "To open the Parliament, or a court of law. This was

anciently done in name of the sovereign, by the use of a particular form of words."

Line 2557—*Thocht reif, &c.* "The allusion here, is to the great expedition, in 1529, to Liddisdale, and Euisdale, when so many thieves were hanged: Yet, something more was necessary *to speed the plough.*"—CHALMERS.

At line 1702 Lyndsay had used a similar phrase: *Be suir that mair belangis to the pleuch.*

Line 2573—*How Prelatis heichtis thair teinds.* "Old Sir Richard Maitland lived to reprobate Lyndsay's reformation, which produced the grievous oppression of the commons, by their *temporal* masters:

> Sum commouns, that hes bene weill staikit,
> Under *kirkmen*, ar now all wrakit;
> Sen that the teind, and the kirk landis,
> Came in great *temporal* mennis handis."
> —CHALMERS.

It might rather be stated, that the greed of the rapacious courtiers, having obtained grants of church lands, which were erected into temporal lordships, proved most detrimental not less to the cause of education, to the support of the poor, and to other purposes set forth in the First Book of Discipline, than to the progress and success of the Reformation.

Line 2594—*And he war spaird.* "If he should be spared. All this had been done by James V. in 1529: Cockburn of Henderland, Scot of Tushiclaw, two lairds, were tried and executed; the Earl of Bothwell was imprisoned; and other great examples were made. Lesley; Pitscottie. At least fifty thieves, with Johnny Armstrong, were hanged in Euisdale."—CHALMERS.

Line 2596—*Sir, I complane upon the idill men.* There

was but too much truth in the severe sarcasms of John the Commonweill on the prevailing corruptions.

Line 2652—*The infetching of Justice Airis.* "The introducing of justice airs. *Justice airs* were very antient in the Scotish jurisprudence. In 1528 it was enacted by 3 Parl. of Ja. V. c. 6, that the maister suld answer for his man in the *justice aires*. In 1535, justice aires were made *peremptour at the second diette* 4 Ja. V. c. 83, which recited an act made in 1525, 'anentis the setting of justice aires to the seconde aire.' But, what *the infechting of justice airis* alludes to, I know not. The Statute-book is the best answer to Lyndsay's *Complaynts*, whereof there seems to be no end.— CHALMERS.

The word given by Chalmers *infechting* is not so intelligible as *infetching*, introducing, bringing in. But the correct word perhaps occurs in Bannatyne's MS., *misusing*. See Various Readings, p. 357.

Lines 2766, 2767—*Lyke rams . . . unpysalt.* CHALMERS explains this phrase, Like rams at large, at liberty, and points out that Lyndsay repeats these lines in the "Monarchie."—See Vol. iii., lines 4701, 4702.

Line 2816—*I tak ane Instrument.* "Make a protestation: The Parliamentary Record is full of such protestations."— CHALMERS.

Line 3227—*My craig (or neck) will wit quhat weyis my hippis.* My neck will know the weight of my hips.—CHALMERS.

" This seems a translation of the noted line of Villon the French poet, who wrote about 1450,

Sçauroit mon col qui mon cul poise."—PINKERTON.

Line 3243—*Micht I him get to Ewis-durris.* "Ewes-doors is the name of a narrow pass between Teviotdale and Ewesdale. The river Ewes, a small and very clear stream, runs a short course between two ranges of green hills, and falls into the Esk at Langholm. An alarming account of this defile may be found in Thoresby's Diary, vol. i., p. 105, Lond. 1830, 2 vols, 8vo."—IRVING's Hist. of Scotish Poetry, p. 379, note.

Line 3249—*Throuch Dysert Mure.* "The Moor of Dysert, a town in Fyfe, between the Earl of Rothes' house and the ferry at Kinghorn."—CHALMERS.

Line 3256—*The Water of Annet.* "Annet (says Chalmers) for the rhyme: the Water of Annan, Dumfriesshire." This is not a satisfactory explanation, if we think how far Common Thift after crossing the Forth would have to ride had he stolen Lord Lyndsay's horse. The river of Annan falls into the Solway Firth seventy-nine miles from Edinburgh. It is much more likely that Lyndsay referred to the stream or rivulet named Annat, or Cambus, which flows into the Forth nearly a mile above the town of Doune, and which takes its rise in the mountainous district of Perthshire. This, at least, was not half the distance of the other, and the horse-stealer might reckon himself as safe from pursuit in that quarter as in the borders of England.

Line 3308—*The Mers suld find me beif and kaill.* "The Mers, which frequently suffered from the depredations of the Liddisdail thieves: *See* Sir Richard Maitland's Complaint 'Aganis the theifis of Liddisdaill,' Maitland Poems, p. 331."—CHALMERS.

Line 3367—*Ane cowclink.* "A harlot. It appears from several passages in the old English drama, that the *courtezans* formerly wore some particular garment, like a *waistcoat.* Dodsley's Old Plays, v. iii., p. 291. There seems to be some allusion to that practise, in the stage direction, which discovers *Ane kirtill of silk under the habite of the Priores.*"—CHALMERS.

Line 3370—*My buttock maill.* "The fine paid by fornicators to excuse their doing penance: So in *M'Gregor's Testament,* "Fra adulteraris to tak the *buttock maill.*"—CHALMERS.

Line 3570—*My coattis,* a modification of the term *quotts,* used in the confirmation of testaments in the Commissary Court.—"The portion of the goods of one deceased, appointed by law to be paid for the confirmation of his testament, or for the right of intromitting with his property."—Dr JAMIESON'S Dictionary, v. Quott.

Lines 3586-3590, also 3593. These lines are repeated by Lyndsay in his "Dialog on the Monarchie."—See Vol. iii., lines 4529-4533, and 4551, 4552.

Line 3628—*Of cowll, and skaplarie.* The old printed copies have *Of coill* and *chaplarie,* and Chalmers retains this reading while correctly enough he explains it, *cowl, and scapulary.* That is, part of the Friar's dress, the cowl or hood, and the scapulary, which consisted of two narrow pieces of cloth, worn by friars or monks over the rest of their dress. At line 4271, the words are accurately given.

Line 3729—*Ye salbe curst and gragit with buik and candill.* "*Gragit,* excommunicated. The Ecclesiastical law of England directed that certain articles should be explained in English, with *bells tolling* and *candles lighted;* that the ceremony may cause the greater dread. Johnson's Eccles. Law, v. ii. We may infer, from Lyndsay's sarcasm, that a similar ceremony existed in the Scotican Church. The Bastard cries out in King John:

'*Bell, book*, and *candle*, shall not drive me back,
When gold and silver becks me to come on.'"
—CHALMERS.

Line 3804—*It is devysit*, &c. "In those times, and long before, there was a practice of passing an act of Parliament during every session, at least, at the commencement of of every reign, providing that 'The freedome of Halie Kirk suld be keeped.'—Skene."—CHALMERS.

Line 3813—*In the last Parliament*. "Upon consideration of the whole context, it appears to me, that the allusion here is to the Parliament which was held at Edinburgh on the 7th of June 1535, when many acts 'baith gude and profitabill,' were certainly enacted. See the Black Acts."—CHALMERS.

Line 3822—*Efter the forme of France*. "This seems to have been a very favourite conceit of Lyndsay, that the lands of France were all *freehold*, and not leasehold I doubt. It is a fact which the prejudice of our satirist did not see, that the tenants of the churchmen were by far the freest and easiest in their situations. The poor tenants felt severely their change of masters after the Reformation; as we may learn from Sir Richard Maitland, who had seen many a change.—See his 'Complaint against Oppression of the Commouns.'—Maitl. Poems, 321."—CHALMERS.

Line 3864—*Of the maist cunning Clarks of this regioun*. "In May 1532 there was erected by Parliament 'a College of cunning and wyse men, baith of Spiritual and Temporal Estate, for doing of justice in all civile actionis,' and this was followed by a whole code, for the better regulation of this College of Justice.—See the Black Acts."—CHALMERS.

This collection of Acts of Parliament, printed *in black*

letter at Edinburgh, 1566, has long been known as *The Black Acts*, to distinguish it, perhaps, from Skene's volume, 1597

Line 3898—*Esay compaireth plaine till ane dum dogge.* Lyndsay (see Vol. i., p. 54) has the same reference to the Prophecies of Isaiah lvi. 10, in his Complaynt to the King, line 321: "They are all dumb dogs. His watchmen are blind: they are all ignorant: they are all dumb dogs: they cannot bark: sleeping, lying down, loving to slumber."

Line 3910.—From this day furth, thay salbe cleane
        denudit,
Baith of corspresent, cow, and umest claith,
To pure commons, becaus it hath done skaith.

At line 2000, in reference to the exactions of the clergy upon poor cottars, Lyndsay says,
Thair umest clayis, that was of rapploch gray,
The Vickar gart his Clark bear them away.
See also lines 2726-2735.

The *umest* was the uppermost cloth on the bed: *Corse present* was a fine, or funeral gift to the clerk, for supplying any deficiency on the part of the deceased. Lyndsay was not singular in crying out on the hardships these matters entailed. See note in Dr. IRVING's History of Scotish Poetry, p. 375.

Line 3915—*Thair hyrald hors.* See note to line 1991. "Their *heriot.* This duty was formerly a relief, for war, from the tenant to the lord; but, now it is taken for the best chattel that the tenant hath at the hour of his death, be it horse, ox, or any such like.—Blount."—CHALMERS.

Line 3949—*Rehabilit.* "The meaning seems to be, that if any nobleman should marry a bastard of a bishop, as the son of Lord Lyndsay had married the bastard daughter of

Cardinal Beaton, he should be degraded, till, by paying a fine, or obtaining a license from the civil magistrate, he should be re-established in his privileges."—CHALMERS.

Line 4020—*To tell your namis.* "Those are the names of most of the west Border families of that age. In the Paper Office, there is a letter from Thomas Musgrave to Lord Burleigh, in 1583; giving that intelligent statesman a very minute account of the several rivers and dales on that Border, with the several families living on them, together with their marriages and alliances. The Nixons, the Rutledges, the Taylors, the Graymes, the Battesons, the Elliotts, the Armstrongs, the Irwyns, the Forsters, the Nobles, the Pandeurs, the Bells, are very numerous. Some of those who are mentioned by Lindsay, though not in Lord Burleigh's letter, may have been persons that were more noted for their robberies than known for their connections."—CHALMERS.

Line 4040—*Now, in this halter slip thy heid.* "This is '*hand*' in both the ed. 1602 and 1604, but '*heid*' is required both by the sense and by the rhyme. The thief complains immediately after, 'Allace! ye hurt my *cray*,' or neck."—CHALMERS.

Line 4216—*Reavers but richt of uthers realmis and ringis.* "Lyndsay seems to have thought this one of his happiest verses; for, he transferred it more than once to his *Monarchies.* And, undoubtedly, what with the alliteration, and what with the flow, it must be deemed a happy verse, when the sense reechoes to the sound. Spoilers, without right, of other's kingdoms."—CHALMERS.

Line 4281—*Gang serve the Hermeit of Laureit.* "The hermit at the chapel of Loretto, at the east end of the town of Musselburgh, which was a famous place of pilgrimage in the time of Lyndsay, who cries out against it in his Exclamation against Idolatry, in the *Monarchie:*—

> And specially that hermeit of Laureit,
> He pat the commoun pepil in beleif,
> That blynd gat sicht, and crukit gat their feit,
> The quhilk the palzeard na way can appreif."

—CHALMERS.

In "the late Expedicioun in Scotlande," under the Earl of Hertford, in May 1544, among the places brunte and desolated by the Kinges army," we find "parte of Muskelborowe towne, with the chapel of our Ladye of Lauret."

Line 4285—*Quhen fuillis are fow, then are thay faine.* "When fools are *drunk*, then are they *glad*. There is another proverb, Fair words make fools fain."—CHALMERS.

Line 4343—*Now wallie fall that weill-fairde mow.* "Good befall that well-favoured mouth."—CHALMERS.

Line 4399—*Gude Glaiks.* "So, in 'Christ Kirk on the Green,' 'His wife bad him ga hame, *gude Glaiks*.' The term is applied to a thoughtless, foolish fellow, or girl."—CHALMERS.

Line 4418—*I sall break thy pallet.* "Break thy crown, or pate. So, Sir Richard Maitland *On the Malyce of the Poetis:*—

> ——Ye maid of me ane ballet,
> For your reward, now I sall *break your pallet.*"

—CHALMERS.

Line 4434—*With hobling of your hippis.* The next eight lines omitted in the 1602 edition of the Satyre, are supplied from the Interludes in Bannatyne's MS. This Chalmers entirely overlooks.

VOL. II. X

Line 4443—*Swyith! harlot.* "The opprobrious epithet *harlot*, was formerly applied to both sexes."—CHALMERS.

Line 4452—*Than stryk ane hag into the poast.* "Strike a notch in the post; a proverbial expression, meaning record such a transaction as extraordinary."—CHALMERS.

Lines 4469, 4509—*Gude chaffery.* "Wares, merchandise, as in Chaucer: 'Hir *chaffare* was so thrifty and so newe.'"—CHALMERS.

Line 4521—*Bot sailis . . . in Winter.* "In 1535, passed an act, 'that na man sail into Flanders, bot twise in the yeir.' 4 Ja. V., c. 31. In the same session it was also enacted 'that na schip saill with staple gudes, fra Simons day and Judes, quhill Candlemes. 4 Ja. V., c. 25. Such were the *actis* to which Lyndsay alluded."—CHALMERS.

Line 4606—*The prophesie of Merling.* We here see how the prophecies of Merlin were in those days regarded. We also perceive how Lyndsay tried to bring them into disrepute."—CHALMERS.

Line 4622—*To Gillie Mowband I you recommend.* From the Treasurer's Accounts we find that this person was one of the Fools at Court of James the Fyfth. "Item, (the 25th of April 1527) to a fule callit Gillemowband, at the Kingis command ———xx s."

Line 4629—*Famous Pepill, &c.* "The conclusion of *Candlemas-day*, the oldest mystery which is distinctly known in the drama of England, is so like that of the 'Satyre of the Three Estates,' that we might suppose that Lyndsay had seen it, though it is not easy to tell where. The conclusion of *Candlemas-day* is as follows:—

POETA.

Honorable Sovereignes, thus we conclude
   Our matter that we have showed here in your presence :
And though *our eloquence be but rude,*
   We beseeche you all of your paciens,
   To pardon us of our offens :
For oft the sympyl cunnyng that we can,
   This matter we have shewed to your audiens,
In the worship of our Ladie and hir moder Seynt Anne.

Now of this pore processe we make an ende,
   Thankyng you all of your good attendaunce ;
And the next yeer, as we be purposid in our mynde,
   The disputation of the doctors to shew in your presens :

   Wherefore now, ye vyrgynes, or we go hens,
With all your company you goodly avaunce ;
   Also *ye menstralles do'th your diligens,*
And fore our *departyng geve us a daunce.*"
      CHALMERS.

ANE DIALOG BETUIX EXPERIENCE AND ANE COURTEOUR.—Page 223.

Although Part First of the DIALOG is contained in the present volume, the NOTES on this portion (from line 1 to line 1616), will be given in Volume Third, page 173, &c., along with those on the latter and larger portion of the Poem.

APPENDIX.

APPENDIX.

No. I.

THE AULD MAN AND HIS WIFE.

A Preliminary Interlude.

Heir begynnis the Proclamation of the Play maid be David Lynsayis of the Month Knicht, in the Playfeild, in the moneth of [blank] the zeir of God 155 [blank] zeiris.

THE PROCLAMATION MAID AT COWPAR OF FYFFE

NUNTIUS.

RICHT famous Pepill, ye sall undirstand
   How that ane Prince, richt wyiss and vigilent,
Is schortly for to cum in to this Land ;
   And purpossis to hald ane Parliament,
   His Thre Estaitis thairto hes done consent
In Cowpar Toun, in to thair best array
   With support of the Lord Omnipotent ;
And thairto hes affixt ane certane day.

With help of Him, that rewlis all aboue,
   That day sall be within ane litill space :   10

Our purpose is on the Sevint day of June,
   Gif weddir serve, and we haif rest and pece,
   We sall be sene in till our Playing place,
In gude array, abowt the hour of sevin.
   Off thristiness that day I pray yow cciss,
Bot ordane us gude drink aganis ellevin.

Faill nocht to be upone the Castell-hill,
   Besyd the place quhair we purpoiss to play;
With gude stark wyne your flacconis see ye fill,
   And hald your self the myreast that ye may. 20
   Be not displeisit, quhat evir we sing or say;
Amang sad mater howbeid we sumtyme relyie.
   We sall begin at sevin houris of the day :
So ye keip tryist, forsuth we sall nocht felyie.

COTTER.

I sall be thair, with Goddis grace,
Thocht thair war nevir so grit ane prese,
   And formest in the fair;
And drink ane quart in Cowpar toun,
With my gossep Johne Williamsoun,
   Thocht all the nolt sowld rair.   30
I haif ane quick divill to my Wyfe,
That haldis me evir in sturt and stryfe :
   That warlo, and scho wist
That I wald cum to this gud Toun,
Scho wald call me fals ladrone loun,
   And ding me in the dust.
We men that hes sic wickit wyvis,

In grit langour we leid our lyvis,
   Ay dreifland in disciss.
Ye Preistis hes gret prerogatyvis,   40
That may depairt ay fra your wyvis,
   And cheiss thame that ye pleiss!
Wald God I had that liberty,
That I might pairt, as weill as ye,
   Without the Constry Law!
Nor I be stickit with a knyfe,
For to wad ony uder wyfe
   That day sowld nevir daw.

NUNTIUS.

War thy wyfe deid I see thow wald be fane.

COTTER.

Ye, that I wald, sweit Sir, be Sanct Fillane.   50

NUNTIUS.

Wald thow nocht mary fra hand ane uder wyfe?

COTTER.

Na, than the dum divill stik me with ane knyfe!
Quha evir did mary agane, the Feind mot fang thame
Bot, as the Preistis dois, ay stryk in amang thame.

NUNTIUS.

Than thow mon keip thy chestety, as effeiris.

COTTER.

I sall leif chest as Abbottis, Monkis, and Freiris.

Maister, quhairto sowld I my self miskary,
Quhair I, as Preistis, may swyve, and nevir mary?

WYFE.

Quhair hes thow bene, fals ladrone Loun?
Dryttand, and drinkand, in the toun?   60
Quha gaif the leif to cum fra hame?

COTTER.

Ye gaif me leif, fair lucky Dame.

WYFE.

Quhy hes thow taryit heir sa lang?

COTTER.

I micht not thrist owtthrow the thrang,
Till that yone man the Play proclamit.

WYFE.

Trowis thow that day, fals Cairle defamit,
To gang to Cowpar to see the Play?

COTTER.

Ye, that I will, Dame, gif I may.

WYFE.

Na, I sall cum thairto sickerly;
And thow salt byd at hame, and keip the ky.   70

COTTER.

Fair lucky Dame, that war grit schame,

Gif I that day sowld byid at hame.
Byid ye at hame; for cum ye heir,
Ye will mak all the Toun asteir.
Quhen ye ar fow of barmy drink,
Besyd yow nane may stand for stink;
Thairfoir byid ye at hame that day,
That I may cum and see the Play.

WYFE.

Fals Cairle, be God! that sall thow nocht,
And all thy crackis sall be deir coft.   80
Swyth Cairle, speid thé hame speidaly
Incontinent, and milk the ky,
And muk the byre, or I cum hame.

COTTER.

All sall be done, fair lucky Dame.
I am sa dry, Dame, or I gae,
I mon ga drink ane penny or twae.

WYFE.

The divill a drew sall cum in thy throte,
Speid hame, or I sall paik thy cote
And to begin, fals Cairle, tak thair ane plate.

COTTER.

The Feind ressaif the handis that gaif me that! 90
I beseik yow, for Goddis saik, lucky Dame,
Ding me na mair this day, till I cum hame;
Than sall I put me evin in to your will.

WYFE.

Or evir I stynt, thow sall haif straikis thy fill.
 [*Heir sall the Wyfe ding the Carle, and he
 sall cry, Goddis mercy!*

COTTER.

Now wander and wa be to thame all thair lyvis,
The quhilk ar maryit with sic unhappy wyvis!

WYFE.

I ken foure wyvis, fals ladrone loun,
Baldar nor I, dwelland in Cowpar toun.

COTTER.

Gif thay be war, ga thow and thay togidder,
I pray God nor the Feind ressaif the fidder.   100

FYNLAW of the Fute-Band.

Now mary! heir is ane fellone rowt!
Speik, Sirris, quhat gait may I get owt?
 I rew that I come heir.
My name, Sirris, wald ye undirstand,
Thay call me FINDLAW of the Fute-Band:
 A nobill man of weir.
Thair is na fyifty in this land
Bot I dar ding thame hand for hand;
 Se sic ane brand I beir.
Nocht lang sensyne, besyd ane syik,   110
Upoun the sunny syd of ane dyk,
 I slew with my richt hand
Ane thowsand, ye and ane thowsand to,

My fingaris yit ar bludy, lo!
　　And nane durst me ganestand.
Wit ye it dois me mekill ill,
That can nocht get fechting my fill,
　　Noudir in peax, nor weir.
Will na man, for thair ladyis saikis,
With me stryk twenty markit straikis, 120
　　With halbart, swerd, or speir?
Quhen Inglismen come in to this Land,
Had I bene thair with my bricht brand,
　　Withowttyn ony help,
Bot myne allane, on Pynky Craiggis,
I sowld haif revin thame all in raggis,
　　And laid on skelp for skelp.
Sen nane will fecht, I think it best,
To ly doun heir and tak me rest:
　　Than will I think nane ill. 130
I pray the grit God of his grace
To send us weir, and nevir peace,
　　That I may fecht my fill.
　　　　　　[*Heir sall he ly doun.*

THE FULE.

My Lord, be him that ware the croun of thorne,
A mair cowart was nevir sen God was borne.
He lovis him self, and othir men he lakkis,
I ken him weill for all his boistis and crakkis.
Howbeid he now be lyk ane Captane cled,
At Pyncky Clewch he was the first that fled.
I tak on hand, or I steir of this steid, 140

This crakkand Cairle to fle with ane scheip-heid.
   [*Heir sall the Auld Man cum in leidand
   his wife in ane dance.*

AULD MAN.

Bessy, my hairt! I mon ly doun and sleip,
And in myne arme se quyetly thow creip.
Bessy, my hairt! first let me lok thy cunt,
Syne lat me keip the key as I was wount.

BESSY.

My gud Husband, lock it evin as ye pleiss,
I pray God send yow grit honor and eiss.
   [*Heir sall he lok hir cunt, and lay the key
   under his heid: he sall sleip, and scho sall
   sit besyd him.*

THE COURTEOUR.

Lusty Lady! I pray yow hairtfully,
Gif me licence to beir yow cumpany.
Ye se I am ane cumly Courteour,   150
Quhilk nevir yit did woman dishonour.

MARCHAND.

My fair Mistress! sweitar than the lammer,
Gif me licence to luge in to your chalmer,
I am the richest Merchand in this toun:
Ye sall of silk, haif kirtill, hude, and goun.

CLERK.

I yow beseik, my lusty Lady bricht,
To gif me leif to ly with yow all nicht.

And of your guoman lat me schut the lokkis,
And of fyne gold ye sall ressaif ane box.

FUILL.

Fair Damessell, how pleiss ye me ?   160
I haif na mair geir nor ye sie :
Swa lang as this may steir, or stand,
It sall be ay at your command :
Na it is the best that ever ye saw

BESSY.

Now welcome to me aboif thame aw !
Was nevir wyf sa straitly rokkit.
Sé ye not how my cunt is lokkit.

FUILL.

Thinkis he nocht schame, that Brybor blunt,
To put ane lok upon your cunt?

BESSY.

Bot se gif ye can mak remeid,   170
To steill the key fra undir his heid.

FUILL.

That sall I do, withowttin dowt,
Lat se gif I can get it owte.
Lo heir the key! do quhat ye will.

BESSY.

Na than lat ws ga play our fill.
    [*Heir sall thay go to sum quyet place.*

FYNLAW of the Fute-Band.

Will nane with me in France go to the weiris,
Quhair I am Captane of ane hundreth speiris?
I am sa hardy, sturdy, strang, and stowt,
That owt of hell the Divill I dar ding owt.

CLERK.

Gif thow be gude or evill, I can not tell,   180
Thay ar not sonsy that so dois ruse thame sell;
At Pyncky Clewch, I knew richt woundir weill,
Thow gat na creddence for to beir a creill:
Sen sic as thow began to brawll and boist,
The commoun weill of Scotland hes bene loist.
Thow cryis for weir, bot I think peax war best.
I pray to God till send us peice and rest,
On that conditioun, that thow, and all thy fallowis,
War be the craiggis heich hangit on the gallowis.
Quha of this weir hes bene the foundament,   190
I pray to the grit God omnipotent,
That all the warld, and mae, mot on thame wounder,
Or ding thame deid with awfull fyre of thunder.

FYNDLAW.

Domine Doctor, quhar will ye preiche to morne?
We will haif weir, and all the warld had sworne.
Want we weir heir, I will ga pass in France,
Quhair I will get ane Lordly governance.

CLERK.

Sa quhat ye will, I think sever peax is best,

Quha wald haif weir, God send thame littill rest?
Adew Crakkar, I will na langer tary?   200
I trest to see thé in ane firy fary.
I trest to God to see thé, and thy fallowis,
Within few days hingand on Cowpar gallowis!

FYNDLAW.

Now art thow gane, the dum Divill be thy gyd!
Yone brybour was sa fleit, he durst not byid.
Be woundis and passionis had he spokkin mair ane word,
I sowld haif hackit his heid af with my swerd.

   [*Heir sall the Gudman walkin, and cry for Bessy.*

AULD MAN.

My bony Bessy, quhair art thow now?
My Wyfe is fallin on sleip I trow;
Quhair art thow, Bessy, my awin sweit thing,   210
My hony, my hairt, my dayis darling?
Is thair na man that saw my Bess,
I trow scho be gane to the Mess.
Bessy, my hairt, heiris thow not me?
My joy, cry peip! quhair evir thow be.
Allace! for evir now am I fey,
For of hir cunt I tynt the key.
Scho may call me in iuffeane Jok,
Or I swyve, I mon brek the lok.

BESSY.

Quhat now, gudman? quhat wald ye haif?   220

AULD MAN.

No thing, my hairt, but yow I craif.
Ye haif bene doand sum bissy wark.

BESSY.

My hairt, evin sewand yow ane sark
Of Holland claith, baith quhyt and tewch.
Lat pruve gif it be wyid annewch.

    [*Heir sall scho put the sark over his heid, and
    the Fuill sall steill in the key agane.*

AULD MAN.

It is richt very weill, my hairt,
Oure Lady, lat us nevir depairt.
Ye ar the farest of all the flok,
Quhair is the key, Bess, of my lok?

BESSY.

Ye reve, Gudman, be Goddis breid,   230
I saw yow lay it undir your heid.

AULD MAN.

Be my gude faith, Bess, that is trew.
That I suspectit yow, sair I rew.
I trow thair be no man in Fyffe,
That evir had sa gude ane wyfe.
My awin sweit hairt, I hald it best
That we sit down, and tak ws rest.

FYNDLAW.

Now is nocht this ane grit dispyte,
That nane with me will fecht nor flyte?
War Golias in to this steid, 240
I dowt nocht to stryk af his heid.
This is the swerd that slew Gray Steill,
Nocht half ane myle beyond Kynneill.
I was that nobill campioun,
That slew Schyr Bewas of Sowth-Hamtoun.
Hector of Troy, Gawyne, or Golias,
Had nevir half sa mekill hardiness.

    [*Heir sall the Fuill cum in with ane scheip-heid
    on ane staff, and Fyndlaw sall be fleit.*

Wow, now, braid Benedicite!
Quhat sicht is yone, Sirris, that I see.
In nomine Patris et Filii. 250
I trow yone be the Spreit of Gy.
Na, faith it is the Spreit of Marling,
Or sum scho gaist or Gyrgarling.
Allace for evir! how sall I gyd me?
God, sen I had ane hoill till hyd me!
But dowt my deid yone man hes sworne,
I trow yone be grit Gow-mak-morne.
He gaippis, he glowris, howt welloway,
Tak all my geir, and lat me gay!
Quhat say ye, Sir, wald ye haif my swerd? 260
Ye mary sall ye, at the first word
My gluvis of plait, and knapskaw to;
Yowr pressonar I yeild me, lo.

Tak thair my purss, my belt, and knyfe.
For Goddis saike, maister, save my lyfe.
Na, now he cumis for to sla me ;
For Godis saik, Sirris, now keip him fra me ;
I see nocht ellis bot tak and slae :
Now mak me rowme, and lat me gae.

NUNTIUS.

As for this day, I haif na mair to say yow :   270
On Witsone Tysday, cum see our Play I pray yow,
That samyne day is the Sevint day of June,
Thairfoir get up right airly and disjune :
And ye Ladyis, that hes na skant of leddir,
Or ye cum thair, faill nocht to teme yowr bleddir.
I dreid, or we haif half done with our wark,
That sum of yow sall mak ane richt wait sark.

NAMES OF PERSONS IN THE PRELIMINARY INTERLUDE,
Page 321.

Nuntius, *the Messenger.*
The Cotter.
The Cotter's Wyfe.
Fyndlaw of the Fute-band.
The Fuill.
The Auld Man.
Bessy his Wyfe.
The Courteour.
The Marchand.
The Clerk.

No. II.

THE VARIOUS READINGS OF LYNDSAY'S SATYRE, COMPARED WITH THE MANUSCRIPT OF GEORGE BANNATYNE, 1568.—Fol. 168-210.

Lyndsay's "Satyre of the Thrie Estates," so far as can be ascertained, was first published at Edinburgh by Robert Charteris in 1602. There is no evidence, at least, to show that it had actually passed through the press either in the author's life, or in the latter half of the sixteenth century. Manuscript copies must therefore have been prepared for the special occasions when the Play was represented at Linlithgow, Edinburgh, and other places; and the addition or omission of local and personal allusions might readily account for any apparent discrepancies. But no such MSS. have reached our times. In the printed Catalogue of books, 1627, presented by Drummond of Hawthornden to the University of Edinburgh, there is included one entitled:—

"Sir David Lindesay. A Satyre of the Thrie Estates. MS." No date or size is given. It is not likely that this was a mere transcript of the printed edition. Unfortunately no MS. of the kind can be discovered in the Library, nor is it described in any of the old MS. Catalogues.

We may conclude, therefore, that George Bannatyne, in the year 1568, when engaged in transcribing his well-known collections of Scottish poetry, made use of a MS. copy of Lyndsay's Play. Instead, however, of copying the entire Play, he gave it in an abridged form of eight different Interludes. Allan Ramsay in 1724 copied it in this form from that MS. with the intention of including it in his proposed additional volume of his Evergreen. His transcript still exists, but is of no critical value for collation, as, in the words of Sir Walter Scott's "Bannatyne Garland"—

> His ways were not ours, for he cared not a pin
> How much he left out, or how much he put in.

From another inaccurate transcript, Pinkerton in 1792, gave the Interludes as already noticed at p. 297; followed by Sibbald's in 1802. Chalmers, on the other hand, in 1806 adhered slavishly to the old printed copy by Charteris, wholly ignoring the text as preserved by Bannatyne.

It seemed therefore advisable that a minute and careful collation of the only two existing copies should be given in the form of a separate article in the Appendix, in place of interspersing often slight or unimportant differences in the preceding Notes. For undertaking this, I am indebted to Mr JAMES WALKER, who has accomplished his task with all possible accuracy, but mere variations in orthography have seldom been noted, as of no importance.

Chalmers, as already mentioned (page 288), rejects as spurious the preliminary interlude of "The Auld Man and his Wife" (pages 325-340), upon the ground of its local allusions, and the reference to Pinkie, forgetting that the Play was not repeated verbatim on its representation either at Edinburgh, Linlithgow, or at Cupar-Fife. Mr Chalmers, when he refers to Dr George Mackenzie, asserts that Lyndsay, according to this wretched writer, "was not only a composer of tragedies, and comedies, but was likewise a principal actor in them." In his heroic style, my old friend adds, in a footnote, "Time has not yet disclosed any *comedies* of Lyndsay's writing, though some meddler [George Bannatyne] has cut down his drama, entitled *A Satyre on the Three Estates* into *a thousand Interludes*." (Vol. i., p. 110).

At pages 297-298 the reader will find the order or arrangement of the Play, as subdivided into the eight Interludes.

THE SATYRE, &c.—Page 11.

MS., fol. 168.—" Heir begynnis Syr Dauid Lyndsay Play, maid in the Grenesyd besyd Edinburgh, quhilk I [haif] writtin bot schortly, be Interludis, levand the grave mater thairof becaws the samyne abvse is weill reformit in Scotland, praysit be God, quhairthrow I omittit that principall mater and writtin only Sertane mirry Interludis thairof, verry plesand, begynning at the First Part of the Play."

Line 1.—The Fader, foundar of faith and felicitie.
,, 3.—And his Sone zour Saluiour, scheild in necessitie.
,, 5.—With his pretious blude.
,, 13.—For now I begin.—*Pausa.*
,, 14.—Pepill, tak tent to me, and hald yow coy;
Heir am I, sent to yow, ane messengeir,
From ane nobill and richt redowttit Roy,
The quhilk hes bene absent this mony ane yeir.
,, 24.—Howbeid that he hes bene langtyme sleipand.
,, 26.—And innocentis bene brocht upoun thair beiris,
,, 28.—Thocht yung oppressouris at the elderis leiris;
Be now weill seur of reformatioun.
,, 34.—Faithfull folk now may sing.
,, 38.—Thocht he ane quhyle now in his flowris,
Be governit be trumpouris,
And sumtyme to lufe paramouris,
Hald him excusit.
,, 68.—Till that the hevinly knycht Correctioun
Meit with our King, and commoun hand till hand.
,, 74.—Thairfoir till our rymes be rung.
,, 76.—Let every man keip weill his tung.
,, 80.—Eterne rignand, in gloir celestiall,
Unmaid makar quhilk havand no mateir.

Line 94.—I thé requeist, quhilk rent was on the Rude.
,, 98.—I knaw my dayis indeuris bot a drame.
,, 100.—Till gif me grace till use my diadame
To thy plesour, and to my grit confort.
[*Heir sall the King pass to royall sait, and sit with ane grave countenance till Wantones cum.*]
,, 104.—Be glaid, sa lang as ye ar heir.
,, 108.—His banis bitterly, sall I ban.
,, 113.—Haiff ye na doubt.
,, 114.—So lang as your grace hes ws in ceure,
Your prudence sall want na pleseour.
,, 118.—Gude bruder, quhair is Solace.
,, 120.—I haif meruell, be the Mess.
,, 125.—That lattis him to gang.
,, 126.—I left Sollace, that loun,
Drinkand doun in to the toun.
,, 135.—As he war chessit, rynnand fast,
Or fleid for ane gaist.
,, 138.—Na, he is druckin, I trow,
I persaive him weill fow.
,, 145.—With ane mirry noyiss.
,, 149.—That wald my hairt rejoyss.
,, 151.—Thankit be God, I am weill hippit.
,, 168.—For scho hes maid me freindis ane fudder,
Off lawit, and leirit.
,, 173.—Thair ene scho bleirit.
,, 177.—To that yung king.
,, 179.—To pass his tyme cum to this place :
I pray to God to gif him grace,
And lang to ring.
189.—Placebo, my bruder.
[*Heir sall Placebo gif Sollace ane drink.*]
,, 203.—And cled upoun the new gyiss,
It wald gar all your flesche arryiss.
,, 212.—I wald not gif ane slane fle.

APPENDIX.

Line 219.—Quha dois forbid men to be licherus.
,, 222.—The quhilk ye gif me till.
,, 225.—Quhilk is als mekle for till sae.
,, 228.—Or from your vertew for till wyil yow.
,, 237.—First, at the Romane court will ye begyn.
,, 251 to 262 *follow in* MS. line 270.
,, 263.—Schir, send furth Sandy Sollace.
,, 267.—Gif it be syn to tak ane Katy.

[*Heir sall entir Dame Sensualitie with hir ma dynnis Hamelines and Dangeir.*]

,, 271.—O luvaris walk! behald the fyrie speir.
,, 275.—Quhat thay desyre in laitis delicius.
,, 290.—I latt no lovaris pass with sorry hart.
,, 297.—We sall pass in, and sing.
Cum on Sister Dengeir.
,, 299.—Sister, I was nevir sweir.
,, 311.—Sister, to sing this sang we man nat.
,, 320.—Sen syne the feind a man I spair.
,, 324.—That luvis japing als weill as I.
,, 327 to 330 *wanting in* MS.
,, 334. That soverane serene.

[*Heir sall Wantones ga spy thame, and cun agane to the King.*]

,, 336.—Dame Sensualitie, baith gude and fair.
,, 338.—For scho can baith sing, and dance.
,, 341.—Soft as silk is hir lyre,
Hir hair lyk the gold wyre:
My hairt birnys in ane fyre.
Schir, be the Rude!
I think that fre sa woundir fair,
I wait weill scho has na compair,
War ye weill lernit at luvis lair
And syne had hir sene.
,, 360. Schir, tak your plesour.

Line 372.—And sumtyme het as fyre.
,, 380.—I cair for na coist.
,, 381.—Pass your way Wantonness,
   And tak with yow Sollace.
,, 384.—Or ellis I am loist.
,, 385.—Command me to that sweit thing,
   And hir present this riche ring.
,, 388.—Bot scho mak remeid.
,, 392.—And saif me fra deid.
,, 393.—Or ye tuik skaith, be Godis croun.
,, 396.—Nor ten mylis abowt.
,, 408.—And win weill thy wage.
,, 411.—We sall nowder spair for wind nor rane.
,, 416.—Thocht we merche with the mone.
   [*Heir sall thay depairt, singand mirrelly.*
,, 447.—That salbe done, bot yit, or I hyne pass.
,, 451.—Hay! for joy, now I dance,
   Tak thair ane gawmond of France:
   Am I not wirdy till avance,
      And ane gud page?
   That sa spedely can rin,
   To tyist my maister to sin:
   The diuill ane groit he will win,
      Off this mariage.
,, 460.—Nor I had previt hir my sell.
,, 494.—And I sall ken yow the kewis how ye sall do.
   [*Heir sall Sensualitie cum to the King, and say:*
,, 500.—O Venus, Goddes! unto thy celsitude.
,, 512.—And specially quhair zowtheid hes the curis.
,, 516.—Unthrald to Sensualatye.
,, 525.—And moist of curage.
   [*Heir sall scho mak reverence, and say.*
,, 551.—Gif he be wiskand wantonlie,
   We sall fling on the fleuir.

Line 557.—Saif you my senzeouris that givis sic audience.
,, 561.—Quhois petious passioun frome feindis zow defend.
,, 563.—Considder my soveranis, I zow beseik,
The causses moist principall my of heir cumming.
,, 568.—Without my wisdome, micht availl thair weill to awance.
,, 570.—Lordis, for lack of my law, ar brocht till myschance.
And so for conclusion
Quho gydis thame not be gud counsale,
All in vane is thair travell,
And fynally fortoun sall thame faill,
And bring thame to confusioun,
And this I understand.
,, 575.—For I haif maid residence,
With princis of pissance.
,, 579.—Bot, owt of Scotland, allace!
I haif bene banneist lang space,
That gart our gydaris want grace.
,, 590.—In his first begynning.
,, 602.—I purpoiss till repoiss me in this place.

MS. *fol.* 175.—[*Heir I omit the nixt mater following: becaus it is writtin heirefter in the* [fol. 187] *leif, quhair Flatery enteris. Now enteris Dame Chestetie.*

Heir sall Dame Chestity pass and seik lugeing athort all the Spritnall Estait, and Temporall Estait quhill scho cum to the Sowttar and Tailzeour, and say:—

Ye men of craft, of grit ingyne, &c.

(*This Interlude, lines* 1288 *to* 1403, *follows the above, at fol.* 175.)

348 APPENDIX.

MS., *fol.* 187,—[*Heir entiris Flattry, new landit owt of France, and storme sted at the May.*

Line 602.—Mak roum, Siris, that I may rin;
　　　　　　Lo se how I am new cum in,
　　　　　　Begareit all in sindry hewis.
„　606.—And I sall tell yow of my newis.
　　　　　　Throw all realmes cristnit I haif past.
„　609.—Storme sted be sic, ay sen Zule day.
„　627.—Now, am I chaipit fra that fray.
„　629.—Ken ye not, Flattry, your awin fule.
„　633.—Quhair ar my fallowis that wald I feill.
„　635.—How! Falsatt, how!
　　　　　　Wa serve the diuill!
„　646.—Now, be my sawle, bot evin be cace.
„　657.—Lat us ly still baith heir and spy,
　　　　　　Gife we persaif him rynnand by.
　　　　　　[*Heir sall Dissait entir.*
„　659 to line 682 *are not in* MS.
„　689.—How chaippit thow, I pray thé tell?
　　　　　　I slippit in ane fowll bordell.
„　693.—With hochurhudy mang hir howis.
„　696.—Mary! seikand King Humanitie.
„　699.—Now, till our purpoiss, lat ws ga,
　　　　　　Quhat is zour counsale, sa I pray you?
„　703.—And als I pray yow, as your bruder.
„　706.—In evill, and gude, to tak your part.
„　731.—Is this I, or nocht I, can ye not say.
„　733.—And war my hair up in ane how,
　　　　　　The feind a man wald ken me now!
„　741.—A freir, quhairto? thow can not preiche!
　　　　　　Quhattrak, bot I can flattir and fleiche.
„　743.—Peraventur cum to that honour.
„　780.—For we mon change all thrie our names;
　　　　　　Cristin me, and I sall bapteiss thé.

Line 792.—Bot zet I wat not quhat to call the.
,, 794.—Sapience, Sapience, a Goddis name.
,, 802.—We thre may rewll a haill regioun.
,, 805.—For thow sall crak, and thow sall clattir.
,, 815.—Steir nocht, bruder, bot hald us still.
,, 828.—Howbeid ye gat that ye desyrit,
   Or I was temprit ye was tyrit.
,, 830 and 831 *in* MS. *come before lines* 728, 729.
,, 863.—Quhat aillis thé can not schaw it now.
,, 869.—Sir, gif ye pleiss to let me say,
   Forsuth his name is Sapientia.
,, 884.—I trow thir thrie come in a happy hour.
,, 889.—Soverane, I sweir you, be Sanct An.
,, 891.—Money a craft, Syr, I can.
,, 927.—War ye in harnes, I think na wounder.
,, 937.—Ze ar all wylcum, be the Rude!
   Ze seme to be thre men of gude.

MS. *fol.* 191.—[*Finis of this Interlude and pairt of Play.*
Heireftir sall Gud Counsale appeir and salbe hostit away, and Lady Chestetie and Verretie sall be put in stokis, and Sensualitie sall gyd the zung King for a tyme.

,, 943.—That salbe done, be Godis breid!
   We sall him bring owdir quick, or deid.
,, 945 to 955, *not in* MS.
,, 956.—That zone awld Carle be Gud Counsall:
   Bruder, I think that counsale ressone.
,, 964.—Awld berdit mowth! gude day, gud day!
,, 975 and 976, *not in* MS.
,, 979.—To speik bot thre wordis with his Grace.
,, 987 and 988, *not in* MS.
,, 1002.—That sall I not, be cokkis woundis!

Line 1019, and on to 1077, *not in* MS.

  MS. *fol.* 193.—[*Heir sall Veretie entir and pass to hir place, quhair Flattrie sall spy hir with feir.*

„ 1084.—His heich honour, and gloir, I sall avance.
„ 1085.—*Sancte Pater!* quhair haif ye bene?
„ 1095.—Hes spokin manifest heresie.

  MS. *fol.* 193.—[*Heir the Vycis gais to the Spritnall Estait and lyis npoun Veretie, desiring hir to be put in captivitie; quhilk is done with diligence.*

  (*In the MS. the First Interlude occurs at fol. 175.*)

„ 1097, *and on to line* 1152, *not in* MS.
„ 1162.—This nicht ye sall bedryt ane pair of stokkis.
„ 1167.—A hundreth thowsand sall ryss in thair place.
„ 1170.—On thame quhilk dois tramp doun thyne hevinly word.
„ 1173.—Suffer thame not, no moir to be mollest.
„ 1175.—With thyne unfreindis lat me not be opprest.
„ 1176, *not in* MS.
„ 1184 to 1199, *not in* MS.
„ 1204.—Thocht I haif past all nicht fra place to place.
„ 1215.—Amang the rest of Spritualitie.

  MS. *fol.* 194.—[*Heir sall scho pass to the haill Sprituall Estait, and scho sall not be ressavit bot put away.*

„ 1288.—Ye men of craft of grit ingyne.
„ 1304.—Fill in, and drink abowt.
„ 1308.—Mynny, how! mynny, mynny.
„ 1310.—Jenney, my joe, quhat dois thy daddy.
„ 1314 and 1315 *not in* MS.
„ 1339.—In cumpany, with ane yung cowcling.
„ 1340.—Gif thay haif done sic dispyte.
„ 1350.—Bot, my gudeman, the trewth I say thee till.

APPENDIX. 351

Line 1358.—I mak ane vow to Sanct Crispynane,
    I salbe wrockin on thy graceles game.
,, 1360.—And to begin the play, tak thair a platt.
,, 1378.—Send for gude wyne, and hald ws blyth and mirry.
,, 1389.—Quhat and the paddois nipt my tais.
,, 1393.—I will go be the Castell hill.
,, 1395.—Sa ye haist yow, go quhair ye will.
   [*Heir sall thay depairt, and Diligence sall say—*
,, 1396.—Madame quhat garris yow gang sa lait.
,, 1401.—That gart me stand frome thame afar.
,, 1403.—And flemit me moir and less.
  MS. *fol.* 177.—[*Finis of this First Interlude; and followis the Peurman and the Pardonar.*

  MS. *fol.* 177.—[*Heir followis certane mirry and Sportsum Interludis, contenit in the Play maid be Sir Dauid Lyndsay of the Month Knycht, in the playfeild of Edinburgh, to the mocking of abusionis usit in the countre be diverss sortis of Estait.*

  [*Heir sall entir the Peurman.* See line 1932.
,, 1412 to 1419 *not in* MS.
,, 1424 to 1428 *not in* MS.
,, 1428.—Now, lat me sie quhat this mater ma mene.
,, 1431.—Sir, scho and I ma not byd in a place.
,, 1440 to 1443 *not in* MS.
,, 1451.—Into the stokkis your bony feit mak fast.
,, 1463.—Bot, hyd me, in the mirke.
,, 1466.—And mekle of the rest.
,, 1468.—And hes directit hir command.
    That I sowld be opprest.
,, 1472.—Thocht I be now opprest.
,, 1480.—Is new landit, thankit be God our Lord.

MS. *fol.* 195.—[*Heir sall entir Correctiounis varlet for reformatioun and say*—

Line 1481.—Schiris, stand abak, and hald you coy.
,, 1189.—I will refer to yow that jugement.
,, 1506 to 1511 *not in* MS.
,, 1528.—I will be treittit, as ye ken.
,, 1547.—Now, quhill the King is sound sleipand.
,, 1550.—That sall I do incontinent.
,, 1555.—It may weill mak us landward lairdis.
,, 1559.—Wald God we war owt of this place.

[*Heir sall thay cast away thair conterfit clais.*

1562.—Latt us now part this pelf among ws,
Syne, hestelly, latt ws depairt.
,, 1574.—Upoun thy clof tak thair a clowt.
,, 1578.—Thy feit sall be wirth fourty handis.

MS. *fol.* 196.—[*Correctioun enteris: I tak heir bot certane schort pairtis owt of the speichis, becauss of lang proces of the Play.*

,, 1580 to 1620 *not in* MS.
,, 1629.—Till all faithfull and trew men of this regioun.
,, 1648.—The merchandmen, thay have resset Dissait.
,, 1653.—Purposing to begyle the Spirituall Estait.
,, 1658.—Unmercifull memberis of iniquitie,
Dispytfully hes ws, my Lord, supprysit.
,, 1676 to 1700 *not in* MS.
,, 1712.—For that self syn, war brint rycht crewally.
,, 1723.—But thay repent, I put thame to rewync.
,, 1731.—I lat yow wit my bewty thair will blome.
,, 1732 to 1752 *not in* MS.
,, 1752.—My Lord, sen ye ar quyt of Sensualitie.
,, 1759.—Thairfoir, with thame, mak ane perpetuall band.

[*Heir sall the King ressaif the thre Vertewis.*

APPENDIX.

Line 1760 to 1776 *not in* MS.
,, 1781.—To all vertew, I salbe consonable.
,, 1785.—Agane proclame the parliament.
,, 1795, 1796, 1797, *not in* MS.
,, 1819, 1822 *which in the text are transposed, in the MS. read correctly,*

> All nicht I had samekle drowth,
> I micht not sleip a wink:
> Or I proclame ocht with my mowth,
> But dowt I mon haif drink.

,, 1834 to 1840 *not in* MS.
,, 1841.—So ye gif ws ane fre remissioun.
,, 1852 to 1859 *not in* MS.
,, 1861.—And Discretioun was nyne tymes war.
,, 1872.—That dastard quhilk ye call Discretioun.
,, 1876.—I mak ane vow to sweit Sanct Fillane,

> Get I thame thai sall beir thair paikis:
> I se thay playd with me the glaikkis.

,, 1882 to 1908 *are not in* MS.

> MS. *fol. 195, in the margin.*—[*Ane Proclamatioun, to be tane in eftirwart, of the Parliament. Heir sall Messinger Dilligence say.*

,, 1908.—At the command of King Humanitie.
,, 1923.—That michty drink confortis a dull ingine.

> [MS. *fol. 195.*—*This verss eikit, quhilk is in the first Proclamatioun.* (See p. 13, line 70, &c.)

> Prudent Pepill I pray yow all,
> Tak no man greif in speciall,
> For we sall speik in generall,
>   For pastyme, be my ffay.
> Thairfoir till our rymes be rung,
> And our mistonit sangis be sung,
> Lat every man keip weill a tung,
>   And every woman, tway.

And ye Ladeis, that list to pische,
Lift up your taill, stcill in a dische;
And gife your quhislecaw cry quhiche,
　　Stop in ane wisp of stray.
Latt not your bleddir birst, I pray yow,
For that is evin annewch till slay yow,
Becauss thair is to cum, I say yow,

Line 1930.—　　The best pairte of our Play.

[*Heir sall entir Correctiounis varlet for Reformatioun, and say:*

Schiris, stand abak, and hald your coy, &c.
See line 1482.

MS. *fol.* 177.—[*Heir sall entir the Peurman.*—(*In the MS., the name Pauper, is written Peurman, or Povertie.*)

Line 1932.—Off your almous, gude folkis, for Goddis luve of hevin,
　　For I haif moderles bairnis outhir sax or sevin.

,, 1943.—The divill a word ye get of sport or play.

,, 1945.—Quhae devill maid you a gentillman wald not stow your luggis?

,, 1946.—Quhat now! methink this cullroun cairle begynnis to crak.

,, 1948.—Cum doun, or be Godis croun, theif loun, I sall slay thee.

,, 1950.—Quhat say ye be thir court knavis be thay gett haill claiss,
　　Sa sone thay leir to ban, to sweir, and trip on thair taiss.

,, 1955.—Yet I sall drink or I ga, thocht thow had sworne my deid.

[*Heir he takkis away the ledder.*

APPENDIX.

Line 1961.—Thow art ower pert to spill the proces of our Play.
,, 1962.—I will not gif for your Play nocht a fulis fart :
For thair is littill play this day, at my hungry hart.
,, 1966.—Quhair dwellis thow dyvour? or quhat is thyn entent?
,, 1970.—To seik law in Edinburgh is the narrest way.
,, 1985.—Nane tydiar hyne to the toun of Air.
,, 1988.—Than scho deit to within ane olk or two.
,, 1995.—Was deid, fra hand he tuke fra me ane uther.
,, 2001.—The vicar gart his clark cleik thame away.
Quhen that was gane, I micht mak no debait.
,, 2005.—How am I brocht to this miscritic.
,, 2009.—That gart me want my sacrament at Pess.
,, 2018.—Thay haif na law except ane consuetude.
,, 2025.—And the thrid cow, he tuke for Meg my moder.
,, 2052.—My pardonis and my prevelage.
,, 2055.—This wofull wicket new testment.
,, 2057.—Sen lawit men knew the veritie.
,, 2064.—Richt weill informit be a freir.
,, 2072.—Wander be to thame that it wrocht.
,, 2076.—Bullengerus and Melanctoun.*
,, 2084.—My potent pardonis, ye ma see.
,, 2087.—Thocht ye haif no discretioun.
,, 2096.—Heir is the coirdis baith grit and lang.
Quhilk hangit Jonnye Armestrang.

* Line 2076.—Pinkerton says this line is deleted in the MS. It would have been more correct had he said his transcriber was unable to read it.

Line 2108.—Withowt he be with Belliall borne.
,, 2141.—A filland flag a flyric fuff.
,, 2150.—Theif cairle, thy wordis I hard full weill.
,, 2166.—Suppois the swyngeour nevir swyve.
,, 2174.—My decreit and my finall sentence is.
,, 2179.—I pray yow, Sir, forbid hir for to fart.
[*Heir the Sowtar sall do the lyk.*
,, 2183.—Schirris, saw ye evir mair sorrowles depairting.
[*Heir sall his boy Wilkin cry of the hill, and say :*
,, 2184.—How! maister, quhair ar ye now, &c.
,, 2189.—Upoun Thome Flescheris midding.
,, 2192.—Gude for the fevir cartane.
,, 2194.—All haill the wyvis will kiss and kneill.
,, 2220.—I pray you speid your heir.
,, 2223.—I dreid your weird ye wary.
[*Heir sali the begger ryiss, and rax him, and say.*
,, 2225.—I haif been dronand and dremand on my ky.
,, 2241.—Now haly maister, quhat sall that pardoun cost?
,, 2254.—Thow hes ressavit my pardoun now all reddy.
,, 2263.—In Sanct Androis and summoned you to their senzie.
,, 2275.—Na than maister, gif me my grote agane.
,, 2278.—And heir ressaif my money in this steid.
,, 2286.—When wilt thow cum my bailis for to beit.
,, 2293.—Or, be Goddis breid, Robene sall beir an rowt.
MS. *fol.* 182.—[*Heir sall thay fecht togidder and the Peurman sall cast doun the burd, and cast the rellikis in the watter.*
[*Heir endis this Interlud, and followis ane uthir Interlud of the samyne Play.*

MS. fol. 182.—[Heir enterris Folie.

Gude day, my Lordis, &c.—See line 4283.

Lines 2298 to 2394 not in MS.

MS. fol. 199.—[Heir sall the Thre Estaitis compeir to the Parliament, and the King shall say.

Line 2395.—My prudent Lords, &c.

,, 2403 to 2417 not in MS.
,, 2430.—Quhair, trest ye, sall I find zone new maid King.
,, 2432.—Now Godis braid benisone licht upoun that face.
,, 2434.—I man rin fast in dreid I gett ane cowp.
  [Heir sall Johne ryn to lowp our the water, and he sall fall in the middis of it.
,, 2413 to 2448 not in MS., fol. 200, which has these lines:

CORRECTIOUN.—Johne, quhome upoun complene ye or quho makis yow debaitis.
JOHNE.—Schir, I complene upoun the King and all the Thre Estaitis.

,, 2449.—As for our reverend Faderis of Spritualitie Ar led by Covettyse and this cairle and Temporalitie.
,, 2477.—Bruder, upoun thay harlottis, lay on your handis;
  Ryiss up Lowry, ye luik evin lyk a lurdane.
,, 2488 and 2490 transposed in MS.
,, 2488.—Thou art ane stif knaif I stand ford.
,, 2491 to 2553 not in MS.
,, 2553.—My wirdy Lordis, sen ye haif on hand.
,, 2562.—For quhy, my Lordis, this is my ressone lo.
,, 2564.—Go, in the battell, formest in the brount.
,, 2568.—Or, be my faith! the realme will be begylit.

APPENDIX.

Line 2573.—How kirkmen heichtis thair teindis, it is weill knawin,
　　　　That husbandmen nowayis may hald thair awin.
,, 2577.—Thus mon thay pay grit ferme, or leif the steid,
　　　　And sum ar plainly hurlit out be the heid.
,, 2583.—Or I depairt, I think to mak gud ordour.
,, 2585.—For, how sowld we defend ws agane Ingland.
,, 2589.—War I ane king, my Lord, be cokkis woundis!
　　　　Quha evir held common theivis within thair boundis.
,. 2601.—And bene to vertewis labour laith.
　　　　Qui non laborat non manduceth.
　　　　This bene, in Inglis toung, to treit.
　　　　Quho labouris nocht he sall not eit.
,, 2607.—Thir juglaris, jestouris, and ydill hensouris.
,, 2615.—For than, thay trucouris' man be treitit,
　　　　Or ellis, thair quarellis ar undebaitit.
　　　　And munkis, preistis, channonis, and freiris.
,, 2621 to 2649 *not in* MS.
,, 2652.—The grit misusing of justice airis.
,. 2668.—Prolixt, corrupt, and pertiall.
,. 2685.—Mair attour, my lord Temporalitie.
,. 2689.—Bot nocht to jynkyne gentill man,
　　　　That nowdir will he wirk or can.
,, 2691.—Quhairby that pollecy may incress.
,. 2700.—Ye salbe puneist, be sweit Sanct Geill.
,, 2708.—Quhat ever ye pleis us to command.
　　　　[*Heir sall thay sit doun and ask grace.*
,, 2723.—Flyt on thy fill, Fule I defy thé.
,. 2727.—The peur cottar, lyand to die,
　　　　Havand small bairnis, two or three.
,, 2731.—With the gray coit, that happis the bed.
,. 2736.—With hir peur coit of roploch gray.

APPENDIX. 359

Line 2746.—The thrid cow, he tuik, for Meg my moder.
,, 2751.—And thocht thay want the preiching sevintene yeir.
,, 2753 to 2827 *and* 2835 to 3052 *not in* MS. *fol.* 202.
,, 3053.—Scryb.—Ye gar me wryt mony sindry act,
And to me ye nevir cast in a plack.
,, 3054.—Ha! my lordis, for the holy Trinitie.
,, 3060.—Mary! I lent my gossop my meir, to fetche in coilis.
,, 3072.—Bot, or thay come half gait *ad concludendum.*
,, 3092 to 3102 *not in* MS. *fol.* 203.
,, 3103 *the* MS. *here passes to* line 3202.
,, 3212.—For I had nevir na uther chift.
,, 3213.—To gar him lauss our field and furris.
Mycht I him get now Ewis the durris.
,, 3266 *not in* MS.
,, 3275.—And mak to me ane sober band.
,, 3282 to 3297 *omitted in the old printed copies, have been supplied from* MS. *fol.* 204.
,, 3322 to 3614 *not in* MS. *fol.* 204.
,, 3614.—Correctioun.—I counsale yow, schyr, now fra hand.
,, 3620.—Zone flattrand knavis, withowttin fable,
I think thay ar nocht proffitable.
,, 3638.—Now, quhat is this, thir monstouris meinis.
,, 3660.—First Sarjand.—Cum on, syr Flattry, be the Mess,
We sall leir yow to dance,
Within ane bony littill spaice,
Ane new paven of France.
,, 3663 to 3686 *not in* MS.
,, 3711.—All freiris, and preistis, of this regioun.
,, 3714.—And als, thay ar all haill contrair.
To Johne the Commonweill.

(*The* MS. *fol.* 205, *omits lines* 3716 to 3772.
Also lines 3798 to 3972.)

Line 3779.—That he is naikit, lene, and disagysit.
  „ 3797.—And Common-weill, be tirrandis, trampit doun.

(*After line* 3797, *at fol.* 210, *is this note.*—[*Heir I omit the Actis maid at this Parliament with the reformation of the Sprituall Estait becauss the same is prolixt and sa passis to the Conclusioun.*])

(*The* MS. *fol.* 205, *then proceeds with line* 3973.)

  „ 3973.—Now I beseik yow for All Hallowis,
Gar hang Dissait, and all his fallowis.
  „ 3990.—Schir, in gud faith, I am beschittin.
  „ 4001.—All murdressaris, and strang transgressouris.
  „ 4009.—Adew! my brethir commoun theivis,
That helpit me in my mischevis:
Adew! Grossaris, Niksonis, and Bellis,
Oft haif we fairne owtthruche the fellis:
Adew! Robsonis, Hawis, and Pylis,
That in our craft hes mony wylis,
Littillis, Trumbillis, and Armestrangis:
Adew all theivis that me belangis;
Tailzeouris, Erewynis, and Elwandis,
Speidy of feit and slicht of handis.
The Scottis of Eisdaill and the Grames,
I haif na tyme to tell your names:
With King Correctioun be ye fangit
Beleif richt seur ye will be hangit.*

---

* The variations in the above passage are not very important, but the list is curious, Thift, referring to his brethren in Annandale as "common theivis,"—meaning Border freebooters; the Johnstons, Grahames, Scotts, Littles, Turnbulls, &c. Pylis is the most uncommon, and it has been suggested

Line 4026.—It is schame to pische in a widdy.
  [*Heir sall Flattry hang Thift.*
,, 4061.—Your craftines, gif Correctioun knew.
,, 4076.—The blude rowyall of Cowpar toun.
,. 4080.—My absens sair will rew.
,, 4087.—Ye young merchandis may cry, allace!
  Lucklaw, Welandis, Carruderss, Dowglace.*
,, 4102.—Mony ane wicht man haif ye wrangit.
,, 4138.—Talzeour Beverage my sone and air.
,, 4146.—Get he gud mat and meill.
,, 4156.—A cukroun quene a laithly lurdane.
,, 4172.—I neid not leir you ony lessonis.
,, 4175.—Adew! the stinkand cordeneris.
,, 4179.—With mony ane crafty cast.
,, 4200.—Or ellis strecht way till hell.
,, 4222.—*Not in* MS.
,, 4275.—Ane wolf cled in ane lambis skin.
,, 4282.—And leir him for to flatter.
  (*The* MS. *fol.* 209 *proceeds to line* 3774.)
  MS. *fol.* 182.—(*The following Interlude or Sermon of Folly, occurs here.*)
  [*Heir enteris Folly.*
,. 4283.—Gude day, my lordis, and God sane!
,. 4290.—But gif I cowd lie.
,, 4296.—Mary! cunand down thruch the bony gait.
,, 4310.—Schir, be All Hallowis!
,, 4331.—Or ellis byt baith the bagstanis fra me;
  Gif ye be king, Syr, be Sanct Anne.

that one of that name had migrated to the South, in Lancashire, and eventually became the founder of the Peel family.

* Pinkerton supposes this line, 4088, in the old printed copy may have been omitted to avoid offence, and supplied as in the text, p. 198.

Line 4351.—Hes thow, Foly, ane wyf at hame?
,, 4363.—Scho riftit, ruclit, and maid sic stends.
,, 4366.—Syne, all turnd till a rak of fartis.
,, 4369.—Scho puft and ziskit with sic riftis,
That verry dirt come furth with driftis.
,, 4381.—(*This line not in* MS.)
,, 4386.—Will scho nocht drink.
,, 4399.—Cum heir gud Gukkis, my dochter deir.
,, 4403.—Cum heir, Stulty, my sone and air.
,, 4406.—Cry lyke the gorbettis of ane kae.
,, 4410.—Now bumbalary, Bum, Bum.
,, 4414.—Thow sall want thy wallat.
,, 4420.—Hald doun your heid, ye ladroun loun.
,, 4435.—(*The eight lines enclosed with brackets omitted in the old printed copies, are supplied from the* MS.)
,, 4479.—Fond Foly, I will be thy clark.
,, 4490.—Peranter, ar all guckit fulis as I.
,, 4510.—Till ony fule that lykis to by.
,, 4512.—Quhilk gart thame gang, as ye ma se,
Bakwart throuche all the cuntre.
With my cramery, gif ye list mell.
,, 4527.—Quhome to myndis thow to sell that hude.
,, 4536.—And bindis with hir in mariage.
,, 4550.—Syne sendis thair awin sawls to the Deill.
,, 4556.—*Ex fructibus eorum cognoscetis eos.*
,, 4559.—Speik on, Foly, I gif the leif.
Than have I remissioun in my sleif.
,, 4563.—Ye are ail fulis, be Goddis passioun.
,, 4569.—Quhilk is not ordanit for dringis.
,, 4576.—Thay care not schedding of cristin blude.
,, 4602.—Ga thow and parte it, richt amang thame.
,, 4616.—Mary that is ane evill farr'd (or saird) mess.
,, 4622.—The Divill mak cair, quhilk of them tynt the feild.

APPENDIX. 363

Line 4628.—That his sweit sawle may be aboif in hevin.
MS. fol. 187.—*Finis of this Interlude.*
(*The concluding lines 4629 to 4652, terminate the text of Bannatyne's MS.*)

,, 4629.—Famous Pepill, heartlie I you require.
4637 to 4644 *omitted in the old printed copies, are supplied from the* MS.

,, 4651.—I pray to God Omnipotent,
To send yow all gude rest.

MS., fol. 210.—[*Heir endis the schort Interludis of Sir Danid Lyndsayis Play, maid in the Grensyd, besyd Edinbur*t. *in anno* 155-. (blank in MS.) *zeiris.*

NOTES TO THE INTERLUDE.—*Page* 327.

Lines 11 and 271.—The mention of Whitsun Tuesday as falling on the 7th of June, shows that Easter was the 17th of April, and this fixes the date of the Interlude to the Year 1552.

Lines 176 and 1238.—Fyndlaw or Fynlaw of the Fute-Band, or the Guard of Infantry. See Pinkerton's History. vol. ii., p. 428.

Line 182.—Pyncky Clewch, to the east of Musselburgh. The battle of Pinkie was on the 10th of September 1547.

Line 277.—From Bannatyne's MS., fol. 164-168.

www.ingramcontent.com/pod-product-compliance
Lightning Source LLC
Chambersburg PA
CBHW020317240426
43673CB00039B/833